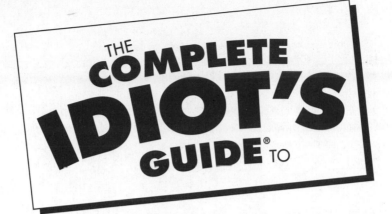

THE COMPLETE IDIOT'S GUIDE® TO

Motivational Leadership

P9-DGU-151

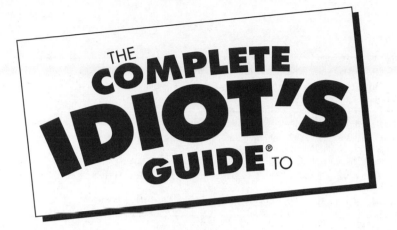

THE COMPLETE IDIOT'S GUIDE® TO

Motivational Leadership

by Scott Snair, Ph.D.

ALPHA

A member of Penguin Group (USA) Inc.

ALPHA BOOKS

Published by the Penguin Group

Penguin Group (USA) Inc., 375 Hudson Street, New York, New York 10014, USA

Penguin Group (Canada), 90 Eglinton Avenue East, Suite 700, Toronto, Ontario M4P 2Y3, Canada (a division of Pearson Penguin Canada Inc.)

Penguin Books Ltd., 80 Strand, London WC2R 0RL, England

Penguin Ireland, 25 St. Stephen's Green, Dublin 2, Ireland (a division of Penguin Books Ltd.)

Penguin Group (Australia), 250 Camberwell Road, Camberwell, Victoria 3124, Australia (a division of Pearson Australia Group Pty. Ltd.)

Penguin Books India Pvt. Ltd., 11 Community Centre, Panchsheel Park, New Delhi—110 017, India

Penguin Group (NZ), 67 Apollo Drive, Rosedale, North Shore, Auckland 1311, New Zealand (a division of Pearson New Zealand Ltd.)

Penguin Books (South Africa) (Pty.) Ltd., 24 Sturdee Avenue, Rosebank, Johannesburg 2196, South Africa

Penguin Books Ltd., Registered Offices: 80 Strand, London WC2R 0RL, England

International Standard Book Number: 978-1-59257-679-1
Library of Congress Catalog Card Number: 2007928971

09 08 07   8 7 6 5 4 3 2 1

Interpretation of the printing code: The rightmost number of the first series of numbers is the year of the book's printing; the rightmost number of the second series of numbers is the number of the book's printing. For example, a printing code of 07-1 shows that the first printing occurred in 2007.

Printed in the United States of America

Note: This publication contains the opinions and ideas of its author. It is intended to provide helpful and informative material on the subject matter covered. It is sold with the understanding that the author and publisher are not engaged in rendering professional services in the book. If the reader requires personal assistance or advice, a competent professional should be consulted.

The author and publisher specifically disclaim any responsibility for any liability, loss, or risk, personal or otherwise, which is incurred as a consequence, directly or indirectly, of the use and application of any of the contents of this book.

Most Alpha books are available at special quantity discounts for bulk purchases for sales promotions, premiums, fund-raising, or educational use. Special books, or book excerpts, can also be created to fit specific needs.

For details, write: Special Markets, Alpha Books, 375 Hudson Street, New York, NY 10014.

Publisher: *Marie Butler-Knight*
Editorial Director: *Mike Sanders*
Managing Editor: *Billy Fields*
Acquisitions Editor: *Michele Wells*
Development Editor: *Michael Thomas*
Senior Production Editor: *Janette Lynn*
Copy Editor: *Marta Justak*
Cover Designer: *Kurt Owens*
Book Designer: *Trina Wurst*
Indexer: *Brad Herriman*
Layout: *Ayanna Lacey*
Proofreader: *John Etchison*

To my parents, Joseph and Lucille, continual sources of leadership and wisdom.

Contents at a Glance

Part 1:   Set an Image and Routine   1

    1   Learn the Science of Motivational Leadership   3
        The advantages of exploring motivational leadership as a science and a method.

    2   Recognize the Motivational Leader   17
        The specific things that make a motivational leader stand out above others.

    3   Develop the Mindset   31
        The way a motivational leader thinks, reacts, prepares, and follows up.

    4   Grow Within the Organization   43
        How to learn the needs of the organization and help to create a vision to satisfy those requirements.

Part 2:   Gain Entrusted Power from Others   55

    5   Understand What the Experts Say   57
        Notions on power and its origins from authorities past and present.

    6   Understand Organizational Behavior   71
        The psychology and collective behavior of people in groups.

    7   Use Ownership and Accountability   83
        Promoting personal responsibility to manage others and to stimulate innovation.

    8   Utilize Rewards and Discipline   95
        The theories behind motivation, counseling, and reprimand.

Part 3:   Offer a Vision, Manage Communication   109

    9   Develop a Vision That Serves as a Beacon   111
        Get people to imagine a better way of doing things and head in that direction.

10 Serve as Cheerleader for Your Team   127
Spread enthusiasm throughout the group,
one person at a time.

11 Establish Relationships   141
Learn about team rapport, collaboration,
and what makes for genuine, two-way
communication.

12 Understand Why Meetings Don't Work   153
Learn why the standard workplace meet-
ing is often a broken, unfixable way of
doing business.

Part 4:   Use Inspiration over Intimidation   165

13 Provide Heartfelt Encouragement   167
Appreciate what makes people tick and
work to build a team atmosphere.

14 Establish Trust and Credibility   177
Learn about the empowering nature of
delegating and the importance of honesty
and mutual expectations.

15 Practice Charisma and Inspire Others   193
Influence people by improving personal
appeal.

16 Be Someone's Guru   203
Understand why mentoring is an impor-
tant part of motivational leadership.

Part 5:   Manage Change and Adversity   219

17 Be a Cheerleader for Change   221
Use tactics for bringing about necessary
change.

18 Choose a Transformational Outlook   233
Learn how motivational leadership brings
out the hidden gifts in others.

Appendixes

A The Motivational Leader's Checklist   247

B Suggested Books on Motivational Leadership   253

C Suggested Biographies and Autobiographies of Motivational Leaders   257

D Glossary   261

Index   269

Contents

Part 1: **Set an Image and Routine**   **1**

1 **Learn the Science of Motivational Leadership**   **3**

Know Why It Pays to Step Up.................................... 4
Learn It as a Science Instead of an Art...................... 6
Know That Leaders Are Made, Not Born.................. 8
Consider This Brief History 10
   Traits Theory.. *10*
   Situation Theory... *10*
   Behavior Theory *11*
   Influence Theory *12*
   Self-View Theory.. *12*
Assess Your Strengths and Weaknesses 13
Commit to a Whole New Outlook 15

2 **Recognize the Motivational Leader**   **17**

Use an Energetic, Inspiring Persona 18
Exercise Precise Decision-Making 20
Utilize Clear Communication 22
Employ Superior Listening.. 23
Maintain a Planner, Set the Agenda 25
Be Firm but Fair... 27

3 **Develop the Mindset**   **31**

Apply Shameless Self-Promotion 31
Take the Blame, Share the Accolades........................ 34
Radiate Confidence and Enthusiasm......................... 35
Groom Yourself... 37
Set the Example... 39
Make Promises and Follow Up 41

4 **Grow Within the Organization**   **43**

Discover Your Organization's Needs 44
Make Your Skills Fit the Needs................................. 46
Don't Be Shy 48

Embrace Your Organization's Vision...........................50
Gather Input from the Team 51
Balance Your Loyalties 52

Part 2:   Gain Entrusted Power from Others   55

5   Understand What the Experts Say   57
Consider Experts' Thoughts on Power......................58
Max Weber *59*
Frederick W. Taylor *60*
Peter Drucker..*60*
Peter Senge..*61*
Know the Different Types of Power 61
Position Power *61*
Personal Power *63*
Appreciate That Power Is Necessary 64
Use Entrusted Power, Not Seized Power 66
Know Where Negotiation Fits In 67
Steer Clear of Power Abuses 68

6   Understand Organizational Behavior   71
Understand How People Behave in Groups..............72
How and Why We Behave Differently in Groups *72*
So What's Wrong with That? *73*
Know a Group's Dysfunctional Attributes 74
The Polarizing Nature of Groups..............................*74*
Birds of a Feather *75*
Watch Out for Groupthink..75
Examples of Groupthink *76*
Ways to Avoid Groupthink..*78*
Know Your Organization 79
View People as an Asset 80
Get People to Believe in the Program 81

7   Use Ownership and Accountability   83
Seek an Endangered Species: Accountability............84
Identify Where the Buck Stops 85
The Power of Veracity...*86*
Don't Foster a Culture of Blame *87*

Use Ownership as a Tool 88
Promote Ownership as a Reward 89
Follow-Up 90
Keep in Mind Who Is Ultimately Responsible.......... 92

8 Utilize Rewards and Discipline 95

Learn the Theories of Motivation.............................. 96
What Turns People On?.............................. *96*
What Points People in a Certain Direction? *98*
What Keeps People Charged Up? *98*
Understand What Motivates the Individual.............. 99
The Human Motivators.............................. *100*
A Word About Punishment.............................. *101*
The Limitations of Pizza and Soda 101
Carrots vs. Sticks 103
Counsel Before Disciplining.............................. 104
The Verbal Warning 104
Carry Out Appropriate Discipline.............................. 106
The Motivational Traits of Discipline.............................. 106

Part 3: Offer a Vision, Manage Communication 109

9 Develop a Vision That Serves as a Beacon 111

Get on Board with "the Vision Thing".............................. 112
Set a Vision for the Team.............................. 114
Get People to Buy What You're Selling 116
The Role of Hope *116*
Steps to Selling Your Vision.............................. *117*
Define Your Winning Motivational Vision 118
How to Create a Vision Statement for Your Team..... *119*
A Model Vision Statement *120*
Turn Your Vision into Priorities.............................. 121
*How to Write a Mission Statement with Your
  Team* *122*
A Model Mission Statement.............................. *123*
Manage by Objectives 123

10 Serve as Cheerleader for Your Team   127

Act Enthusiastic and … 128
Know That Corny Often Works 129
 Examples of Corniness That Worked *130*
 Expressions That Work, Even Though They
   Look Corny in Print *131*
Get Dirty 132
Know When Some Things Are Beneath You 134
Consider One-on-One Management 135
 Time Efficiency *135*
 Steps Toward Becoming a One-on-One Manager *137*
Read These Cheerleading Stories............................137

11 Establish Relationships   141

Know What Rapport Means....................................142
Know Why Rapport Matters 142
Get Out the Word...143
Develop Teamwork 145
Encourage Collaboration 146
Know the Ways to Encourage Collaboration 147
Know that Good Communication Goes Two
  Ways..148
Keep the Lines of Communication Open 149

12 Understand Why Meetings Don't Work   153

Avoid "A Nightmare on Meeting Street".................154
A National Pandemic 155
Know If a Meeting Is *Really* Necessary 156
 Some Signs a Meeting Is Necessary *156*
 Ten Things to Ask Yourself....................................*157*
Understand Why Most Meetings Fail......................158
Use Alternatives to Meetings..................................159
 Some Meeting Alternatives....................................*159*
 A Big-Time Executive Who Limited His Meetings...*160*
Don't Film the Movie Without a Script...................161
Run That Rare, Successful Meeting.........................161

Part 4:   Use Inspiration over Intimidation   165

13   Provide Heartfelt Encouragement   167

Understand Human Needs 168
Consider What Else the Experts Say 169
Abraham Maslow 169
Victor Frankl 170
David Burns 170
Dale Carnegie 170
Respect the Fragile Nature of People 171
Value the Encouraging Word 172
Build a Sense of Community 174
Appeal to the Tough Audience 175

14   Establish Trust and Credibility   177

Understand Why You Should Delegate 178
Know the Process of Effective Delegation 179
Steps for Effective Delegation 180
Some Pointers for Effective Delegating 181
Know the Paradox of Effective Delegation 183
Add the Overlooked Ingredient: Integrity 185
Discover the Multiplying Effect of Trust 187
Learn That Credibility Is Contagious 190

15   Practice Charisma and Inspire Others   193

Know That You Weren't Born with Charisma 194
Ten Steps for Being More Captivating 195
Treat Someone Like the Person of the Moment 196
Be More Inspirational 197
Champion the Grand Ideal 198
Read These Inspirational Leader Stories 199

16   Be Someone's Guru   203

Know What a Guru Is... 204
Define Yourself Through Your "Grasshoppers" 205
Be the Hidden Advocate 207
Promote Job Enrichment.. 211

Expect Something Back—It'll Come.........................213
   Be a Guru to Yourself..................................*213*
   More Specific Ways That Being a Guru Benefits
     You..*214*
Encourage Formal Mentoring................................215

Part 5:   **Manage Change and Adversity**   **219**

  17   **Be a Cheerleader for Change**   **221**

Appreciate That People Dread Change 222
Know How to Introduce and Launch Change 223
Don't Change Just for the Sake of Change.............226
Measure Your Team's Change Success 227
Get Comfortable Managing Crises 229
Work the Margin Between Good and Great 231

  18   **Choose a Transformational Outlook**   **233**

Go from Motivational to Transformational 234
Traits of the Transformational Leader 235
Have People Work Just to Impress You 236
Take the Tough Initial Stand 238
Sell Destiny..239
Be the Remembered Leader 241
Some Final Thoughts on Motivational
   Leadership 243

Appendixes

  A   **The Motivational Leader's Checklist**   **247**

  B   **Suggested Books on Motivational Leadership**   **253**

  C   **Suggested Biographies and Autobiographies of**
      Motivational Leaders   **257**

  D   **Glossary**   **261**

      Index   **269**

Introduction

A common thread runs through most personal success stories—these winning people are able to take charge of their lives, and, when necessary, they are able to take charge of and motivate others. From business owners to project managers to sports coaches to teachers, setting a course, working with people, applying techniques of self-confidence, and getting results from others serve as mutual routines in their daily lives.

This book offers a systematic approach to establishing one's image as a motivational leader, gaining entrusted power from and influencing others, offering a vision and managing communication, using inspiration over intimidation, and, when necessary, directing change and drawing out the best from people in an organization.

Just this year, the American Psychological Association published a special issue of their professional journal, dedicated entirely to leadership. The issue made three important observations: 1) the need for strong leaders in organizations cannot be overstated, 2) the study of leadership, from a psychological, scientific approach, should be continued and even expanded, and 3) somewhere out there, a model for motivational leadership exists. It is a group of actions, anticipated behaviors, and situations that, if researched, studied, and applied, will someday take all prospective leaders down the appropriate decision-making path. In other words, motivational leadership is a science and a skill to be learned—not some sort of nebulous art form or inborn gift.

Make no mistake about it. In this world of indecision, self-victimization, poor social skills, and corporate butt-covering, bold leaders are in high demand and in dramatically short supply. If you learn the craft of motivational leadership and you step up to the plate, you set yourself apart from millions of other employees and team members. And you instantly make yourself important and impressive.

How to Use This Book

The Complete Idiot's Guide to Motivational Leadership is broken down into five parts, each covering a major area in the study of motivational leadership.

Part 1, "Set an Image and Routine," considers, in detail, the activities and attitudes of today's successful motivational leader. It considers those specific things you can do to make others respect you and want to follow you.

Part 2, "Gain Entrusted Power from Others," reviews some important psychological theories on power, group behavior, and incentives. It delves into why people act the way they do at work, and how to channel these tendencies in productive ways.

Part 3, "Offer a Vision, Manage Communication," considers how today's motivational leader gets people to look toward a brighter future and strive for it. It looks at practical ways you can encourage your team and keep them focused on the big goals.

Part 4, "Use Inspiration over Intimidation," considers motivational leadership attributes such as trust, credibility, charisma, and mentorship—not in a deep, emotional way, but from the vantage point of sincere and practical methods for relating.

Part 5, "Manage Change and Adversity," looks at the motivational leader as an agent for necessary change within the organization. It looks at realistic ways of drawing out hidden skills and the very best of team member talent. It looks at ways to permanently change people and teams for the better.

Extras

Along with the chapter-by-chapter reading, this text contains four special features to guide you through the concepts behind motivational leadership.

Best Voices Forward

Best Voices Forward boxes offer helpful quotations from the motivational leaders and consultants of yesterday and today.

One Step Back

One Step Back items provide suggestions on what situations and practices you should avoid as the motivational leader.

def•i•ni•tion

Definition sidebars further define or explain words that appear in the regular text. Since motivational leadership is a science, it's important that you understand and appreciate the terms.

Repeated Excellence

Repeated Excellence is added advice on a particular topic that enhances the essentials throughout the chapters. These proven, practical tips add to your arsenal of motivational leadership tactics.

Acknowledgments

I am deeply grateful to the people who brought me this project and saw me through to its completion. At Penguin Alpha: Michele Wells, my very supportive, inspiring acquisitions editor; Mike Thomas, a smart, resourceful development editor; Jan Lynn, a great senior production editor; and Marta Justak, a highly competent copy editor. At Sheree Bykofsky Associates: Janet Rosen, my wonderful, caring agent, and her colleagues, Sheree Bykofsky and Caroline Woods, all exceptionally considerate and professional people.

Many thanks to those who have helped me approach motivational leadership as a scientific and academic endeavor. At Seton Hall University's College of Education and Human Services: Joseph De Pierro, Charles Mitchel, Joseph Stetar, Martin Finkelstein, and Philip DiSalvio. At Seton Hall University's Stillman School of Business: Karen Boroff and Brian Greenstein. At New Jersey City University's College of Professional Studies: John Collins. At Rutgers University's Office of Continuing Professional Education: Edward Lipman and Carol Broccoli. At Davenport University: Julia VanderMolen, Sherry Roslund, Linda Crosby, Laura Pipenger, and Barb Huston. At Thomas Edison State College: Esther Taitsman, Sonja Eveslage, Jamie Priester, Anne McKithen, Patricia Memminger, and Susan Fischer. And to my great bosses at the U.S. Military Academy Preparatory School: Tyge Rugenstein, Stephen Jacobs, and William Krug.

A very special thank you to my wife, Mary-Jane Snair, a mental health clinician wrapping up her Ph.D. in clinical psychology, for reviewing and offering advice on some of the psychological stuff mentioned in this text.

I appreciate all the love and support from the Gebhardts and the Snairs, who cheered me on and tolerated me as deadlines approached: Roy, Jane, Roy, Leah, Joe, Lucy, Patti, Andy, Kenny, and Jimmy. And thank you, once again, to my brilliant wife, Mary-Jane, and to my terrific daughters, Patti and Katie.

Trademarks

Part 1

Set an Image and Routine

The overriding leadership challenge is to develop an image, lifestyle, and workstyle where the leader controls people and events rather than the other way around. Along with inspiring people, the goal is to be *pro*active as a leader instead of *re*active. By manipulating the nature and flow of tasks, leaders establish their environments. If, on the other hand, they find themselves existing day by day and simply "putting out fires," they become overrun by minutiae and, in essence, lose control.

The effective leader designs a routine and controls the daily and long-term tasks connected to the mission.

The effective leader is defined by his or her persona and actions more than by words or corporate policies. As such, self-definition—shaping one's image—becomes the ultimate way to influence an organization. This personal re-characterization includes developing an air of fervor and confidence. It means keeping a cool head. It means staying well-groomed and dressing nicely. It means getting known as someone who makes few promises but always follows up on them and keeps those promises.

1

Learn the Science of Motivational Leadership

In This Chapter

- ◆ Stepping up to the motivational leader's plate
- ◆ Learning the discipline of motivational leadership—it's not a creative art form
- ◆ Reviewing the academic study of motivational leadership
- ◆ Conducting a personal inventory of motivational leadership attributes
- ◆ Creating a new image and attitude

Motivational leaders recognize that they fill a unique role. Their challenges are sometimes enormous, but their rewards are equally grand. Motivational leaders enjoy control of their people, their careers, and their lives. In this chapter, we'll consider why motivational leadership is a set of skills to be learned and practiced rather than a simple set of traits one is born with.

Know Why It Pays to Step Up

Why on earth would anyone want to be in charge? First, it's a thankless task, best left to the self-important person or the person who doesn't know how to say no. Second, by avoiding responsibility for a team, you avoid the self-imposed punishment of unwanted attention and extra work, the aggravation of dealing with other people, and the potential for blame. Third, being in charge—not to mention trying to serve as an example and an inspiration for others to follow—is basically a lot of energy and drudgery with very little reward.

Right on all counts?

Wrong!

Although choosing the part of *motivational leader* is by no means an easy life preference, it is considerably rewarding for all sorts of reasons. Make no mistake about it: it pays to seek the role of leader and to accept it if you're offered it.

First, filling the role of a motivational leader is the ultimate internal triumph. Even though there are undoubtedly better measures of a person's success—for example, money, fame, status, virtue, love— there aren't many compliments in life or signs of accomplishment more fulfilling than when someone says, "You're a fine leader." It's a deeply rewarding praise coming from your elders or your peers, and it's especially gratifying to hear it from someone you've led. Forming a team and leading it toward a common goal gives you a personal sense of worth, control, and (when done effectively) achievement like no other experience can. Knowing you possess the reputation for getting things done as an inspiring manager is a wonderful feeling.

And speaking of those other, more external success measures, consider how each of them ties in with the ability to lead. For example, if the best avenue to more money is through promotion at work, then demonstrating you are able to manage others surely translates into a better existence financially. The richest people in the world, like Bill Gates of Microsoft and Ingvar Kamprad of Ikea, are not simply owners and movers of stock, but also inspiring, hands-on leaders of their companies. Being out in front involves being noticed as *important* by important people, meaning some degree of fame and enhanced status is attributed to you. Being responsible for others, setting a good example for them, and doing right by them (making their lives better) not only makes you a virtuous person, but it also sets up good karma that comes back to you in a hundred different ways. Although leadership does not convert necessarily into love (especially the one-to-one, companionship type), being a good boss makes you feel better about yourself and about approaching other people—two qualities that make you infinitely more attractive and likely to live life in a less lonely fashion. It also gives your partner (present or prospective) another reason to be proud of and admire you.

def•i•ni•tion

What is a good, working definition of **motivational leader?** I like the wonderful description that the faculty of Thomas Edison State College (New Jersey) teaches in their graduate-level course "Foundations of Leadership and Management." They define a motivational leader as "someone who uses the process of inspiring and persuading others with a compelling combination of actions, attitude, and persona."

Furthermore, learning tangible ways to take charge and become a motivational leader provides you with two key ingredients to your sense of well-being—a perception of belonging and a feeling of control.

Abraham Maslow, the famous humanistic psychologist of the 1940s and 1950s, suggested that, next to water, food, shelter, and the desire to procreate, there is no human need greater than the yearning to belong to a family or a group and to receive the approval of others. You only have to look at the powerful influences of family pressure and peer pressure to appreciate the innate desire to be a part of a team and to receive the respect and approval of others on that team. Although respect and approval don't come automatically, one thing is for sure: if you form the team and serve as its motivational leader, you are unquestionably an important part of it, and your sensation of belonging is healthy.

If most anxieties and phobias begin with a perceived loss of control, then being at the helm of a team—with heightened levels of control and influence—is conversely one of the more mind-pleasing reasons for taking charge. Being in control means, well, being in control. If you're going to be saddled with a project at work, why not volunteer to lead it and set the agenda for tackling it? Calling the shots can be very soothing and invigorating "mind candy."

Hey, the bottom line is that it's good to be the king. There are enough tangible and subliminal prizes for being a team's motivational leader to make it well worth the effort it takes to pursue a leadership role. Embrace it and celebrate it once you have it.

Learn It as a Science Instead of an Art

When roaming through the leadership section of any bookstore, you might initially think you're in the wrong aisle and that you have inadvertently wandered into celebrity autobiographies. Many of today's leadership books have as much to do with the life stories of quirky but successful personalities as they do with step-by-step methods for channeling people's energy and loyalty. On the other hand, these celebrity books are quite entertaining and, admittedly, often thought-provoking. So when pondering the general theme of these books, you might wonder if, perhaps, motivational leadership is more of a creative talent—a personality-based art form—involving some sort of hit-and-miss inventiveness or "the-stars-are-in-alignment" luck.

Seeing photos of wealthy, famous people on those book covers adds to the notion that leadership might be more alchemy (magical powers) than reputable science. Standing in front of those success-story books might also remind you that great leaders do seem rare and elite. In fact, many leaders—such as good professional baseball pitchers—make an insane amount of money because the demand for those people far outweighs their supply.

Finally, good motivational leadership has a certain "I know it when I see it" quality to it. It's easy to oversimplify or reduce it to something very straightforward because of the ease with which many admired bosses seem to carry out their duties. We marvel at their effort because it seems so, well, effortless. With the veneer of simplicity comes an on-off switch misconception: Either I *am* a motivational leader or I'm *not*, and there's little I can do about it and little territory between the two extremes.

And don't expect the leaders to clear things up for you. The image they convey and the influence they possess come from having you believe all the things I just mentioned.

But the less glamorous (yet more fortunate for you) truth is that leadership is a science, not a mystical or confidential art. Over the years, leadership theory has managed to identify, classify, and measure those very specific things that inspire groups of people and channel them in the direction you need them to go. If you take nothing else away from your interest in the study of motivational leadership, know that it involves unambiguous concepts and practices that can be learned and applied by nearly anyone.

> **Repeated Excellence**
>
> Method-based and knowledge-based research on leadership concepts has only been around since about the beginning of the 1900s, coinciding with the beginning of social psychology.

Learning about motivational leadership means understanding some of the academic concepts behind it (covered in this text), such as the traits and behaviors of a leader, what types of situations a leader is placed in, different kinds and sources of authority, and how leaders help people learn about themselves. It means knowing human behavior patterns when people interact within a group, and how they inherently yearn for clear direction and communication. It also takes into account human psychology and intrinsic human flaws, such as the tendency to rely on useless meetings and to yield to "groupthink" (more on groupthink in Chapter 6).

The science of motivational leadership includes understanding how power works, how it is efficiently and ably applied, and how organizational politics help facilitate it. It involves polishing one's image and creating a unifying vision that the group can relate to and rally around.

Motivational leadership, as a science, entails quantifiable procedures, such as assessing work team efficiency, calculating absenteeism and undesired employment turnover, and looking at worker productivity and balance sheet data.

Finally, the study of motivational leadership, like most sciences, implies an observable phenomenon—which means it pertains to the real world, and not some sort of hypothetical or simulated, academic world. It recognizes that leadership situations are not sterile and clear-cut, but generally dynamic and always a bit messy. Motivational leadership is studied against the backdrop of each manager's organization, recognizing that each person must gauge what works best for his or her individual situation. And it's also critical to assess a group's strengths, weaknesses, and idiosyncrasies, recognizing that motivators that might work for one person don't necessarily work for another.

Know That Leaders Are Made, Not Born

Why is it that expressions like "leader" and "born leader" are used interchangeably? When we call someone a *born leader*, we don't mean that he was born with a clipboard in his hand, barking out commands in the delivery room as soon as he came into the world. What we really mean is that the person is simply a good leader, successful at managing people to the point where he makes it seem natural. But perhaps there's something more here. More likely the term "born leader" carries with it an underlying premise—that someone who does an exceptional job directing others was born with the talent. And, even more importantly, it implies that people without that talent at birth won't get it.

Unfortunately, we don't seem to mind the implication. After all, assuming that great leaders are that way from birth makes our tendency to idolize them all the easier. Not only are we inclined as humans to excessively adore great leaders, but we often go further by identifying important historical events with the leaders of the time. Is it possible to separate George Washington from the American Revolution or Dwight Eisenhower from War World II? The good news about such worship is that it rightfully assumes these individuals held a strong influence over the people and events that surrounded them. The bad news about this idolization is that it keeps us from considering the learning process that made them great. The result? An expression such as "born leader."

From an academic standpoint, there is one area of study that supports the notion that motivational leaders are, to a large extent, born with the tools that will make them such leaders. It's called the "traits theory of leadership" (discussed in the next section). The underlying assumption of this theory is that effective leaders have certain inborn qualities and mannerisms, and that ineffective leaders don't.

I don't really subscribe to the "traits theory," and I think it's important, as we discuss leadership development, that you get past it. Instead, let's consider this important question before continuing on: Are motivational leaders born or are they made?

> **Best Voices Forward**
>
> Leadership guru Warren Bennis suggests that leadership personality traits and leadership actions are not easy to separate—nor should they be. In his *Learning to Lead* workbook (written with Joan Goldsmith), he says: "Leadership *is* character. It is not just a supervision question of style, but has to do with who we are as human beings, and with the forces that have shaped us."

The question relates somewhat to the nature versus nurture argument in the field of psychology. As science and behavior studies advance, psychologists—especially researchers, such as biological and social psychologists—find themselves learning more and more about how you behave in reference to what behavioral traits are part of your DNA and what traits you pick up from observing the people who surround you. The current school of thought seems to throw out the nature versus nurture argument in favor of a nature PLUS nurture line of reasoning. That is, if someone inherits, in layman's terms, a "worry gene" from her father, but she also observes her father constantly worrying throughout her childhood, then the two conditions probably compound to make her a worrier.

My argument is this, regarding motivational leaders being born versus made: 10 percent are born and 90 percent are made. Here's why. Even if we subscribe to some parts of the traits theory, we're assuming that human behavioral attributes are handed down from generation to generation. That means we're also assuming that how people react to motivational stimulation and how people behave within a group are also inborn, predicable qualities. Therefore, if people can be influenced and directed in such a predictable way, then learning how to do so makes a person, in essence, an effective motivational leader.

So if you tend to accept the predictability of people, as many motivational leadership theorists do, and that this predictability can be used to trigger people in a productive way, then you've purchased the right book. And if you believe that there's a big difference between a manager and a motivational leader, then you've purchased the right book. Unlike simply administering procedures and projects, the knowledgeable (or "made") motivational leader knows how to create an array of influences (vision, motivation, harmony, synchronization, synergy), using methods that are learned and not simply skills acquired at birth.

Consider This Brief History

Before delving into the more practical aspects of becoming a motivational leader, it's worth taking a brief moment to consider the human theories behind the practice.

There are generally five main bodies of theory when it comes to motivational leadership.

Traits Theory

Mentioned in the last section, the "traits theory" is probably the oldest theory set regarding leadership, going back to the early 1900s. The traits theory suggests that motivational leaders share the same personal attributes, many of which they were born with. These characteristics include intelligence, composure, lots of energy and enthusiasm, and (depending on the theorist) even physical attractiveness.

Again, I generally lean away from the traits theory. Much of it, in recent years, has been countered with studies suggesting that good leadership has little to do with inherited traits or physical features (even though, statistically speaking, tall, attractive people *do* get hired into leadership positions more often). Instead, I prefer those theories that celebrate a person's adjusting to the situation, learning, and growing as a motivational leader. Read on.

Situation Theory

The "situation theory," which is also called the "contingency theory," is an academic philosophy suggesting that motivational leaders are most successful when they modify their leadership styles based on the different situations they are placed in. In other words, this theory suggests that one size does *not* fit all.

The situation theory includes specific research on motivation. For example, in 1974, Robert House and Terence Mitchell created the "path-goal model," suggesting that groups are more motivated when they are given clear, well-described paths to their desired outcomes. House and Mitchell's work remains important because it reveals that groups can be motivated collectively, as one.

Repeated Excellence _____

In 1988, Kenneth Blanchard (who wrote the famous *One-Minute Manager* books) and Paul Hersey produced the "situational leadership model," matching certain types of motivational leader styles to different group situations. For instance, if leader-group rapport was low but the task understanding for the group was high, Blanchard and Hersey suggested a "telling" style, with very specific instructions and rigid monitoring of performance. If the leader-group rapport was high but the task understanding was low, they recommended a "participating" style, where the leader and the group shared in the decision-making.

The situation theory includes the notion of tracking and reacting to group responses to leadership. For example, if a group reacts well to a particular style of leadership and perceives that style as "good leadership," then the boss should appropriately take the cue and use the same style. Sure, in some ways that's the "tail wagging the dog," but if motivational leadership is results-driven (and it is), then it's worth watching what works as you continuously adjust your leadership style.

Behavior Theory

The "behavior theory" attributes much of an organization's success or failure to the actions of its leader. Does a leader behave in an autocratic way when a democratic style might have worked better? Is the leader delegating enough?

Individual studies within this academic point of view vary widely, as do their findings and recommendations. But their prevailing principle is that the things a leader says and does affect the organization dramatically, and that it is possible, in charting these leadership behaviors, for us to create a model for any motivational leader to follow. A criticism of the behavior theory is that it gives the leader too much credit and pays too little attention to organizational behavior and different leadership situations.

Influence Theory

The "influence theory" looks at power—its origins, its uses, and its impact. This is probably the most interesting theory set when it comes to considering how people rise to power and how they lose it. (Chapter 5 discusses the concept of power at length.)

The influence theory is interesting in that it often considers power as something of a constant within an organization. In other words, this philosophy says all organizations have X amount of power. Some people within the group have larger slices of the power pie, and some have smaller slices. Sometimes, people combine their slices into coalitions for more power. But there's never more or less power collectively in the organization—it just gets moved around in a dynamic game of politics, alliances, and give-and-take.

Self-View Theory

The "self-view theory" is my favorite type of leadership teaching. This philosophy looks at how a motivational leader inspires people by helping them improve how they view themselves. For instance, highly charismatic and inspirational leaders not only set lofty goals for their followers, but they also convey a high level of confidence in them. In the right setting, the outcome is often a dramatic, positive impact over large organizations.

These types of motivational leaders often put out grand plans and visions, generating an emotional involvement from the group. Such leaders often appear and become powerful (and often save the day) in times of crisis. Winston Churchill was a good example of a leader who succeeded by convincing his countrymen that they were capable of weathering staggering challenges and rising to new heights against a formidable enemy. He was the personification of the self-view theory.

The self-view theory celebrates the transformational leader who convinces people that they are part of something bigger than themselves and then encourages them to accomplish things outside the scope of their own self-interests. Charismatic, idealistic, visionary, trusting, and loyalty-provoking—that's what the motivational leader is all about.

Assess Your Strengths and Weaknesses

The first step toward becoming a motivational leader is conducting a personal inventory of your motivational leadership attributes. The point of answering the following questions is to develop a self-awareness of where you are, where you'd like to be, and what things you need to do to get there.

This survey is descriptive, not diagnostic. That is, there is no right or wrong answer to each of these questions. After you privately write down your answers, consider them and mull them over. Collectively, they should paint an accurate portrait of your abilities, successes, or inclinations regarding motivational leadership.

1. Are you running events at work and in your life, or are the events running you?

2. Are you delving into these questions and reflecting on your answers, or have you decided to skip past this section as a waste of time?

3. Do you personally "own" your life situations, or do you find yourself blaming others (or blaming bad luck) for your lot in life?

4. Do you spend more time working toward long-term goals (yours or the team's) or "putting out fires"?

5. Do you consider yourself self-confident? If so, do you believe that other people sense it?

6. Are you comfortable with the idea of being in charge of others?

7. Has there ever been a time when you positively influenced a group of people, whether or not you were in charge? If so, what happened?

8. Do you handle change well? Have you ever had to help a group handle a difficult change? How did it go?

9. Do you enjoy going to work? Why or why not?

10. Do you prefer inspiring and encouraging people over threatening them?

11. Do you consider concepts like "team" and "encouragement" and "inspiration" corny or important?

12. Have you ever considered ways to improve your outward image or your self-image? If so, what did you do? Do you feel that it worked?

13. When is the last time you tried to be more charming? What did you do? How did it go?

14. How is your grooming? Your wardrobe?

15. Do you generally keep your promises to your superiors? Your peers? Your team?

16. When is the last time you listened to someone, nodding and taking notes, for at least two solid minutes without interrupting?

17. Are you able to, at this moment, write down the five most important needs of your team? Of your larger organization?

18. Who are you more loyal to—your superiors or your team?

19. Do you know where power comes from? Do you have any? If so, how do you use it?

20. Have you ever seen a really bad idea, in a meeting, take on a life of its own? What did you do?

21. What is your "vision" for your team? For your life?

22. Do you know what it means to manage by objectives? If so, do you consider yourself someone who manages this way?

23. When is the last time you handled a conflict between (or among) people on your team? What happened? How did it go?

24. Do you prefer one-on-one encounters over team meetings?

25. Are you comfortable delegating some of your projects or parts of a project?

26. Have you ever taken a talented, promising team member "under your wing"?

27. Do you consider yourself a cheerleader for your team? For the larger organization?

28. Have you ever had someone do something for you for no other reason than to win your approval or appreciation?

29. Do you consider yourself in demand? If so, why? Is it because of your knowledge and skills? Your ability to take charge? Your reputation for getting the job done?

30. Are you comfortable or uncomfortable with these questions?

Commit to a Whole New Outlook

After privately considering your responses to these personal inventory questions, lock them up and then reconsider them the following day. Upon reconsideration, you might decide that you like what you see, or you might decide that you are interested in projecting yourself differently.

Sometimes, becoming a motivational leader means committing yourself to a whole new outlook—on goals, people, image, and personal vision. You don't want to become a different person, of course. No one likes or trusts a phony. The idea is to change your outlook in ways that make people think to themselves, "Hey, what is it about this person that has changed? I can't quite put my finger on it, but I like what I'm seeing and what I'm hearing. I see myself taking this person more seriously. I notice others doing the same, seeking this person's attention and approval, and I'm impressed by it."

Wanting to become a motivational leader, as well as desiring to change in ways that bring it about, is an important first step involving ownership of your circumstances and your life.

The Least You Need to Know

- Taking on the role of your team's motivational leader brings with it many tangible rewards, such as status and recognition, and intangible rewards, such as personal triumph and a sense of control.

- Motivational leadership is a science more than it is an art, involving both academic and real-world concepts, such as human psychology, human needs, organizational behavior, communication, power, and politics.

- Although some leadership theory suggests that people are born with leadership talent, the more common teachings—along with the predictability of human nature—argue that motivational leadership is an ability that can be learned and improved on over time.

- Leadership theory considers the traits and behaviors of successful leaders, the situations they're placed in, the power they exert, and, most importantly, the influence they have over how team members view themselves.

- A personal inventory of your motivational leadership attributes is an important first step toward understanding where you are as a leader, where you'd like to be, and what things you need to do to get there.

- Sometimes, becoming a motivational leader means committing yourself to a whole new outlook—on goals, people, image, and personal vision.

2

Recognize the Motivational Leader

In This Chapter

- ◆ Finding a motivational leader's energetic, rousing quality
- ◆ Providing the team with prompt and unambiguous decisions
- ◆ Getting the message out in a way that's understood and earns a response
- ◆ Perfecting your listening skills
- ◆ Organizing a daily schedule and calling the plays
- ◆ Developing a reputation for handling others with resolve and evenhandedness

When a motivational leader walks into the room, everyone knows it. There's an instant crackling in the air—the electric energy of high enthusiasm. This boss makes people feel important and good about themselves and convinces them that they're part of something bigger than any one of them. In this chapter, we'll look at what makes a leader truly motivational, from firm but fair treatment of others, to acceptance and flexibility regarding people and situations, to showing genuine interest when team members are talking.

Use an Energetic, Inspiring Persona

It's possible to be a good boss without being a motivational leader. Showing up for work, keeping payroll current, vacations covered, work accomplished, and controversy at a minimum—that's sometimes all organizations ask for and all a boss needs to deliver. But many times, a mission or a new endeavor requires more. Sometimes, a unique, exciting person is required to pull a team (or even a country!) out of its routine or its doldrums and set it down on a new, important path. Sometimes, a new idea requires someone who can lead people into scary, uncharted waters. And occasionally, this interesting, rousing person becomes not only a conduit for the team's success, but also a major part of the success story itself. What are the qualities of this motivational leader, and what is it that sets this leader apart from other supervisors or other people on the team?

The first thing about a motivational leader is that she does not show up for work simply to go through the motions. When people are around her, they're interested in and excited about where the team is headed next. Wherever she's going, they want to tag along. More importantly, they want to support her and be a part of what she has planned. They want to be characters in the great story that's being written and a part of the history that's being made.

Another thing about the persona of a motivational leader: it doesn't include grumbling. Rarely does one hear a motivational leader complaining about the organization or its priorities. If there's a problem, she's more likely to offer suggestions and serve as the remedy rather than to surrender to the problem or be bitter about it. If she has high-level criticism, it takes place behind closed doors, so that she can remain loyal to the organization's vision once the doors open.

In that same vein, the motivational leader doesn't offer a "you and me against the world" message to her team. That is, she doesn't seek loyalty from her team by suggesting that the team is always right and the organization is always wrong. To be sure, she balances her loyalty to her team with her loyalty to the larger organization. And she doesn't pander to the more selfish needs of her team members, especially if they run contrary to the greater needs of the organization and its mission.

Best Voices Forward

What could be more inspiring than saying "Let's go to the moon—literally!"? If there were ever an exciting, motivating persona, it was U.S. President John F. Kennedy. At a time when a single computer occupied the entire wing of a building, Kennedy proclaimed that America should lead the world technologically by being the first country to put a man on the moon. Kennedy suggested in 1962 that "no nation which expects to be the leader of other nations can expect to stay behind in the race for space." He dared Americans to test their creative limits, saying, "We choose to go to the moon in this decade and do the other things, not because they are easy, but because they are hard … space is there, and we're going to climb it!" His rousing challenge carried six years past his assassination, as Americans Neil Armstrong and Buzz Aldrin landed on the moon in July of 1969.

Once her team buys into a vision for itself with a larger plan in the background, the motivational leader is a champion for that vision. She sells them on the notion that they are a part of something bigger than themselves and keeps them locked on that motivational idea.

The motivational leader gives off the impression of a high-energy person. Is it an act? Sure—sometimes. After all, sometimes life gets us down, and we can't all be perky all the time. But the motivational leader puts on a positive front for the benefit of her team. And, curiously enough, by acting enthusiastic, she finds that the act often becomes reality for her, meaning that a positive front often seeps inward and cheers and motivates the leader who is in the process of motivating others.

That rousing quality of a motivational leader not only makes people admire her, but also inspires them (openly or not) to be like her and to carry themselves in the same enthusiastic, professional manner.

Exercise Precise Decision-Making

The motivational leader sets himself apart from other bosses by being boldly decisive. There are a lot of words to describe the motivational leader, but "wishy-washy" is clearly not one of them. People know and respect this person who is at the helm—for his resolve and his confidence. As with many other leadership attributes, this self-assurance is contagious, as others on the team seek to be a part of this straightforward way of living and working.

When the motivational leader makes a decision, everyone knows it and most people understand it. There is not a gray span of time when people are drifting rudderless or acting tentatively. The decision generally includes solid, working guidelines and, when necessary, specific work instructors. Team members are guided by a *commander's intent*, asking themselves, "What would my leader do?" before acting autonomously. As a result, the motivational leader is comfortable pointing people in a direction and simply letting them go on their way without feeling the need to micromanage or baby-sit them.

def•i•ni•tion

Commander's intent refers to a top boss's explanation of what needs to be achieved, why it needs to be achieved, and what forces exist that might keep it from happening. A commander's intent message is meant to allow second- and third-tier managers to operate within a holistic set of guidelines that still permits independent decision-making and innovation. The concept of a commander's intent ties in with the philosophy of the U.S. Army Infantry School: "We will teach you *how* to think, not *what* to think."

This decisiveness is not rash. On the contrary, the motivational leader often takes everyone's input into account before making a decision. He often goes to each team member, soliciting input and advice, trying to incorporate as much of it as possible so that the entire team buys into the ultimate verdict.

It's worth noting that asking for input does not translate into getting bogged down in meetings. How many times have you watched an indecisive boss simply schedule another meeting rather than make a decision? Conversely, the motivational leader does not equate meetings with decision-making. In fact, he understands that a meeting is just as likely to create an atmosphere for groupthink, where a bad decision tends to take on a life of its own and where people get on board for all the wrong reasons. Bottom line: a good leader understands that more meetings do not mean better input or better decision-making. Another thing about the decision-making process of the motivational leader is that it's practical. Sometimes, when we think of the quintessential leader, we think of grand plans and lofty aspirations. And to be sure, it is the purpose of a leader to take a team to greater heights. However, underneath the hype and the glory is often a very utilitarian, nuts-and-bolts plan, unhampered by frills and complications. If the KISS option ("Keep it simple, stupid") is available, the motivational leader is the first person to select and refine it.

The motivational leader's practicality carries over into the philosophy behind his decision-making. His choices are driven by the desire for meat-and-potatoes results and not by dogma or some zealous political stance. How many times have we watched a politician who could have done the responsible, practical thing but chose not to because it went against some silly overriding political viewpoint? Choosing the matter-of-fact reasoning over a stubborn creed makes the motivational leader clear about and comfortable with his decisions.

This leader also understands that "decisive" doesn't mean "pig-headed." Is your initial decision starting to look like the wrong one? Hey, it's okay to change your mind. In fact, it's what everyone prefers. As a cannon platoon leader in the U.S. Army, I was in charge of making sure that cannon-fired rounds landed on targets miles away from where we were firing. When the rounds were not on target, we had to adjust the cannons. Our philosophy: "Make *bold* corrections!" That is, it was better to shift where the rounds were landing dramatically at first and then dial them into the target, rather than to make tiny corrections and take forever to nudge the rounds where they needed to be. The same goes for adjusting a bad decision. Make bold corrections as you find the right path to your target.

Utilize Clear Communication

With all the technology that exists today, you would think that people would have an easy time communicating. The truth is that passing a single, clear thought from one human mind to another is probably as tough as it has ever been, if not tougher. The unfortunate side effect of instantaneous, electronic transmission is that people are inundated with information—much of it trivial or unrelated to the project at hand. It's no wonder that many school districts, for example, have banned cell phones in the classroom. Many parents and teachers would rather give up quick access to their students in favor of having them a lot less distracted and more inclined to listen in the classroom. The same goes for computers and phone messaging in the evening: it is a major interruption to old-fashioned family living and communicating.

Consequently, it is the first-rate, motivational leader who can push through this noisy static and resonate clearly and comprehensibly with her team. Through a clever combination of low-tech, one-on-one interaction, body language, and listening skills, she is able to connect with her team in a way that makes them shimmer with a feeling of togetherness and sameness of purpose. There are two things that make people feel important—hearing their names and hearing requests for their input. The motivational leader articulates both, loudly and often, and people individually feel good about being part of a team.

It's easy to spot an organization with a great communicator for a leader: everyone seems to know what's going on. The information tends *not* to vary from person to person. People are aware of the big picture, and they understand each person's individual responsibility in making it happen. If you walk into such a work environment and ask what's going on, several people will approach you to inform you.

Having an entire team on the same wavelength and all possessing the same amount of info is not just a rarity— it's not even something all managers are comfortable with. Information is power, and the weak-minded manager doesn't always want to share it. Don't you hate the boss who has just learned some important, pertinent information but chooses to dribble it out in tiny doses to the team? What a childish power play, and yet it goes on every day. The motivational leader, on the contrary, gladly shares information with the team the second she gets it, rather than hoarding it for leverage. She's at ease with her role as team leader, and she isn't threatened with the notion that others might have access to relevant data and might offer their own great ideas along the way.

The motivational leader knows what she wants and states it plainly for the team, one priority at a time. A couple of major projects, with reflecting talking points and objectives for the team—that's how a real leader gets the word out and makes big things happen.

Does the motivational leader follow up on her requests? You bet, and, when making a request, you can expect her to tell you *exactly* when she's going to follow up on your progress—the date and the time. When it comes to following up, she leaves little to the imagination.

She's demanding, but not cruel. The motivational leader comes across as approachable. Assuming she's an important and busy person (and, of course, we know that she is), she's not always going to be easily reached. But if you can find time on her agenda, you'll find that she doesn't hide behind her title. Chances are, to subliminally demonstrate her interest in your concern, she'll sit at a conference table rather than the official boundary of a large desk. She'll absorb what you have to say, take down notes, and ask related questions. You'll leave feeling like you got to speak your piece.

Does it sound like clear communication involves large doses of good listening? Sure. Indeed, the incomparable leader is a champion at it.

Employ Superior Listening

If you think for a moment about the best bosses you've ever worked for, you're likely to remember what great listeners they were. Active, caring listening is so rare these days that we instantly revere and admire the supervisor who makes use of it.

It is difficult to put a finger on whatever happened to good (or even just courteous) listening, as well as when it might have vanished. Was it television, cell phones, instant access to Internet information, web instant messaging? Since the brain can process words so much more quickly than the voice can generate them, and since modern technology seems to have shortened our attention spans dramatically, today's culture tends to allow—even condone—the midsentence interruption more than ever. If a person asks a question today, it's often *not* because he desires an answer, but because he is introducing his own next statement, and *your* response better not keep him from doing it!

The motivational leader sets himself apart from other managers, dramatically so, by listening to his team members, often one-on-one, with a sincere show of interest and an inclination to retain the information from other people's responses. The motivational leader nods his head, "mirrors" some phrases back to the person (to provoke more revelations), and asks the person follow-up questions. The motivational leader demonstrates interest by jotting down an important point or two in his daily planner.

One Step Back

If you're formulating your retort while someone is still speaking—hoping to respond the second that person pauses for a breath—then you are definitely *not* practicing the art of good listening. Instead, try to listen to the person's full statement, nodding your understanding. Perhaps wait a second or two before formulating your response. Or better yet, respond with a question, to help clarify the person's contention. If people know you are actively listening, they are more likely to give credence to your reply and support you as their leader.

Over the years, I have worked in the military, in sales, manufacturing, logistics, and in education. By far, the toughest people to deal with as leaders are college professors. They're often cantankerous, disorganized, self-absorbed, and marching to beats of a hundred different drummers. So when I worked at Seton Hall University, it was a pleasure to watch a motivational leader, Charles Mitchel, work his magic on a daily basis, gaining consensus from his unruly bunch of faculty and administrators. Mitchel, the chairman of the Department of Education Leadership, Management, and Policy, made a point every morning of walking from office to office, shaking hands, and asking people about their families and their concerns at work. Later in the week, he would follow up with questions about something he had heard on a previous day or with information someone had requested. He was a genuine, thoughtful listener and a true pleasure to work for (and learn from).

If he managed to gain consensus on a plan or issue at a meeting later in the day, I'm certain that it was largely due to the rapport he had gained from walking around and skillfully listening to his team, one-on-one.

Professional counselors are taught early in their training that active listening and repeating (what famous psychologist Carl Rogers called "the reflection of attitudes") not only helps people relate their concerns to others, but it also helps people reflect on themselves and find answers to their own problems. It is the superior listener who can make this happen.

Maintain a Planner, Set the Agenda

You can always tell the motivational leader or aspiring leader at a meeting. She's the one with the notebook, page planner, or electric organizer, jotting down notes, scheduling follow-up items, and recording crucial events on upcoming dates.

Keeping a planner doesn't just keep you organized; it sets you apart from lots of other people in a lot of positive ways. The next time you attend a meeting, notice how many people show up with nothing in their hands—except, perhaps, a cup of coffee and a pastry. Essentially, what they're saying is, "There's nothing I'm going to hear today that's worth writing down." And maybe that's so—meetings can be a huge waste of time. But assuming, during an hour-long meeting, one important event and one important new policy is going to get mentioned, you show yourself as a prospective leader by bringing along the resources to record and keep track of them.

One Step Back

If you keep an electronic organizer, you better back up your memory cards frequently. A colleague of mine lost all the information on his organizer (including his electronic phone book and information regarding an important, yearlong project) due to a glitch in the device. Sadly, he didn't learn his lesson. After tracking down much of the lost information through phone calls and transcribing handwritten notes, he didn't back up his electronic memory and lost it all again that same month! As with many things in life, when it comes to electronic organizer memory, you'd better back it up.

There are other reasons why the first-class motivational leader maintains a planner. First, it offers her the opportunity to plan her day and her week, rather than fall victim or puppet to events happening around her. Time is your most important resource, so making the effort to apportion it makes you smart and efficient. A planner keeps you focused. It's easy to get caught up "putting out fires" or allowing problem people to get you off track. By creating and following a schedule, you're more likely to stay focused on the big-picture items of the day.

A second reason for keeping a planner is that it shows your team that you care. A great motivational leader I worked for some years ago was Chris Mallon, a paper mill manager at International Paper Company. Mallon recommended that I always have on hand a notebook or, at the very least, a clipboard with a notepad on it. "When a team member approaches you with a concern," he said, "write it down. It shows people that what they tell you isn't going in one ear and out the other." I followed his advice for three years, always jotting down issues involving the paper machine, pay, time off, or general gripes. It didn't make me the perfect boss, but it helped me get support from a crew that hadn't been easy for others to manage.

A third reason for maintaining a planner is it shows your boss that you care. As mentioned previously, if you're at a meeting and you're the only one taking notes, you're saying, "I'm concerned enough about what's being discussed to take notes." And if you're not yet in charge, you're also saying, "Some day, I hope to be in charge."

Fourth, while showing your boss that you care by writing down things he says, a planner sends the subliminal message that "You're on my time," rather than the other way around. It's not a disrespectful message—after all, we're all busy people. But when a boss asks you for something and you enter it into your planner, you are—again, in a gentle, respectful way—reminding him that your time is limited and that you budget it well. Perhaps the underlying message will help cut back on his asking for things on a dime or on a whim.

Fifth, having a planner offers you a place to carry and read your long-term ambitions. Says Chuck Ahner, senior vice president for a major loan services company and occasional candidate for Congress: "Have your written goals and objectives posted in your planner, so that you can see them whenever you refer to it."

Finally, maintaining a planner allows you to quietly portray yourself as an important person. When you carry a planner with you—everywhere—you represent yourself as something of a gatekeeper. The planner is the gate to someone asking for your time. It's the gate to information about upcoming, crucial events. It's also the gate to a record about recent happenings. ("Gee, when did we say we were going to start submitting daily reports?" "I have it right here in my planner. We agreed to daily reports at a meeting on Wednesday, the 8th.") When you're reading something out of a planner, it's tough to dispute, especially when all your counterpart is holding is a cup of coffee.

Be Firm but Fair

Up to this point, the characteristics of a first-class motivational leader might be misconstrued as the traits of a first-class softy. Phrases like "inspiring persona," "clear communicator," and "superior listener" could easily be linked to the pampering boss, eager to please everyone and vulnerable to a team that takes advantage and eventually becomes out of control.

In fact, a top-notch motivational leader understands that niceness has its limits, that people must be given parameters within which to work, and that they must be held accountable for actions and responsibilities. He also recognizes that most people appreciate the necessity of authority and that they respect the boss who handles others with resolve and evenhandedness.

A controversial study at Yale University during the 1960s certainly suggested that people have an inborn yearning for direction and guidance. In the psychological experiment, two people were taken into a room. One was seated at a table with a set of lists and a control panel with a dial and a button, and the other, a "learner," was hooked up to wires behind a screen. The person at the table was asked to read the lists and have the learner recite them in order. Whenever the learner got the order wrong, the person at the table was asked to press a button and administer shocks to the learner, turning a dial and increasing the voltage of the shocks as the experiment went on!

As it turned out, the "learner" was an actor, in on the experiment, and not being zapped at all. People at the table, administering the shocks and listening to the "learner" howl in agony (and, in some instances, pretend to pass out), very often simply went on with the horrible testing, with little more than the gentle prodding of the lab technician, saying things such as "please continue" or "you must go on." Years later, the experiments were criticized for placing people in such an unnerving situation under false pretenses. But the results were clear: people inherently seek guidance, and they often do what they're told.

The motivational leader plays into this human condition by being demanding, quick with counseling or a disciplinary word when necessary, but equally quick to compliment and recognize a task that's completed successfully. This control is administered fairly, ignoring for a moment the mentor-student relationships or the personal friendships that might exist outside the workplace. People might initially resent the firm feedback, but they invariably appreciate the fairness in which it's administered. The most consistent compliment I have ever heard people give a boss behind his or her back was that the supervisor was "firm but fair."

The motivational leader recognizes that people inherently yearn for guidance and clear direction and offers this type of leadership without being gruff or cruel.

The Least You Need to Know

◆ Motivational leaders set themselves apart from other bosses by displaying high energy and high enthusiasm and serving as cheerleaders for a vision, convincing the team it's part of something bigger.

◆ Being gallantly decisive—while remaining approachable and flexible—is one way to define yourself as a special leader.

◆ Connecting with people, one person at a time, with big-picture information and concerns, puts the team on message and instills a sameness of priorities.

◆ Employing skillful, considerate listening on a team, one member at a time, results in a high level of rapport for the leader.

- ◆ Keeping a notebook planner or an electronic organizer helps you plan your life rather than allowing events to plan it for you, and it portrays you as an important, organized, and caring person.

- ◆ People inherently yearn for strong leadership and the sure hand of a resolute boss, as long as fairness goes with the firmness.

Chapter 3

Develop the Mindset

In This Chapter

- Selling yourself as a leadership product
- Owning the team's faults, but sharing its praises
- Displaying self-assurance and a passion for the mission
- Dressing professionally
- Serving as a model for others to admire and follow
- Limiting promises but following up on them

Motivational leaders display themselves as something of a product that everyone wants to have around. These professionals know how to present themselves in words and deeds, in grooming and dress, and in how they represent their teams. In this chapter, we'll examine how to act, dress, think, and react in a motivational way.

Apply Shameless Self-Promotion

If you want to be a motivational leader, you had better check your meekness at the door. Certainly there's a place for humility when it comes to assuming a leadership role: for example, seeking the opinions of people on your team or admitting when you don't have an answer are both appropriate exercises in humility. But if you have a difficult time tooting your own horn, you'd better learn how, because the odds are against anyone else's tooting it for you. The motivational leader is an expert at self-promotion.

"Selling yourself" to your superiors, your colleagues, and your team is a significant part of motivational leadership. Your image as a success story in the making, or as someone people expect to make a difference, is as much a management tool as anything else you offer the organization. Self-promotion also has a nice way of tapping into a self-fulfilling prophecy. A leader promotes himself as a winner, his bosses bring the important project to him, give him the best people to help him with it, and—surprise of surprises—he successfully accomplishes a crucial assignment for the company. And the positive cycle continues. Unfortunately, the cycle of defeat works the same way; you can avoid that sequence at the outset by letting others know you prefer the winning track.

Publicizing yourself in a triumphant light involves more finesse than simply announcing, "Here I am, and you're going to love me!" An unchecked ego, especially one that's not backed up with a solid record, is an annoyance to all. Instead of the unpleasant aroma of self-centeredness, why not give off the more pleasing scent of friendliness, confidence, enthusiasm, and ability?

Well-known leadership and marketing consultant Jeffrey J. Fox offers a novel thought in his job-seeking book, *Don't Send a Resume*. He claims that any aspiring leader should look at himself like a box of cereal. The notion is that, within an organization, you are a product, and you are competing for attention at any given time with other people—other "products," so to speak. "You are a box of corn flakes competing with every other cereal to catch the eye of the customer," he writes, "to get plucked off the shelf, to get purchased." The idea is that your employer and your team should feel good about *buying* what you're *selling*, and that—more often than not—the thing you're selling is you. An employer should feel good about hiring or promoting you the same way he might feel good about purchasing a new photocopier. And a team should feel good about subscribing to you, the leader, the same way they might feel good about subscribing to a useful and informative magazine.

> ### Best Voices Forward
>
> Has there ever been a motivational leader better at selling himself as a product than American football great Joe Namath? First, he overcame a series of knee injuries to establish himself in the 1960s as the new American Football League's star rookie quarterback. Then he outrageously guaranteed that the fledgling New York Jets would defeat the National Football League's dominating Baltimore Colts for the world championship—a guarantee that shocked the sports world by becoming true. He trademarked his flamboyance by wearing a long fur coat and sunglasses on the sidelines during football games. And he established himself as part of popular culture by advertising shaving cream and, of all things, pantyhose on television! His team and his fans were constantly inspired and charged by this intriguing character. Namath understood early in his career about the leadership impact of presenting himself as a "product" as much as a person.

As with all big "purchases," it essentially comes down to comfort. People have to feel comfortable having you in charge. And, as with all economic transactions, both the buyer and seller should come out of it feeling better off. By sending out success signals to those around you, you're telling them, "Hey, you've made a great buy."

Here's an example of self-promotion. Shortly after I signed a contract for this book, toward the end of a staff meeting, I said, "I hope you don't mind my sharing some recent good news. I just signed an agreement with a major publisher to write another management book. It's due to hit bookstores sometime next year." Nothing fancy or too self-aggrandizing. But had I not said anything, no one would have ever known, unless, a year later, a colleague came across the text in a store or noticed it in my office. Similar announcements regarding the completion of a college degree, obtaining some type of license or certification, receiving an award, or meeting a company objective all are worth mentioning in a nonbragging "can I share with you some good news?" manner. The idea is to make people feel proud to have you around and, if you're in charge, proud of (and at ease with) following you.

Take the Blame, Share the Accolades

The "blame game" seems as much a part of American life as anything else these days. It's a part of our culture—particularly our work culture—to blame everyone for our problems except ourselves. People hold a sense of entitlement, of wanting "what's in it for me," and when they don't get it, they want someone to pay. The result? Hard feelings and lawsuits abound. It's difficult if not impossible to get rid of incompetent employees. Proposed organizational changes get caught up in arguments over what norms and values are acceptable. Political correctness overshadows everything. Sheesh! Is anything getting done?

Unfortunately, in a lot of organizations, the answer is no, not much *is* getting done. The idea of people individually taking possession of their own actions and problems is, indeed, a rare event. No wonder that the motivational leader sets herself apart from others by having a mindset that includes taking responsibility for her decisions and her actions and admitting to and correcting her mistakes along the way.

I have the privilege of teaching research and writing skills to U.S. Army soldiers who are preparing to attend the United States Military Academy at West Point. I keep a banner at the front of my classroom that reads, "An expression of maturity, character, and ownership: *No excuse, sir!*" *No excuse* is not only a phrase taught early on at West Point, but it is also a philosophy instilled in all military leaders—that they need look no further than themselves in determining who is responsible for their own successes and failures or the successes and failures of their team. It is a wonderful, unique encounter whenever one of these young adults says to me, "No excuse, sir." Perhaps he or she is simply reading the banner, knowing what I want to hear. Or maybe, just maybe, this young cadet candidate is embracing the idea that a genuine motivational leader owns his or her own destiny.

As if owning your own actions weren't tough enough, owning the actions of your team is even more difficult. It is human nature, when asked by the big boss "Why did things go so wrong?" to want to share the individual mistakes of people on your team. After all, you *did* tell them what you needed, and they *did* let you down. However, a captain is responsible for everything that happens on her ship, and owning the collective letdown of your team is adopting the mindset of the true motivational leader.

One Step Back

Don't ever explain to your superior why your team fell short on a task by itemizing the individual failings of your team members. Fairly or unfairly, that boss will look at those failures as a reflection back on you, the leader. It is better to "own" those weaknesses and letdowns yourself and to tell your boss which things will be done better next time. You will immediately establish yourself as a responsible, accountable manager. And you will further confirm yourself as a motivational leader when your team hears through the grapevine that you accepted the hit rather than sell them out.

So if you take all the blame for mistakes, then you get to take all the credit for your team's triumphs, right? Wrong. On the contrary, when you are complimented as a leader for your team's success, you should— *must*—share the credit. "Great job on that project, Joan." "Thank you, sir. I'll let the team know."

Does sharing the accolades amount to just being a good guy? No, although it is very much a "good guy" thing. But more importantly, complimenting your members to your superior has an interesting way of coming back to you threefold.

A psychological study was done a few years ago that speaks volumes about why you should share the credit and compliment others whenever you can. People, having heard criticisms and compliments about others, were questioned about the people who had relayed that information to them. A very interesting outcome: people tended to associate those attributes relayed about the other people with the deliverers of the information. In other words, if you say critical things about other people, those who hear the criticism will tend to relate those unfavorable comments to you. On the other hand, if you say highly complimentary things about other people, those who hear what you're saying will tend to remember flattering things about you. What you say about others is projected onto you, the motivational leader.

Radiate Confidence and Enthusiasm

The mindset of the motivational leader includes a calm but noticeable self-assurance and a passion for the mission at hand. Don't expect your boss or your team members to walk up to you and say, "Hey, don't be down on yourself. We know you can do the job." Oh, it may happen, but once you've displayed your hesitation, you might be leading from a place of disadvantage. Starting off a project by exhibiting a quiet confidence in yourself puts you in a position where people are more likely to respect you, follow you, and offer you their support.

Such confidence can't be hollow or unsubstantiated. That is, don't say you can do it if you're sure you can't. Know your limitations ahead of time by taking an inventory of your skills, especially as they relate to what you suspect you're going to be asked in your role as motivational leader. On the other hand, if you have a reasonable grip on the situation and you're ready to step up to the plate, let people know. Your superior will feel good about relying on someone who feels good about himself.

It's also good to begin a project by showing confidence in your team and voicing it loudly and often. Let them know you're happy to be a part of the team and that they're the best ones for the job. Say it often enough, and people will start to believe it. As you walk around in the morning, talking to each team member one on one, let each of them know that it's good to see him or her, and that you're glad to have him or her on board. Offering the personal, kind word to the individual teammate is an important way to maintain a sense of exhilaration within your team. "I'm lucky to have you on this team," you say. Is it corny? Sure. But if you say it like you mean it (and you should mean it), then people will believe it, and they will appreciate your considerate words and your trust in them.

If slightly exaggerating confidence in yourself or in others is okay, then exaggerating your enthusiasm is grand. On any given day and at any given moment, you should portray yourself as a few notches more motivated than you really are. During the toughest, filthiest, most physically and mentally demanding tasks I've ever been on, there was always some team leader shouting with glee, "Man, you gotta *love* this stuff!" Sure, everyone shook his head and laughed at the silliness of the statement. But, you know, it *did* make the task easier and the day go by more quickly. If you have a job that occasionally involves being in the driving rain, you really have two choices: a) be miserable, or b) laugh and sing and convince yourself (and others) that it's a ball. I know which choice I prefer.

At U.S. Airborne School at Fort Benning, North Carolina, in 1986, the school commander, Lieutenant Colonel Leonard B. Scott, was always on the morning runs, or at the parachute staging sites or the drop sites, shouting "Ya gotta love it, crazy!" We all thought he was nuts, but again, his enthusiasm and confidence in us made a tough Army school more bearable, and it was a privilege to have our Airborne wings pinned on by Colonel Scott at the end of the course.

Incidentally, since I'm bringing up enthusiasm, it's worth posing the question here: If the larger organization desires your enthusiasm and the enthusiasm of your team, shouldn't they just pay you all more money? That is, doesn't more money generate more enthusiasm? The answer is essentially no. Money can be used to reward a good person for long-term, consistently good performance. And money can be used to entice a person onto the team or entice someone good from leaving a team. But the idea that you can create an enthusiastic team through pay raises, except perhaps for the shortest of short terms, is false. Even if you could make them all rich, it probably wouldn't work. Psychologists have researched and demonstrated pretty consistently that wealthy people are often unhappy people. Studies also suggest that workplace happiness is often related to things such as feelings of personal worth to the organization, being appreciated, having a say in what goes on, having options for personal and career development, and working in an environment that's fair and respectful.

There is plenty more throughout this text about keeping the team stimulated and in high spirits. But in regard to the motivational leader's frame of mind, it's worth noting that the confident, enthusiastic personality holds lots of sway over the team.

Groom Yourself

Is the world too superficial? Sure. But you can't consider entering the elite club of truly motivational leaders without taking into account how you groom and dress yourself. It's more than simply cleaning up to the point where people feel comfortable with you. The motivational leader immediately identifies herself as a winner by dressing and presenting herself professionally. It is part of the way a motivational leader thinks: "How can I present myself to others in a way that conveys credibility and command before I ever say a word?"

Let's not kid around. Just because you decide you want to become a leader doesn't mean that everyone is going to step back and let you assume control. It's a very competitive world out there. By dressing perhaps one level above the pack and maybe a little bit nicer than what your office protocol dictates, you tell people that you've got your stuff together and that, in one way or another, you're in charge.

Repeated Excellence

There are ways to dress appropriately without spending a lot of money. However, you might not want to take bargain chances with your shoes or your watch. Often, without realizing that they're doing it, people tend to measure your "dress for success" quotient by your shoes and your watch. That's right—people do look at your shoes. Lots. So if you work a job where dressing professionally matters, consider spending a little extra on a couple pairs of comfortable-fitting leather shoes and a nice watch.

Dressing well goes back to the initial, important point in this chapter: you are, as a motivational leader, offering yourself as something of a product to your team and to the larger organization. Marketing consultant Jeffrey J. Fox agrees. "Appearance is an important part of the packaging of your product," he notes, "and the product is you."

Whatever your workplace uniform or clothing protocol, consider going up one degree. If jeans are okay, consider only wearing slacks. If a tie is the order of the day, consider a tie and a jacket. If you're a woman, try a business suit instead of just slacks and a blouse. Avoid extremes. Stylish but not ostentatious is the order of the day. Demonstrate through your dress the seriousness of your work ethic and self-image.

Incidentally, from a financial perspective, it's possible to fake it 'til you make it. My brother, Andy, is a full-time professional artist who meets with his clients daily. At any given time, he is very nicely dressed. And yet, in his closet, along with very expensive jackets are $5 jackets he picked up at the local consignment shop or thrift store. It's tough to tell the difference, because he's good at selecting generic items that fit nicely, are fashionable, and generic enough to mix and match. There are some exceptions to thrift or discount shopping. For example, more expensive silk ties seem to hold a stylish knot better than the cheaper ones.

There are ways to balance the necessity of professional conformity with the independent style of a confident leader. Again, avoid extremes. Keep jewelry to the point where it doesn't clink and clatter. Look in store windows and see how the fashions jive with what you've been wearing. Wear a trademark perfume or cologne, but wear it sparingly. Use breath mints. Keep your hands washed and your nails clean, manicured if you have the time and cash.

Larry Nykwest, a technical service manager in Pennsylvania, cautions that, at some point, you're going to have to live up to the good first impression that a nice suit makes. He suggests, "Make sure the suit is not all there is!"

The key is not only to present yourself well, but also to enjoy the mental lift that dressing well gives you.

Set the Example

There are places in this world for management "generalists"—people who manage all types of people and all types of different projects and know a little bit about everything and a whole lot about nothing. And they often do quite well tying together loose ends, meeting deadlines and budgets, and getting assigned to new projects as the old ones are concluded. They might fit the strict definition of successful managing, but unless they have a particular area of expertise and a passion that they can apply at some point in the process, they are probably not motivational leaders.

The motivational leader sets himself apart from the ho-hum managers of the day by being so technically capable within his realm that he finds his team asking him for specialized advice, rather than the other way around. The motivational leader not only sets the example through his professionalism and sense of responsibility, but he also serves as a model by knowing his stuff to the point of being the team expert.

As a leader, you should set the example for technical proficiency by learning the craft and immersing yourself in it. Attend professional training when it's available. Stay current on the profession. When something new and controversial is happening within your line of work, share it with your team and discuss its ramifications. If you're good at writing and have done something innovative in your profession, write an article for a trade journal. Become the guy who knows what's going on, maybe even the guy who is asked to speak at functions in a particular area. Share the spotlight by having one or more of your team members co-present with you.

Have your expertise bleed into your personal work code. You want people to ask not just "What would Joe do?" but, more importantly, you want them to ask "What has Joe done in this regard, and how can we emulate it?" In both your professional conduct and your workplace know-how, you want to always be the example for others.

It's worth mentioning again that being the expert doesn't mean hiding away information so that other experts can't be created. The motivational leader shares information, teaching others when he's the expert on a particular topic, or opening a topic for discussion and perhaps his own personal learning when he knows just enough to understand that someone else can probably teach him something on the topic.

Setting the example also carries into personal behavior, as the motivational leader puts himself on a slightly higher tier of conduct and deeds so that other people may do good things based more on his manners and mannerisms than on his words. His performance sets the tone for the team and the standard for other, aspiring motivational leaders.

One Step Back

The words *hypocrisy* and *leadership* don't go together. If you passionately push a workplace standard or philosophy, make certain that you have the personal control to follow that same rule. The quickest way for a motivational leader to fall from grace is to get caught violating his own strict standards. If you find yourself in a hypocritical situation, own up to the hypocrisy and make a highly visible, immediate correction. If you prefer the "do as I say and not as I do" viewpoint, then you are, in all likelihood, something of a hypocrite, and you're in for a difficult road ahead as a manager.

Possessing the outlook of a motivational leader means defining yourself by your actions, including limiting how many promises you make and who you make them to, but fervently following up on those promises.

Make Promises and Follow Up

Your time, energy, and resources (including your abilities and the time, energy, and abilities of your team) are limited. You know it and accept it. So should other people. Therefore, do whatever you can to politely limit the promises that you make. However, when you do make a promise, follow up on it religiously. In other words, don't promise the world, but when you do promise something, deliver it to the point where you gain a reputation for doing so.

The limited-promises, unlimited-reliability philosophy ties in nicely with the persona of a motivational leader. Just as a leader gravitates to a few major talking points and objectives at a time, taking care of and aggressively following up on a few promises defines you as someone who focuses on the important issues and people (namely, those around you) of the day.

Repeated Excellence

If you're going to limit the workplace promises you make (and you should), why not occasionally select your promises and projects based on your job expectations? If you plan on going the extra mile at work, tie some of your promises to areas that can later be reflected on your supervisor's yearly appraisal. Like many companies, your organization might allow you to submit an annual list of contributions as a "state your case" supporting form toward your yearly evaluation. If you have channeled your above-and-beyond promises toward factors related to your job description and your stated professional development, and if you have followed up on your promises the way you should, then you have not only helped others, but you have also efficiently created a nice bullet-point list of personal contributions you can submit in support of your annual evaluation.

The mindset of the motivational leader suggests that, if you're going to regulate your promises, you should channel them to what you're known for. "Hey, from what I hear, you're the person who knows best how to polish a business plan. Mind if I brief my proposed plan to you sometime?" Keeping your limited time focused on something you're good at reinforces your reputation in this regard. Also, odds are that if you're good at something, it's probably because you enjoy it. Feeding your promises toward something you like will make the time go by in a good way.

One more thought on limiting your promises. Saying no to people every now and then isn't a pleasant thing, especially when so many people depend on you as the team's motivational leader. However, much more unpleasant is putting so much on your plate that you have a difficult time, well, eating and digesting. Not to use too many clichés in one paragraph, but don't be the workhorse that's worked to death. Occasionally say no, buck the rider, eat a cube of sugar, and take a breather. But when you *do* say yes, be the workhorse that plows the field in a way that impresses all the animals on the farm.

The Least You Need to Know

- Proudly and confidently endorse yourself as a product that your team members and your larger organization can feel comfortable with "buying."

- Own your mistakes and the mistakes of your team, but share compliments with your team that you receive as team leader—it makes you a unique, "no blame, no excuses" type of leader.

- Calmly display confidence in yourself and your team, and show— even exaggerate—a contagious enthusiasm for the duties and projects your team is working on.

- Groom and dress yourself in a way that's stylish, not extreme, and a cut above the rest, giving yourself the mental boost that comes with good attire.

- By learning one aspect of your job better than anyone else and by setting a high standard of words and deeds, serve your team as a model for others to admire and follow.

- Limit the promises you make, keep them reasonably connected to your job goals and company review goals, and then follow up on them unfailingly.

4

Grow Within the Organization

In This Chapter

- Uncovering a group's deficiencies
- Matching expertise with perceived need
- Exploiting brashness as an advantage
- Backing the larger organization's vision
- Calling on team members for involvement
- Defining the delicate dance of loyalty

Motivational leaders make a point of matching their skills to the needs and the vision of the organization. In this chapter, we'll check out how these matches are made, how teams become involved, and how loyalty comes into the picture.

Discover Your Organization's Needs

What causes bad or ineffective leaders to step down and gifted motivational leaders to step up and assume command? In my opinion, the difference between the two is that the inferior leader is a stagnant leader who becomes unaware of how an organization or a climate is changing—or perhaps he *is* aware of his changing surroundings, but he refuses to grow along with the company. The gifted motivational leader is one who understands that the only thing constant within a particular setting is that it's always changing and that, to be successful and to make a difference, he must adapt and improve on the way to greatness.

Repeated Excellence

Tom Wilson is a workplace safety consultant for the New Jersey Department of Labor and Workforce Development. His job includes inspecting places of employment for unsafe conditions, and he trains managers and workers on how to change those conditions to make them safe. Interestingly, Wilson initially comes at an unsafe situation from the angle of needs-skills motivation. That is, he identifies the safety needs, he makes it known through his extensive manufacturing experience that he has the skills necessary to help the organization address these needs, and he works with the company to make it happen. "I feel like I have a small window of opportunity to gain their confidence and respect," says Wilson. "If I expect to motivate people beyond their current outlook, I must show confidence in myself and my abilities to assist them in achieving these goals. I must present myself as a professional in my field and knowledgeable of the information I am discussing." Wow! Wilson easily could barge into a company like an overbearing government enforcer. But instead, he sees the benefit of making people safer by first convincing them what he's saying is right and making them *want* to incorporate his suggestions.

If you want to offer yourself as a transformational leader to your organization, start by discerning where it is, where it's going, and where your profession as a whole is headed. What's the buzz? Check the lobby in your building or the waiting room in your office—there's probably the company's Annual Report sitting on a table. It's the pretty book printed on glossy paper, and it says all kinds of nice things that might not have anything to do with your location. But borrow it, read it, and learn. Stockholders want to know where your outfit is headed—you, as a motivational leader, should want to know, too.

As your organization continues to grow and change, see if you can uncover its new needs or deficiencies—its growing pains, so to speak. If you're already in charge of a team, consider the big picture's impact on your team. Let them know what's going on in the "outside world" and how you see it affecting them. Find out what they already know: you might be surprised—sometimes, the most unlikely people are *farsighted* and well read.

def•i•ni•tion

Someone who is **farsighted** can see the long-range impact of new happenings in a profession or in an organization. Farsightedness is the ability to predict the long-term effect of things such as hiring and policy trends, through staying educated and informed and keeping a hand on the pulse of an institution. By seeing a few moves ahead, the farsighted leader might bang heads with those advocating the short-term solution, but successful leaders often promote and push forward the long-term, big-picture resolution.

When you're returning the company's Annual Report to the lobby, check out and borrow a few recent trade journals. Read up on them, and see what kinds of trends or new phenomena are happening within the industry. Don't assume that your bosses know about the latest and greatest (or latest and most threatening) marvels that are going on out there. Very important people are often very busy people, and sometimes they get lost in the trees while other people are watching the forest. Some of them appreciate when they're told about new events from employees who are paying attention (just as you, the busy motivational leader, appreciate it when your teammates tell you about something new and interesting).

Learn about this new trend or new need. Study up on it. Improve or modify your skills so that someday you might address it. And then watch for the chance to segue this new trend or new need into a new opportunity for you, the leader who's willing to step up and be the expert.

> **Best Voices Forward**
>
> Leadership consultant and salesman extraordinaire Brian Tracy (BrianTracy.com) suggests that there's a close connection between the sometimes imprecise concept of charisma and the more clear-cut notion of matching needs to skills in a nonconfrontational way. When you convey how your skills match the needs of the organization, Tracy says it generates positive emotions toward you. This perceived harmony of needs and skills translates into an aura or halo effect. Such an effect, says Tracy, generates magnetism "to the people who look up to you, who respect and admire you, the members of your family, and your friends and coworkers." This attractiveness often converts to charisma, the ultimate creation of positive emotions around you.

There's a saying among salespeople: "No need, no sale." That is, if a prospective customer doesn't perceive a need for the product, then the salesperson has little chance of selling it. The same goes for big-impact leadership: if the organization or the team doesn't feel there's a need for a strong personality in charge, you may be relegated to the role of caretaker or paper shuffler. But if the organization senses a weakness that you can help remedy or an important, long-term goal that you can help them aim for, then the odds of your "selling" yourself as a transformational leader, as well as serving that role successfully, dramatically increase. More thoughts on the selling of your skills as a motivational leader …

Make Your Skills Fit the Needs

While you may agree or disagree with the politics and political legacy of Ronald Reagan (as with the legacy of Kennedy, discussed in Chapter 2), it's difficult to argue that Reagan was anything other than the consummate motivational leader, especially when it came to "selling" himself to the American people during the years leading up to and comprising his U.S. presidency. Sensing that the country had lost its sense of strength, optimism, and opportunity, Reagan sought, through his easygoing and straightforward message, to assume a position of national, motivational leadership and to see the country forward to a renewed perception of greatness. During his "auditioning" for the job of president, he boasted about his successes as California governor, his experience as the head of a major union, and his ability to gather a star team of idealists anxious to make a difference in the White House. In sum, he sensed what the country needed, and he fit his skills as a no-nonsense bureaucrat and chief administrator in selling his capacity to transform the nation. It was the model of matching skills to perceived needs. If you didn't subscribe to Reagan's political and economic view-points, I hope it won't keep you from purchasing a book or two about his rise to power: he knew as well as anyone how to grow as a motiva-tional leader within the political and national landscape.

As you sense your organization's growth and progress, consider your potential with the outfit. Inventory your strengths; then write them down and think about them. Write a short sentence describing each strength in an exciting way. These sentences will be your talking points, at the ready, when organizational needs come along. Note that you're not interested in presenting yourself as a jack-of-all-trades, master-of-none. Instead, you prefer to have a few easy-to-state, easy-to-summarize tools that you can bring to the table. Periodically, you might conduct a *SWOT analysis* of your organization. When you see a need or two develop within your shifting work backdrop, jump at the chance to declare these strengths and offer yourself as a possible solu-tion.

def•i•ni•tion

A **SWOT analysis** is a simple method for assessing where your organi-zation is. "SWOT" is an acronym for the four things you look at with this planning tool—your organization's strengths, weaknesses, opportunities, and threats. Strengths and weaknesses are considered internal factors; opportunities and threats are considered external factors. The SWOT analysis was created in the 1960s by Albert Humphrey at Stanford University.

Inspiring leaders whom I've studied or worked with over the years have said it a hundred times in a hundred different ways: if you want to take charge, just ask. Presenting your thoughts and suggestions and pre-senting yourself as a willing leader separates you from the pack. Your enthusiasm might not take you where you want to go right away—but, then again, it might. If you're inclined *not* to ask for the opportunity, not only is it much less likely to happen, but you might find yourself stepping aside for the person who eagerly asks for the leadership role instead of you.

Incidentally, don't be one of those aspiring managers who conveniently creates an organizational weakness to fit their areas of expertise. Make sure that, when you present yourself as a potential leader, you are submitting yourself as the answer to a real problem and not a fabricated one. If you work for a business that doesn't have problems, first, pinch yourself, because you might be dreaming. Then, second, think of ways that you might be able to take this great company to a new, better level, how you might be a vehicle for making it happen, and present yourself that way.

Don't Be Shy

There's nothing wrong with a dose of humility. After all, Clint Eastwood had a point when his movie character Dirty Harry said, "A man's got to know his limitations." However, there's a difference between humility and meekness. If you want to take charge of and inspire groups of people to do wonderful things, the last thing you want is an unassuming nature. There is a distinct advantage to brashness. It's not arrogance, but a type of assertiveness that, when combined with courtesy and personal concern for others, serves to classify you as someone willing to take charge and assume large responsibilities.

Being brash doesn't mean assaulting the big boss on the elevator in the morning. ("Good morning, sir," you shout, as you press every button on the panel for maximum face time. Naw, that's just obnoxious.) But it does mean occasionally "standing in the traffic" of important people. Where do the influential people in your organization go for lunch? Is there a "regular spot"? Go there. You don't have to worm your way into a conversation. Just be seen there on occasion. Say hello. Carry yourself professionally.

I have worked at several locations where there were huge disconnects among the meat-and-potatoes employees, the operations people, and the administrators. (At various times in various jobs, I have served in each group.) To close the gap and, at the same time, make myself visible, I ate in the employee cafeteria. In some jobs, I have consistently been, for example, the only nonoperations person in the room. But I promise you one thing: the operations people always approach me for conversation and my opinion. And if I ever need an operations-type favor, it is much easier to ask someone with whom I have dined and conversed. What are the odds that one of those operations people could be my boss someday, or that one or more might be on a team that I manage? Who knows? But it is a very small world, and I put myself in a position of advantage by not being shy or unsociable.

One Step Back

Don't ever brag about your scores on an IQ test or standardized management proficiency test as a way of asserting your leadership skills. Jeff Fuchs, management trainer and president of Neovista Consulting, LLC (NeovistaConsulting.com), says he has seen many an embarrassing situation where an aspiring leader "played the intelligence card" in an attempt to pull rank on others. "Sometimes the score comes up, sometimes it's indirectly referred to," he says. "But in both cases, it's very embarrassing and certainly counterproductive to developing a good leadership relationship." Fuchs suggests that there are so many different types of work proficiencies—fiscal, logistical, mechanical, emotional—that if you consider yourself leader-worthy or better than others simply because of a good standard proficiency test score, you're probably being too self-centered. More importantly, you're overlooking the important proficiencies that others have to offer the team.

When I was a lieutenant in the U.S. Army at Fort Bragg, North Carolina, I was being considered for something called a target acquisition battery command. Sound important? Maybe it was, maybe it wasn't, but it sure seemed appealing at the time, and I was very interested in the position. Anyway, I sized up who I considered to be my biggest competition—a good friend and colleague named John. I remember asking myself, "How do I get myself noticed over John?" I decided that the best way was to starch a uniform, spit-shine a pair of jump boots, and show up at brigade headquarters under the flimsiest of excuses. That is, I wanted to "stand in the traffic" of important people. And so I showed up the next day in a perfect uniform and, as soon as some paperwork needed to go to headquarters, I eagerly volunteered to deliver it.

As I entered brigade headquarters, who do you think was leaving? That's right—John, his uniform as crisp as ever, was on his way out. We nearly bumped into each other, laughed at what we both knew was going on, and continued on our ways. Who got the job? A different person altogether, who I'm sure had done an even better job at selling himself for the mission.

Embrace Your Organization's Vision

Just as your profession and your company change with the times, so does the vision of the organization. As you attempt to match your skills and strengths to the needs of the company, you should also try to fit them to this vision. As mentioned previously, the motivational leader is the ultimate cheerleader for a company's vision, and keeper of its long-term ideal of where it wants to be. As the organization grows, you, the motivational leader, increase your part and your impact fighting for this grand plan.

That's an important point: toward the top of a business's list of critical needs is the need for people who will embrace, promote, and carry out its vision. As you show willingness to learn about your company and where it wants to go, you identify your importance.

The term *company person* can have different connotations. It can be used in a negative fashion to describe someone who is too eager to please the big boss, perhaps at the expense of or disregard for her team. The phrase can also be used in a positive light, to describe someone who is "into" the company and stays tuned into company happenings, successes, expansions, and future goals, and who wants to advance as the company develops. I suppose I've been called a company person in both regards. That is, at different times, people have meant it unflatteringly and approvingly. But, to be sure, I strive for the latter meaning. The point is to serve as the company vision personified—a walking version of what the company is all about and the philosophies that it encourages.

If you strive for that second, admiring definition of company person, make sure that, as you grow within the company as an advocate for its vision, you bring your team into the experience as much as possible.

As emphasized throughout this text, remember that you have as much to learn from your team as anyone else, and you should never discount other people's experience and know-how. For that matter, as you advance and help to form your organization's vision, why not have your team members offer their input? When I was an employee some years ago for Bell Atlantic (now Verizon), we were taught about "the shadow up," meaning that all employees had the capacity to help the company develop and plan and chart its course. I thought it was a novel idea—that influence did not have to always be top-down but could sometimes be bottom-up, as people bought into the vision and hoped to be a part of making it happen.

Gather Input from the Team

Speaking of team influence and "the shadow up," I can't stress enough that growing as a motivational leader within an organization means convincing your team members that it's worth it to share important information with you. First, sell your team on your abilities and your interest in them the same way you sold the larger organization on your leadership potential. Tell them what you offer them. Explain your plan if a plan is called for. Let them know (one at a time, if necessary) what's in it for them if they support you. You don't have to bribe them—your promise might be no more than offering mature, steady management, some knowledge, and a voice to the higher-ups when required.

Again, don't be the foolish boss who thinks that the highest-ranking people in the company are the ones who always know what's best for the organization. Of course, don't ignore them—they're the ones paying your salary and, in all likelihood, setting the parameters for you and your team to follow. But high-ranking people spend a lot of time in meetings, often talking about doing things instead of actually doing them. Your team members—well, they're doing the doing. And, therefore, they probably know about the doing. Dig into that knowledge and experience as much as you can.

Some organizations formalize this input, using feedback tools such as *360 evaluations*, where leaders are obliged to listen to opinions and advice from all sides and all tiers. The idea is to make a leader humble enough to open himself up to criticism and comment and to indoctrinate himself to the notion that all assessments, regardless of their sources, are worth considering.

def•i•ni•tion

A **360 evaluation** is a motivational leader's method for gathering criticism and advice from all levels surrounding the leader—above, below, peer, and even self. The 360 evaluation form often includes comments about a leader's capacity to give direction, offer encouragement, and consider the opinions of others. These evaluations are generally better received when they involve leadership development, rather than determining promotions or raises. The most common criticisms of 360 evaluations are that they generate too many piles of paper (unless they're done electronically), that they're not confidential enough, and that higher-level managers don't actually do them.

It should be mentioned here that the trend at this writing seems to be away from lots of formal leadership development, such as 360 feedback and training in organizational effectiveness. Some consultants I keep in touch with recently have lamented that longtime corporate clients have cut back on leadership development and some of the multitiered appraisal systems mentioned. What a shame that the art of leadership might be getting underestimated or devalued just when academic and professional studies suggest the value of having good people in charge. "Not all management teams are looking for 'carpenters,'" said one mournful consultant. "Some of them just want people with hammers!"

Balance Your Loyalties

Unless you're running your own company or your own operation, you have two groups of people to answer to as a motivational leader—the people above you and the people below you. As you grow as a leader within the organization, be sure to balance those loyalties. It's not an easy task. In fact, it's a very dynamic, circuslike undertaking. But to be a truly effective leader, at any given time, your loyalty "down" must equal your loyalty "up." If you only exercise loyalty up, your team will recognize you as too much of a corporate partisan, and you will lose their support. On the other hand, if you only exercise loyalty down, the company will consider you too much of a panderer to your team and not true to the vision of the larger organization. Again, it's a tough balancing act and the situation is very fluid, but at the end of any work-day, you should ask yourself, "Was I as loyal to my team as I was to my supervisor, and vice versa?"

The inventor of computer software, the late Grace Hopper, gave speeches on leadership into her eighties and was known for speaking to audiences about the need to balance loyalties. "Loyalty up equaling loyalty down—that's the key," she'd say. A math professor who revolutionized technology by getting computers to understand English, Hopper was passionate about a team leader's allegiance to both the project *and* the team members who were being asked to make it happen. From her perspective, you couldn't have one without the other. That's a pretty emotional, "right-brained" (feeling, holistic) standpoint from someone whose background and fame was for something as "left-brained" (logical, mathematical) as computer pioneering.

Best Voices Forward

Following his "You're hired!" victory on NBC-TV's *The Apprentice*, Kelly Perdew, a venture capitalist, worked for Donald Trump for a year. Perdew says he was amazed by how many people had been working for Trump for 20 years or more. When Perdew asked Trump what he looked for most in his employees, Trump answered, "More than anything else, loyalty." Perdew points out that, when a company hires a new CEO, that new leader often brings over his or her own team. Why? Because they bring with them their loyalty to this leader—valued above all else.

Incidentally, when I once spoke about complementary loyalties before a large group of corporate leaders, the mid-level manager of a water treatment company raised his hand and suggested that I was leaving out an important part of the balancing act. "You're forgetting about loyalty to one's peers," he said. "If you don't network with colleagues on the same level, both inside and outside the company, you're in trouble. Without friends, management becomes a very lonely, difficult job." His point was well taken. Managers are like soldiers: their experiences are unique and challenging, and the distinctiveness of these shared events fosters a certain brotherhood/sisterhood/kinship that's worth translating into work-related friendships. The occasional dinner or golf outing with other motivational leaders on the same professional tier, with the goal of sharing stories, seeking advice, or simply letting off manager steam, makes lots of sense. And if you're ever looking for a new leadership opportunity, such a network serves as a "first response" phone list.

Being able to balance your loyalties is another tool in the image-and-routine toolbox that makes you a motivational leader. It's part of the image and everyday life practices that make you one of those people who control their surroundings and their experiences, rather than being controlled by them.

The Least You Need to Know

♦ The motivational leader accepts the volatility of any profession or organization, reads up on trade journals and annual reports to seek new trends and new organizational needs, and becomes the expert on those things, hoping to someday match his expertise to these new necessities.

♦ An aspiring motivational leader inventories her strengths and creates a short, exciting sentence for explaining each one, ready to state them as a solution whenever an organizational need makes itself evident.

♦ The would-be leader is not shy: he offers an assertiveness that doesn't quite cross into arrogance and combines it with genuine conscientiousness and concern for others.

♦ An organization's list of critical needs includes people who are eager to learn about, embrace, promote, and carry out the organization's vision.

♦ Growing as a motivational leader means tapping into one's team members, after selling them on the benefits they'll get for supporting and, in a sense, teaching their boss along the way.

♦ As the leader grows within the organization, she needs to ensure at any given time that the loyalty she shows her superiors is equal to the loyalty she shows her team, and vice versa.

Part 2

Gain Entrusted Power from Others

The effective and inspirational leader knows the different sources of power, how to utilize them, and how people are persuaded. She appreciates the limitations of formal power and the unlimited potential of personal power. She knows how to blend rewards with counseling or appropriate reprimands and how to channel her team toward common goals.

The leader is also aware of the politics in her organization and the power that her political connections can bring about. She keeps track of connections and personal favors—without becoming too caught up in such things. Notably, she blends politics with a heavy dose of personal consideration, personal accountability, an aura of openness, caring, and courtesy.

Chapter 5

Understand What the Experts Say

In This Chapter

- ◆ Understanding the nature of power
- ◆ Highlighting various forms that power takes
- ◆ Showing an organization's need for power
- ◆ Learning the difference between seized power and entrusted power
- ◆ Understanding politics and quiet negotiating
- ◆ Avoiding misuses of power

Motivational leaders know the true meaning of the word *power* and from where it originates. They understand the different types of power and how these types are combined to work best. Motivational leaders appreciate the necessity of power in all kinds of organizations and the importance of someone who is in charge. They know that power is most effective when it is granted, or entrusted, to the person at the helm by the larger team or organization. They respect the role that politics and above-board negotiating plays in garnering power. And motivational leaders know how to keep power from taking on an unfortunate life of its own. In this chapter, we'll learn what real power is, what it *isn't*, and why the most imposing boss isn't always the most effective.

Consider Experts' Thoughts on Power

It's difficult to discuss the word *power* without feeling a little uncomfortable. After all, if your team is to be inspired by you, the motivational leader, the last thing they want to hear (or overhear) is a conversation about power and how it can be used to wield influence over others. Imagine walking by a conference room and hearing *your* bosses conversing about how much power they have and how successful they've been at manipulating *you*!

I can't help but recall that medieval movie classic, *Conan the Barbarian*, with Arnold Schwarzenegger in the title role. James Earl Jones plays the evil ruler, Thulsa Doom. In one scene, Schwarzenegger and Jones's characters are discussing the concept of power. "There, on the rocks—that beautiful girl," says Jones, motioning to a young lady (one of many) high up at the edge of a cliff. "Come to me, my child," he shouts up to her. Hypnotically, she happily steps towards him, dropping off the cliff to her death. Jones looks to Schwarzenegger and states *"That* is power!" (I wonder if Schwarzenegger brandishes such influence over his staff as governor of California.)

Unfortunately, when most of us hear the word *power*, those are the images conjured up: primordial dominance, repression, restraint, manipulation—even destruction. Interestingly, the word's origins have little to do with any of those things. The definition of power dates back to the fourteenth-century Middle English term *pouer*, which means "to be able," and even farther back to the Latin word *potis*, which means "able." In other words, power, in its purest, most original form, is not really about oppression at all, but rather it's about the ability to get things done without disruption or disturbance from others. When you "empower" others, you're not really handing them the Sword of Conan, you're simply saying, "I'm giving you the freedom to accomplish your task without my meddling or the meddling of others whom I control." And that's how you need to consider power—as not only the capacity to direct others, but also the freedom to reach goals without unnecessary holdups from your team members or your supervisors.

Power—as well as the things that help give you power, like status and a keen sense of negotiation—is important to any business, because getting things done almost always involves dealing with both people you supervise and people you're not formally in charge of. By exerting some type of influence over all these people, and by maneuvering in such a way that you avoid their obstacles, you are able to accomplish things in ways that set you apart from others.

Let's consider for a moment what some experts over the course of history have had to say about power.

Repeated Excellence

In the 1960s, behavioral psychologist David McClelland suggested that, although power is one of three basic human interaction desires, not everyone desires it equally. He said that while some people crave high levels of power and all that goes with it, others prefer to seek high levels of achievement or high levels of affiliation (relationships) with others. His theory is considered useful in recognizing why some people seek power and others don't. McClelland noted that this craving could be useful to organizations and that companies should provide motivational leaders who seek high levels of power with the opportunity to manage others. His theory also suggested that there are ways to lead other than seeking unrefined dominance over others.

Max Weber

Max Weber was a German socialist at the dawn of social psychology in the early 1900s. His "Protestant Ethic" thesis suggested that religious principles and ideals created capitalism as an economic concept and practice among nations.

Weber argued that power is formed during a crisis. He suggested that strong personalities rise to the forefront as people seek resolutions and as they become willing to go along with the sometimes radical new vision of a leader. He also noted that workers tend to react well to rewards—an original concept at a time when workers were simply fired or punished for poor performance, rather than being rewarded for doing good work.

> **Best Voices Forward** _____
>
> There's an old saying: "Those who can't do it, teach it." Is that a truthful statement? *Fugheddaboudit!* Max Weber wasn't just some crusty old sociology professor in Germany, writing and lecturing about power and leadership. Weber left university life to serve as a director of army hospitals during World War I. He was also a chief negotiator for Germany at the Treaty of Versailles, which ended the war. Weber once said that when people became more preoccupied with procedural trifling than with simply getting things done, they reached an unfortunate state he called the "polar night of icy darkness."

Frederick W. Taylor

Frederick W. Taylor is often called the Father of Scientific Management. He was an industrialist in the early 1900s. While Weber was doing his thing in Germany, Taylor was doing his thing in Pennsylvania. When American universities began offering business degrees during that time, they based large parts of their curricula on the management theories Taylor had developed as a machine supervisor at Bethlehem Steel.

Taylor believed that every job could be broken down and optimized by each task. That is, he believed that management should be approached as a science (an argument I wholly subscribe to). More importantly, Taylor believed that power within an organization works best when it is shared between management and the workers. He believed that, since supervisors and workers essentially need each other, they should both hold sway over how an organization runs and how jobs are set up—a pretty novel and ground-breaking way of thinking a hundred years ago.

Peter Drucker

Whereas Taylor is often referred to as the Father of Scientific Management, Peter Drucker is often called the Father of Modern Management. This economist and author was given access to General Motors in the late 1940s, and he wrote and consulted extensively on how the company could improve the way it managed itself. Taylor was fascinated with how work was evolving in such a way that workers were becoming smarter, in a sense, than their bosses.

Like Taylor, Drucker believed that power was best shared between managers and workers, and that managers were most powerful when they advocated a sense of community among their employees. A writer of dozens of books still highly referenced to this day and a columnist for *The Wall Street Journal* into his eighties, Drucker suggested that the most powerful leaders are the ones most willing to purge themselves of old thinking and embrace new, innovative ways to achieve success.

Peter Senge

An engineer and an MIT professor, Peter Senge became well known in management circles with his 1990 text *The Fifth Discipline*, still on bookstore shelves and still very much referenced today.

Senge argues that the most powerful leader is a highly adaptive leader and that, subsequently, the most successful organizations are ones that grow and learn along the way in similar fashion. He also suggests that the most powerful leaders are ones who can sell a vision of great things to come to their team members.

Know the Different Types of Power

If we consider power as the capacity to get things done, unhampered, then it's worth looking at the various ways that this ability is provided to the motivational leader.

There are fundamentally two ways that you acquire power: it is either given to you in one manner or another by your supervisor or your organization, or it is garnered by you through something that you do for yourself. In the early 1960s, psychologists John French and Bertram Raven offered a now-famous catalogue of the different types of power and how it is acquired in the two ways just mentioned. The following discussion draws heavily from their studies.

Position Power

Position power is the power you acquire through the way your management position is set up within the organization. There are six types of position power.

The first type of position power is *legitimate power*. This is essentially the formal authority, written out in your job description. It is power that is handed to you by your superiors with their blessings to use it. The key word here is *legitimate:* this is a power that is rightfully yours. That is, with this power, you have the right to exercise influence over someone else as provided by your company.

def•i•ni•tion

John French and Bertram Raven suggested that the two main categories of power were **position power** and **personal power**. Position power relates to a manager's job description and the formal authority that he or she is handed in that job. Personal power, on the other hand, is power that is gained through personal attributes, such as expertise and the ability to make friends, demonstrate loyalty, and stay politically astute.

The next type of position power is *reward power*. Reward power is your capacity to get things done by offering company-sanctioned rewards. For example, when I was a shipping supervisor some years ago, I was allowed by my boss to release my workers whenever the last truck of the day was loaded and still pay them for eight hours of work. Amazingly, we went from taking about eleven hours to load a dozen trucks to about six and a half hours to load a dozen trucks. Yes, we were paying an hour and a half worth of income to a crew that was no longer around, but we were saving all kinds of overtime pay—three hours to several workers at time-and-a-half. The reward of leaving early and remaining on the clock clearly outweighed the benefit of slowing down and milking the trucks for overtime. Plus, the administrators were happy (which is a wonderful thing) because they could leave at an earlier time.

Besides time off, other types of power-generating rewards include pay increases, bonuses, meaningful gifts, and promotions. It's worth mentioning that the amount of reward power is often correlated with not only the value of the rewards, but also the *perceived* value of those rewards. If you're offering free cars but no one knows how to drive, even this seemingly valuable reward might not generate much power.

French and Raven suggested that another type of position power was *coercive power*. Whereas reward power is offering incentives to get jobs done, coercive power is applying negative reinforcements with the same goals in mind. Coercive power is power that is generated by the ability to apply punishment, withhold awards, or reduce awards. Although it's the power many of us see the most often in life, it is also considered by many experts to be the least effective type of power, because it fosters resentment and creates an environment where people only work and act responsibly when the boss is around.

In the later years of their work, French and Raven and their protégés added two more types of position power to the list—*informational power* and *connectional power*. Informational power is power derived by one's control over information. By having first access to data, you can decide who gets it, and you can interpret the data before handing it out. Of course, the motivational leader does not ration information to prop up his or her influence, but instead keeps all lines of communication open, both to special sources of facts and figures and to the team members who depend upon them. Connectional power is power that is garnered by personal connections. In other words, it's power you get from who you know, how well you know them, and what they can do for you.

There's one more type of position power that French and Raven might not have considered back before the age of computers—what's called *ecological power*. This power is gained by controlling the technical, electronic environment of people. By making information and guidance easily conveyed through, say, e-mail and web access, a leader makes good use of ecological power. In a less technical sense, this type of power is also applied when a manager makes a team's physical surroundings more amenable to work, such as providing better lighting or more sunlight or more comfortable work furniture. Ecological power, at times, is also used to describe how jobs are designed to encourage personal feelings of worth and the potential for success and growth.

Personal Power

Along with the six types of position powers, French and Raven suggested that there were two types of *personal power*.

The first type of personal power is *expert power*. Expert power is the power gained from holding a highly specialized skill or expertise in a particular area. Expert power is not unique to managers: anyone on a team can wield expert power, especially if the skill applies to an important team or organizational goal. Of course, once the need goes away, so does the expert power. Also, once the expertise becomes obsolete or commonplace, the expert power goes away.

The second type of personal power is what I consider to be the strongest of all powers—*referent power*. Referent power is the power to persuade others through charisma, personal interaction, and other personality qualities. In many cases, referent power works simply because the follower wants to identify with and seek approval from the motivational leader. Traits such as likeability, friendliness, trustworthiness, and displayed confidence play into referent power. It also can be gained through other personal attributes, such as attractiveness or those physical things that a particular culture identifies with authority. For example, in the United States, the appearance of health or wealth might add referent power. In parts of Asia, age might add referent power.

Appreciate That Power Is Necessary

So, we've considered what power is, what the experts have said about it, and what forms it can take within an organization. But we haven't addressed an important consideration: is it really necessary? Companies like Microsoft and Google conjure up images of family-like settings, with very creative people chumming around, taking midday naps, and having access to all resources and all people all at once. Doesn't sound like much power-struggling going on there, does it?

The answer, again, goes back to the origins of the word *power:* "to be able to." If today's creative companies portray an atmosphere of chaos, I suggest that you take a good look at their income statements and balance sheets. If there's chaos in those buildings, it's managed chaos. Clearly, some people are ultimately in charge, projects have strong personalities at the helm, and power—the capacity to do things without being hampered—is being utilized, big time. It's not power comparable to the bowing of minions before a grand ruler. But that was never the type of power we were talking about. And, indeed, that's not what power, in its truest form, means anyway, at least not to the motivational leader.

Consider for a moment the example of billionaire businessman and New York City mayor Michael Bloomberg. His mayor's office is not an office at all, but a large, open bullpen space, taking up the entire floor of a public building. There aren't even cubicles—just many desks, circled around his desk, with the appearance of a disorganized, circus atmosphere, much as you might find on a stock trading floor on Wall Street. The setup is meant to portray open access and personal accountability, both to Bloomberg and to his lieutenants. But, for all its disarray, make no mistake about it: there's still someone in charge of that room. It's Bloomberg—one of America's most powerful people.

Best Voices Forward

Why would any successful billionaire businessperson want to step out of the boardroom and into the harsh glare of public service? That is, why would a motivational *business* leader desire to become a motivational *government* leader? Michael Bloomberg, the head of financial information company Bloomberg L.P., was asked if it had been worth spending tens of millions of his own money to get elected mayor of New York. His response: "I've got the greatest job in the world. There's no other job in government where the cause and effect is so tightly coupled where you can make a difference every day in so many different ways and in so many different people's lives. It's a great challenge." That's what motivational leadership is all about—making a difference.

Notice that, aside from coercive power, none of the forms of power mentioned above have much, if anything, to do with compelling or intimidating people. Instead, they have to do with persuading and influencing people, and, in some cases, channeling people in such a way that they no longer function as obstacles. Things like rewards and communication and expertise and friendliness certainly don't *sound* like the items brought up in a conversation about power—at least not the stereotypical notion of power. But that's what power is all about—getting people to allow you to get things done, getting people to do things for themselves, and getting people to move out of the way for your team.

Use Entrusted Power, Not Seized Power

We all enjoy a good story about a corporate power play: the drama, the ruthlessness, the blindsided executive. Hey, it's great drama, and we eat it up. However, keep in mind that there's a big difference between power holders and motivational leaders.

A person can hold power but not be much of a leader (we've all had to answer to *that* person at some point in our lives), and a person can be an extraordinarily transforming leader without having any formal power whatsoever (such as Nelson Mandela, who inspired a nation of apartheid reformers even as he sat in a jail cell for decades). Even when someone successfully seizes formal authority, he isn't guaranteeing himself influence within the company. People do not necessarily follow someone just because he holds a title, and they do not follow rules and decrees simply because they're issued. If you ever find yourself in a situation where you're going to attempt a power grab, even for a noble reason (to save an organization from a ruthless or corrupt director, for example), you'd better make sure you hold the support and high regard of most of the team players before taking the risk.

The fact is that power is invariably mirrored. Very powerful people—even dictators—leverage their dominance with the clout, capability, and favors they provide others. It's a simple matter of numbers: there are more of them than there are of you. And if you don't give people a reason to *want* you in charge, they are going to take it away from you, one way or another, at one time or another.

One Step Back

Avoid assuming a position of power unless you have the support of most, if not all, key players. In 1995, billionaire investor Kirk Kerkorian attempted to buy out the Chrysler Corporation and make it a privately held company. Kerkorian mistakenly believed that Chrysler executives would support the stock purchase offer. Instead, his deal was viewed by the board as a hostile takeover scheme. Kerkorian, caught off guard by Chrysler's aggressive stand against his power leveraging attempt, lost the support of his financiers and eventually withdrew the offer, leaving him to watch as Chrysler later merged with German manufacturer Daimler-Benz.

As a motivational leader, what you need to say to your team is, in essence, "Allow me to be your leader—allow me the power to supervise and to take this team to a good place." Once you have the entrusted power and trusting cooperation of others, you will become formidable in your influence. At that point, you will know the meaning of *real* power—not simply ceremonial power.

Know Where Negotiation Fits In

If it seems like power involves a lot more give-and-take than the word's connotations suggest, well, it does. The most powerful people are invariably the most adept negotiators. These people are consummate politicians, because they use organizational cooperation and compromise to achieve the outcomes they desire. Their tactics include building networks of reciprocity, influence, knowledge, and connections. They portray a lofty status and give off the aura of someone who knows how to get things done—or, more importantly, knows the person who can get it done.

If politicians are such unsavory characters, then why do over 90 percent of them get reelected in any given election? It's probably because people tend to think, "Yes, politicians are sleazy, but I guess *my* elected official is okay. I'm inclined to vote for him yet again." It's not by chance that we feel that way. The shake of a hand, the smile at a rally, the returned phone call regarding garbage pickup, and the thoughtful visit to our children's elementary school class—they're all little things the politician does to melt our ice walls, cube by cube, until we're convinced just enough to pull his voting-booth lever once again.

And behind the scenes, he's equally smooth. But in the case of legislating, the shake of a hand translates to, "I'll help pass your bill if you help pass mine." The smile at a rally becomes the smile at a political fundraiser. The returned phone call turns out to be a call to a powerful lobbyist and advisor. And the visit to an elementary school is for the principal who served on his reelection committee.

Do these images leave a bad taste in your mouth? Well, perhaps they should, but it's a taste you should get used to—kind of like the icky medicine you sometimes tolerate to kill the bug that's buggin' you. The somewhat uncomfortable truth is that behind-the-scenes negotiation is simply the way that large groups make decisions and get things done. Politics, really, is little more than the process of interacting, reaching some type of consensus, and moving forward with a plan. If you don't see yourself ever quietly bargaining or returning a favor, then you might find yourself having a tough time leading people.

Without being too overt or too cavalier about it, keep track of your political connections and the favors done for you and those you do for others. Don't make it a game—just show people that you care, that you pay attention, and that you return favors whenever it's ethical and feasible to do so.

Steer Clear of Power Abuses

People don't really have a problem with power as far as putting someone in control. As referenced throughout this text, not much gets done unless someone's in charge, and most of us don't begrudge a person who takes charge. The problem we have with power is its potential for misuse. That means that we fear power for its ability to corrupt others, to make them feel self-important, and to coax them into doing horrible things to keep from losing power or even sharing it. It's like J.R.R. Tolkien's power-mutated character Gollum says in *The Lord of the Rings*: "I *must* have my *precious!*"

There are some pretty straightforward ways to avoid the toxic nature of power and to ensure that neither you nor someone you empower abuses the privilege of being in charge.

First, keep in mind the reason for power's existence is so that an organization can complete tasks and achieve goals. It does not exist for the self-interest of the person who holds the power (although, if she's doing a great job, she certainly deserves appropriate credit and benefits). If power begins to exist for the sake of its holder or for its own sake, it needs to be diminished. If you're the leader and you feel yourself getting taken over by the mesmerizing, addictive nature of your power, put it in check by spreading it out. It is better to give up some (or lots) of your power than to invite the rebellion that's not good for anyone.

Second, encourage the dissenting opinion. Allow open, healthy debate before reaching a decision. Encourage consensus, but leave the door

cracked open enough so that the opposing voice is still heard and considered.

Third, emphasize and institutionalize ethical behavior in your organization. This includes structural checks and balances, oversight committees, ethics training, and, possibly, leadership term limits. These things
are not just niceties: companies in recent years have paid dearly for the
ethical failings of power-infected, corrupted leaders. Many of these
groups dissolved, unable to weather the damage to their reputations,
their leadership structures, and their bottom lines.

The Least You Need to Know

- ◆ Power has more to do with freeing yourself from the obstacles
  others create than it does with dominating people. Experts
  throughout history suggest that power works best when it is
  shared among people in mutually beneficial ways.

- ◆ Position power is gained through formalities, rewards, punishments, information, acquaintances, and technology. Personal
  power is gained through expertise and qualities that foster likeability and respect.

- ◆ The use of power—that is, influencing people and maneuvering
  around obstacles—is necessary, even in seemingly creative organizations that don't appear on the surface to need structure and
  authority.

- ◆ Power is most formidable when it is entrusted to the supervisor
  through the cooperation of people on the team, rather than being
  seized or forced upon people.

- ◆ Political interaction and negotiation are often an important, if
  uncomfortable, part of leading, and it pays to keep tabs on friendships, connections, favors, and favors returned—assuming they're
  legal and ethical.

- ◆ To make certain that neither you nor someone else becomes corrupted by power, keep the power focused on the needs of the
  organization, keep an open flow of vigorous debate and dissenting
  opinions, and make ethical behavior part of your organization's
  training and foundation.

Chapter 6

Understand Organizational Behavior

In This Chapter

- ◆ Observing the way people conduct themselves in groups
- ◆ Avoiding the inherently flawed nature of groups
- ◆ Avoiding the dangers of groupthink
- ◆ Assessing your team's organizational behavior
- ◆ Knowing what makes your most important asset tick
- ◆ Motivating people without manipulating them

Motivational leaders understand how people conduct themselves differently in groups. These leaders know how to celebrate and utilize the positive aspects of team spirit and membership while watching out for and keeping in check the more unfortunate aspects of group identity. Motivational leaders know what groupthink is and how to prevent it. They understand the importance of tapping into the minds and behaviors of their team members without being dictatorial or manipulative. In this chapter, we'll consider what makes groups work, what makes them fail, and how it is possible to channel them without tormenting them.

Understand How People Behave in Groups

Perhaps nothing interests sociologists, social psychologists, and leadership researchers more than how differently humans act in packs contrasted with how they behave individually. Organizational behavior is a field of study in itself—worthwhile, controversial, and never dull.

How and Why We Behave Differently in Groups

You should be in tune with how and, to some extent, why a person acts in a different way when he or she is physically around others. Part of it has a lot to do with conformity and inherent human tendencies toward compliance, accord, and general obedience. Perhaps a little less scientifically, it's important to recognize that peer pressure doesn't end in the kindergarten sandbox or in the high school cafeteria. Adults are heavily influenced by what people are doing around them. Often it's not pretty, and it's not responsible. But if we can acknowledge peer pressure as a driving force and work against it whenever appropriate, then we are all better off as workers and people.

People behave differently in a group because they often feel a distinctive bond to the group—an unspoken pride and security. You'll find more about the sense of belongingness mentioned in Chapter 13, but for now, just realize that the desire to be a part of a group is a very, very strong, inborn human need. After water, food, sex, and shelter, it is nature's strongest urge for us.

Finally, from a practical standpoint, people behave differently in a group because they have instant, unrefined access to other people's opinions, responses, and information. That is, groups work differently than do individuals because of the corporeal nature of group communication.

> **Best Voices Forward** _____
>
> Yale social psychologist Stanley Milgram unnerved the academic community in the 1960s by showing how easily people could be ordered to administer electric shocks to others. (The shocks, in fact, were faked.) Milgram was criticized for putting his subjects through the psychological discomfort of thinking they were zapping someone at high voltage—although the vast majority of them continued to do so. Said Milgram: "I'm convinced that much of the criticism, whether people know it or not, stems from the results of the experiment. If everyone had broken off at slight shock or moderate shock, this would be a very reassuring finding, and who would protest?" His findings unsettled us into considering who we are and why we are often so easily swayed.

So What's Wrong with That?

At this point, you might be saying, "Uh, Scott, you're writing about these human characteristics like they're bad. But for someone like me who's trying to keep a team in line, I think they're wonderful. Why *wouldn't* I want a group where people kept their mouths shut, conformed, and towed the line?"

That's a very good question. In fact, many aspects of motivational leadership celebrate the urge for conformity, agreement, and group identity. Without the human propensity for wanting to be a part of the group and for following the group, your life as a motivational leader would, indeed, be much more difficult.

However, remember that in the last chapter it was noted that *entrusted* power is the most robust, most resilient type of power. Power and influence drawn from manipulation, including the manipulation associated with aspects of peer pressure and organizational behavior, might result in temporary victories for you as a leader, but the dysfunctional nature of what you'll have established will ultimately lead to bad planning, bad feelings, and your likely end as the team leader.

Know a Group's Dysfunctional Attributes

History is littered with stories of people taken over by the radical stance. Uncompromising regime crafting, fear mongering, political imprisoning, even mass murdering—they're all a sad, unfortunate part of mankind's story. Are humans *really* wired to do those things? On a one-by-one basis, probably not. There's a pretty good argument that each of us is innately a good person. However, placed in groups, we have a tendency to occasionally do some unbelievably shameful things.

I don't mean to discount personal accountability. On the contrary, if this text celebrates anything, it is the power of the individual who steps forward, accepts responsibility, portrays distinctiveness and trustworthiness, and motivates a group of people to charge forward. However, if you as the motivational leader fail to recognize the dysfunctional inclinations of groups, you might find yourself initially abusing those inclinations and ultimately surrendering to them.

The Polarizing Nature of Groups

The most dysfunctional attribute of a group is that it tends to become very polarized in its opinions and actions. Militant, uncompromising beliefs get thrown around until they accelerate and invigorate the group. People, lacking the alternate (and, often, the sane) opinion, become mesmerized and soothed by beliefs and chants. For example, horrific groups that advocate their superiority over other races or religions are adept at banding together like-minded people and encouraging such polarization.

The impaired nature of many groups is fed in part by the loss of a sense of personal responsibility. That is, it's easier for someone to take the extremist position or carry out fanatical undertakings when he feels blended into—or perhaps hidden within—a group. Albert Einstein noted that such hiding is only temporary. "It is only to the individual that a soul is given," was his commentary on the tendency of groups to act collectively and wrongly.

One Step Back

Be wary of the polarizing nature of groups—both the groups you belong to and the teams you lead. If a group you belong to seems too extreme in its opinions, ask yourself, "How will these opinions be considered ten years from now, and will I want to be associated with those opinions in the future through my membership now?" If you're concerned, split. On the leadership side, if your team members become too intense in their opinions and their influence over the more timid members, nip this excess in the bud by encouraging a diversity of opinion and allowing for the quieter, alternative voice. If a team zealot can't stop poisoning the environment, talk to your HR department about ways to change this behavior or replace this person.

Birds of a Feather

Psychologists have something of a chicken-or-egg disagreement when it comes to group mentality. While some subscribe to the notion that a group mindset can take on a life of its own, thus controlling its members, others suggest that the phenomenon might be a bit more basic. Some psychologists argue that groups, by their nature, are simply made up of like-minded people. That's what brought them together, they argue. So if their opinions become uniform and sharpened, say these psychologists, it's more because of whom these people were to begin with. So what came first: like-minded group members or the polarization of their opinions and actions?

It seems to me that the theory and the unfolding of history lean heavily in the direction of the latter argument. That is, groups, in an intrinsically imperfect fashion, tend to distort, regiment, and intensify the opinions and actions of their members. Take, for example, the notion of groupthink ...

Watch Out for Groupthink

Have you ever sat at a meeting and watched a bad idea—a *really* bad idea—take on a life of its own? Chances are that you didn't speak up against the dreadful scheme, because you knew better, based on past experience. Once certain people on your team had their minds made up, well, that was that. It was probably just better to shut up or play along and then watch as the plan was put into action and the slow train wreck commenced.

You're not alone in having experienced such a phenomenon. It's called *groupthink*, and it's more than just a funny foible of doing business. When people in groups go along with a bad idea—in a spellbinding deference to seniority, compliance, peer pressure, and team spirit—the results can be catastrophic, even deadly.

def•i•ni•tion

> **Groupthink** is the experience of belonging to a group, surrendering to conformity, and allowing plans (often bad ones) to develop without dissent. Once a plan takes form, the group often commits to it passionately and completely. The concept of groupthink was revealed as a psychological concept and exhaustively investigated in the 1970s and 1980s by Yale research psychologist Irving L. Janis. His most celebrated book on the subject is *Victims of Groupthink: A Psychological Study of Foreign Policy Decisions and Fiascoes.*

Among psychologists and management theorists, the jury is still out on how groupthink works and what sort of mental effects are happening within the inner workings of group dynamics. Moreover, as with group polarization, some very intelligent people argue that groupthink is an overstated phenomenon. I'm not one of them. (That's right—I'm neither intelligent nor do I agree!) That is, I belong on the side of the argument that groupthink is very real, very mysterious, and plays a dramatic, often ruinous, role in how people behave. Again, it seems to me that there's enough anecdotal evidence throughout history to suggest that the typecasting, group aloofness, pressures to conform, and existence of conformance bullies within any group make smart and good people often behave dumbly and badly.

Examples of Groupthink

In war, politics, and business, examples abound where intelligent, sure-footed team members got together and allowed groupthink to take over. The prominent military example is John F. Kennedy's decision in early 1961 to help 1,500 Cuban exiles launch an attack at the Bay of Pigs, with the impractical notion that this small infiltration would somehow rally the people of Cuba to overthrow Fidel Castro. After training them, the United States helped the exiles mount the attack and essentially left them to death or imprisonment. In later years, several attendees of the Kennedy planning sessions openly discussed the decision-making process. They all agreed on how hypnotically *right* the decision seemed at the time.

One well-studied political example of groupthink is the planning by Richard Nixon and his group of advisors to put together an enemies list and make life difficult for the people on it, as well as to cover up their direct or indirect involvement in the break-in of the Democratic National Committee Headquarters at the Watergate Hotel. Due to the public release of taped, high-level meetings, social psychologists have had a unique opportunity to pick apart the curious way that grown men, as a group, could invoke such childlike paranoia and create such underhanded (and illegal) schemes. Looking back, the misdeeds of a president and his staff all those years ago still make us pause and reflect. But the historically significant aspect of the Watergate scandal is how some very smart people allowed themselves to be entranced by groupthink.

Initially, you might think that business people would not be so easily swayed by groupthink. After all, they're strong-minded workers who often have stockholders to answer to. However, regardless of their backbones and business savvy, corporate personalities are every bit as susceptible to groupthink. Consider the well-known business failings of recent history—huge corporations crumbling behind money-hemorrhaging front companies and false accounting practices, giant investment firms throwing their good names behind profitless dot-coms, behind-the-scenes lending of hundreds of millions of dollars to executives. Throughout these debacles, there were well-documented meetings. At these get-togethers, otherwise talented, insightful, and charismatic people chose not to voice their concerns or objections. How, for instance, could successful, proven business people—the best of the best—get together and decide, as a group, to change the taste of the most popular soft drink in America? In 1985 it happened, and it was, by all accounts, a marketing disaster. To this day, Coke still calls itself "Classic Coke" to remind consumers that they're drinking the good ol' formula and not the one that was tried and failed over 20 years ago.

Ways to Avoid Groupthink

If you subscribe to the notion that groupthink can ruin your organization—and I argue that you should—then you should take some precautions to avoid or dampen the effects of groupthink whenever you can. These steps are similar to the ways mentioned in Chapter 5 for avoiding autocracy.

The first step is to make certain that your group never becomes too exclusive. Good dynamics are fluid. Great people are recruited. Proven performers leave for promotions and better opportunities. Advisors, collaborators, and contractors show up. Ideas and talent are very porous, and appropriately so. When an organization becomes a "good ol' boys club" or a supercilious group of self-congratulating sticklers, it's time to shake things up.

Second, when you delegate a task, allow for the delegating of an opinion as well. In other words, when you hand over a job, don't smother the assignment with directions or with the overriding customs of the group. Let the person inheriting the mission try a different, better way of doing it. Let that person find a new direction.

Third, again similar to a power balance-and-check, encourage dissent before a decision is reached. Of course, once a course of action is set, it needs some sort of consensus and support. But while ideas are being bantered about, alternatives need to be looked at, and the contradictory voice should be celebrated and respected.

Finally, don't overlook history. Just because a group, in its groupthink naïveté, believes a square wheel will roll doesn't mean that it will. If just one team member, not quite so absorbed by group feelings of infallibility, looks at history and says, "Uh, folks, shouldn't we make this wheel round?", then a lot of trouble and embarrassment could be avoided.

Know Your Organization

When you take over a team as its motivational leader, spend some time assessing its bonding characteristics and idiosyncrasies. In other words, from a *social impact* perspective, what kind of baggage is it carrying?

First, consider the big picture. What's going on in the larger organization? What is the company culture? Do groups form and bond because they love it at the company or because they hate it? What is the corporate climate? Is there downsizing or layoffs going on? If so, are groups forming in some sort of circle-the-wagons, self-preservation mode? As such, is your group bonded in a fair, reasonable way, or are they gathered unfairly, in an elitist, petty, or discriminatory way?

def•i•ni•tion

Social impact theory suggests that a person's behavior is influenced by the group he or she is in, with the size of impact depending upon the forcefulness of the people in the group, their proximity to the person, and their number. This theory argues that a large, tight-knit group with powerful opinions holds dramatic control over each group member.

Next consider the team itself. Are its members alike in social status, background, or outlook? (If so, this could be a good thing or a bad thing.) How's their sense of belongingness? Is there high morale and team pride? Is the peer pressure on par or forceful to the point of harassment? Do team members tend to conform and seek a quiet accord, or is there a healthy whirlwind of ideas and opinions bounding off the walls? Are the ideas and opinions diverse, or are they extreme, polarizing, and uncompromising? Once a decision is reached, do the team members tend to support it or collectively undermine it? What's the communication like? After new information is broadcast, do you get the sense that people are walking away with what was said or what they *thought* they heard (if they heard anything at all)? Is there individual responsibility, or has all ownership been lost within, or diluted by, team identity?

How do meetings run for this team? Are there too many of them? (Or, as unlikely as it may seem, too few?) At the typical meeting, what happens? Is there an agenda? If so, does the meeting tend to veer off course rather quickly? Does one person or subgroup dominate the get-together? Do other team members sit there submissively? Does the person running the meeting (possibly you) completely lose control? Or, perhaps, is the person running the meeting the one who completely dominates it, allowing only compliance and nodding of heads?

Does groupthink exist, in or out of meetings? Is there an overshadow-ing force—a combination of blind loyalty, obedience, peer pressure, and fear of persecution—that creates bad ideas and carries them through to organizational failure?

Once you assess what variety of organizational behavior your team dis-plays, you can tap into the good aspects and work to alter the counter-productive aspects.

View People as an Asset

So why all this psychobabble about organizational behavior? Doesn't motivational leadership have more to do with offering sound advice, setting a good example, and promoting esprit de corps? Does psychol-ogy really play all that big a part?

To answer those questions, look at an unfortunate example: the na-tional dictator. Pick up a text that covers a country's surrender to dic-tatorship or a biographical account of the dictator himself. Did this vile ruler begin his rise to power by gathering rifles in his basement? It's doubtful. Did he begin it by gaining control of some natural resource? A bit more likely, but still doubtful. More likely, this dictator ascended to power by initially tapping into the minds of a small group of pas-sionate, fearful followers and then systematically working to control the minds and opinions of the majority of people.

The dictator, in his ruthlessness, understands something that most well-meaning leaders (like yourself) often lose track of: people are an asset to your organization. In fact, they're the primary asset. They may not go on your accountant's balance sheet, and you may not be able to write off the depreciation of their skills on your taxes. But they are clearly the most important component of your organization. Their knowledge and talent are the driving force for your success as a motivational leader. And their capabilities, just like any other good or service, follow the laws of supply and demand. If you are to keep them around and to keep them focused on the big mission (even world domination!), you need to know what makes them tick.

The bottom line: being able to tap into the minds of your team members and the collective mind of your team and reacting in a positive way to what you find is akin to knowing the inner workings of an important machine or vital computer software where you work.

Get People to Believe in the Program

The key, then, to appreciating and constructively applying the concepts of organizational channeling to your team members is to utilize its precepts in a way that motivates your people but does not manipulate them. Get people to freely believe in your program for success without trying to hypnotize them with exaggerated promises or false feelings connected to membership and compliance.

Recognize that people behave differently in groups and adjust your management style accordingly. Encourage team identity, team membership, and team pride without promoting blind obedience or hardhearted regulation. Celebrate your team's doctrine without advancing the extremist view and without hindering individual thinking. Make sure that your team's collective personality doesn't serve to hide the responsibility and accountability of its members.

Enjoy the open, streamlined communication that comes with belonging to a team, but avoid groupthink by giving serious consideration to alternative ideas whenever possible. Don't get drawn in by the really bad plan just become your team becomes mesmerized by it.

Don't play mind games—they'll backfire at some point. But do embrace your knowledge of organizational behavior as you tap into the minds of your organization's greatest asset.

The Least You Need to Know

◆ When in groups, people are more likely to obey, seek harmony, give in to peer pressure, and feel pride and security. Although motivational leaders can take advantage of this condition, they should be wary of its dysfunctional nature.

◆ The negative aspects of a group include its tendency to become very polarized in its opinions and actions, as well as its members' loss of a sense of individual responsibility.

◆ Groupthink can be avoided by keeping the team roster fluid, by seeking input from outside the team, by delegating decisions along with tasks, by encouraging dissent, and by seeing what has worked for others in the past.

◆ When you first assume responsibility for a team, assess its organizational behavior by determining its morale and pride, its type of grouping, its level of conformity and peer pressure, its meeting culture, and the extremism of its views.

◆ Respect for the mindset of your team members—as well as their collective, organizational behavior—shows that you recognize them as a vital asset to your organization's success and that you want to understand this important asset better.

◆ Get team members to believe in your plan for success by promoting team identity and team pride without obstructing original thought or personal responsibility.

Chapter 7

Use Ownership and Accountability

In This Chapter

- ◆ Asking for and taking responsibility
- ◆ Stopping the buck and the power of veracity
- ◆ Utilizing responsibility as a leadership instrument
- ◆ Offering ownership as a reward
- ◆ Keeping track of the ownership and accountability given to others
- ◆ Never forgetting who's ultimately accountable

Motivational leaders stand out in a culture more prone toward *blame* and self-preservation than *accountability* and ownership of circumstances. Motivational leaders seek new areas of responsibility and encourage others to do the same. They don't pass the buck, and they are genuine in their displays of responsibility. They offer ownership to their team members as a leadership tool and, believe it or not, as rewards. They follow up on the ownership they give out, remembering that the motivational leader is the one who is ultimately responsible. In this chapter, we'll consider how ownership and accountability work as powerful management mechanisms, and how a "passed buck" ultimately comes back to you.

Seek an Endangered Species: Accountability

If you had to make a list of the worst characteristics of the worst boss you've ever had, what types of things would be on that list? They probably would have a lot to do with how little he assisted, backed up, and encouraged your team. And, undoubtedly, somewhere on that inventory would be, "He worries more about covering his you-know-what than anything else." In fact, his preoccupation with self-protection probably worked to the detriment of the team and its mission, and perhaps it became contagious as others on your team sensed the "gotcha" nature of what was going on and decided to turtle themselves into a shell as well.

def•i•ni•tion

The words **accountability** and **blame** are often used interchangeably, which is unfortunate. Corporate consultant Rick Brenner (www. ChacoCanyon.com) notes the important difference. "To be accountable means to be responsible for and answerable for an activity," he says. "Blame is something different altogether. To be blamed is to be accountable in a way deserving of censure, discipline, or other penalty, either explicit or tacit." So accountability has to do with owning a situation and helping the team learn from it; blame has to do with finger-pointing, guilt, and censure.

In the early 1990s, political commentator Charles J. Sykes made the controversial argument that America was rapidly turning into "a nation of victims," as people shunned accountability for their own situations, avoided seeking additional responsibility and duties, and felt utterly blameless for anything going on around them. That might have been a bit much, but anecdotally, it does seem as if people are a bit quicker these days to attribute a tough predicament to everything and everyone other than themselves. (Or am I just getting old?)

Does anyone accept responsibility anymore? Sure! The motivational leader does, and that's what makes him stand out. The motivational leader hunts for accountability as if it were a rare animal—not to assign blame or to absorb blame and fall on his sword for the organization, but to create a positive work atmosphere where people own their own situations, where they get credit for jobs well done, where they can make learning-focused mistakes without fear, and where people aren't afraid to step up to new challenges, new roles, and new responsibilities.

Repeated Excellence

In 1993, Attorney General Janet Reno approved a plan to end a stand-off in Waco, Texas, between Branch Davidian leader David Koresh and FBI agents. Unfortunately, the plan, involving rifles, tanks, and tear gas, failed when the compound either caught on fire or was set on fire from inside or outside or both. Eighty of Koresh's religious followers (and Koresh himself) ultimately died during the raid. Reno, only a few weeks on the job, impressed many on Capitol Hill when she accepted responsibility for the tragedy. "I made the decisions," she said. "I'm accountable. The buck stops with me."

Most importantly, the motivational leader, when asked, "Who's in charge here?" or "Who made that call?" doesn't hesitate to answer, "I am" and "I did." *It's my call and my accountability.* For good or bad, that's the mantra of the motivational leader.

Identify Where the Buck Stops

In the old days of poker, if you didn't care to deal, you passed the responsibility on to the next player by handing her the dealer's marker. Over the years, "passing the buck" has come to mean passing along (or refusing to take) any sort of responsibility in any situation. No wonder "Give 'em Hell" Harry Truman, the 33rd president of the United States, gained notice for keeping the sign "The buck stops here" on his desk. Truman, a no-nonsense leader, was considered a straight talker who didn't mince words and who bravely led this country through the end of World War II, the Korean War, and some of America's most difficult times.

How times have changed. More than straight talk these days, we have politicians using the passive voice to say things like, "Mistakes were made." In other words, mistakes were made, but *I* really didn't have anything to do with making them. How sad, and how we yearn for people who own their situation and pin the badge of accountability on their chest. Clearly, the situation has carried into the business sectors, as we watch corporate big-wigs found guilty and escorted to prison, still insisting they didn't do anything wrong!

Be a distinctive motivational leader. Let the buck stop with you. Let ownership and accountability begin and end with you. The saying, "The fish stinks from the head down," holds merit, but a flower radiates from the head down, too. By saying "Bad call on my part" every now and then, you will gain notice as someone willing to own a problem and its solution. You will also be surprised to find how contagious the attitude is. When your team discovers that it's okay to take responsibility, make some mistakes, and learn in a no-excuses zone, they will follow your lead wonderfully.

Aside from assuming responsibility and setting a positive tone for your team, there's also something very freeing about displaying a personal sense of accountability. Passing the buck might seem easy enough, but if it is to become a habit, it takes lots of time and energy—personal resources that you should be using for more productive endeavors. Saying "Hey, it's my call" is very liberating, as if weights were untied from your feet.

The Power of Veracity

There are several reasons why portraying yourself as genuine and accountable brings power with it, aside from the fact that you immediately set yourself apart from hundreds of other ho-hum managers.

By presenting yourself as someone who owns the situation, you portray yourself as someone who also commands it. I have watched many a leader say to her supervisor, "I've got it under control." Whether she did or not (and she mostly did) was almost irrelevant—the supervisor was impressed enough with her ownership of the situation to let her take the reins.

Being the leader who is accountable projects an image of sure-footed control. You come across as someone in control of the situation, in control of the facts, and even in control of your personal life. You come across as one of those enviable people who has his stuff together. Is the projection a bit flawed and a bit unfair? Sure—but you're on the winning side of the altered image.

Not to dwell too much on the military aspects of motivational leadership, but it's worth mentioning that there's a reason corporate headhunters do so well placing former combat leaders in civilian business jobs. It's because these people are perceived as authentic, responsible, and instantly ready to *own* the situation they're handed.

Finally, portraying yourself as accountable also suggests that you are someone willing to go the extra mile. Taking on additional tasks and enthusiastically seizing the responsibility that goes with them tells people that you're ready for bigger and better things—and that perhaps you hold potential for future promotions or special tasks.

Don't Foster a Culture of Blame

Are you helping to foster a culture of blame in your organization? Massachusetts-based corporate consultant Rick Brenner (www. ChacoCanyon.com) suggests there are 10 bad attributes of a work team that indicate you've become part of a blaming culture.

1. **Blame runs downhill in public and uphill at the water-cooler.** You're in a blaming culture if supervisors rarely assign any responsibility to themselves. Blame almost always runs downhill. But water-cooler talk is the opposite—people grumble about management.

2. **You rarely blame processes.** Blame is rarely assigned to equipment, to a process, or to a situation. If something went wrong, human error is the cause.

3. **You usually blame an individual.** Rarely do you assign blame to a group or to several people. One is enough to satisfy the beast of blame.

4. **You "kill" messengers.** Bearers of bad news are especially at risk, because people have a pattern of "killing" the messenger.

5. **CYA is a standard business procedure.** Since you can't be sure when you might need to cover your (ahem!) assets, it's only prudent to take every opportunity to cover your behind.

6. **In response to catastrophe, you apply revised policy retroactively.** When something bad happens, you convene a panel to write or revise policies and procedures. Then you apply them retroactively, and you blame violators.

7. **You never revise policy in response to success.** When something good happens, you feel that your policies and procedures are validated, so there's nothing to do.

8. **You have designated winners.** When good things happen, you usually assign credit to someone who's already an anointed winner. In a blaming culture, heroes are rarely found in the trenches.

9. **You blame people for breaking unwritten rules.** Some policies and rules are written down only in obscure documents, if they're written at all. No matter. People can still be blamed for violating them.

10. **People get sandbagged.** Some people find out about a failure or policy violation for the very first time in their annual review. This is especially maddening when withholding the information prevented the employee from righting a wrong or from avoiding repetition of the error.

As a team's motivational leader, you must seek to avoid bringing about these attributes, and, if they exist, you must work to stamp them out and encourage a climate of ownership and learning. Brenner suggests: "Remember that blame is almost always inappropriate … learning is a far better choice."

Use Ownership as a Tool

Passing along ownership of situations to people on your team is a valuable tool in your motivational leadership toolkit. There's more on delegating in Chapter 14, but for now, know that ownership and accountability are often self-sustaining qualities of a team, and you might find yourself being asked for part of your work once the mood has been set.

People "dig it" when they can avoid the culture of fear and self-preservation that exists in many organizations. So why not cultivate a culture of ownership, at least in your team if you can't bring it about throughout the organization?

Begin the process of using ownership as a leadership apparatus by asking for volunteers. Sounds easy enough. You might not get too many takers initially, but that's okay. When they see the rewards and the autonomy that those volunteers are given (assuming you grant those things), they'll come around.

Offer a long tether, so to speak, to those volunteers. If the situation allows it, have no tether at all, as you show your trust by setting them free to do great things.

Encourage the notion that admitting to mistakes and sharing them with others is okay. Turn the admissions into learning sessions with the group. Of course, no one wants to sit through a "my blunder's bigger than your blunder" gathering, but a brief talk about what someone did—while owning a project—and how they might improve on it in the future is time and energy well spent.

Finally, maintain good records. Make sure that you document who owns what, what responsibilities have been handed out (although the buck ultimately stops with you, remember), and who has accomplished good things along the way. If it's possible to have that information handy at any given time, such as in a planner or organizer, then all the better. This information allows for mentoring, advocating, and following up.

Promote Ownership as a Reward

There are lots of stories these days about workplace creativity and the companies that cultivate it. They do all sorts of interesting things, such as idea empowerment, periodically mixing up people and dissolving departments, and allowing people to take naps in the afternoon to recharge. (I believe I feel one coming on right now.)

(Ah—that was refreshing. I'm back.) A common thread that runs through many of these settings seems to be the companies' willingness to allow people to own their own little pieces of the universe. In these venues, people don't view individual responsibility and project ownership as a hassle, but as a reward.

There are a few ways, even if you have relatively little power over the human resources aspects of your company, to advocate personal ownership in a way that people will tend to seek it out as a reward.

First, loudly fawn over the people who step up. Make a fuss about them. Let everyone hear it!

Second, grant autonomy whenever possible. People often like to be left alone, especially at work, and especially when they're getting important things done.

Third, make the ownership experience seem fun. Remember ol' Tom Sawyer pretending the fence painting was a good time? After his friends saw what they thought was fun, they all joined in and—sure enough—it *was* fun.

Fourth, make the ownership seem like a learning experience, because, as mentioned previously, it surely is. A manager where I currently work allowed two temporary supervisors to plan out a full day of training. They had to present him with their proposed agenda and how they planned to carry it out. The manager noticed lots of things wrong, but none of them were show-stoppers. So he approved it and, without saying anything more, allowed them to learn for themselves what they might have done better.

Fifth, offer incentives to people who assume extra duties and responsibilities (at least to the extent that you can offer such extras). These incentives include pay, recognition, and all the things that make us perk up when they're given to us. You'll find more on the topic of rewards in Chapter 8.

Follow-Up

A myriad of ideas with no follow-up is nothing but fluff. And starting 100 projects without finishing any of them is akin to starting nothing.

The difference between successful motivational leaders and other managers is that successful motivational leaders write things down in a planner and follow up, especially when ownership and accountability are being assigned.

> **Best Voices Forward**
>
> NBC military/political commentator and Medal of Honor recipient Jack Jacobs suggests that a raw, self-centered attitude violates who we are as people. Jacobs received the Medal of Honor for carrying, dragging, or rescuing over a dozen soldiers during one combat mission in Vietnam, in spite of his suffering heavy blood loss while fighting. Jacobs says that throwing your efforts into your team, without losing track of yourself, is what motivational leadership is all about. Jacobs quotes Hillel the Elder, the Jewish philosopher: "If I am not for myself, who will be for me? But if I am only for myself, what am I? And if not now, when?"

Remember that ownership without follow-up (on yourself and on others) loses its value in a hurry and may, if left unattended, lead to lots of things not getting done.

Here are some thoughts for keeping track of and following up on the ownership and responsibilities you give others.

1. **Try to keep your documentation as simplistic and consolidated as possible.** Again, have it near you at all times if possible.

2. **Prioritize the list.** Some large-scale responsibilities might need to be checked frequently. Others don't need to be checked much at all—even once a month if things are getting accomplished.

3. **Just because you write things down, don't become convinced that they're written in stone.** Be willing to add, take away, or modify ownership and responsibility as people show you what they're made of. If you take autonomy away from a team member, counsel the person about what went wrong and when you're going to give it another try.

4. **Let the people know when you're going to ask for progress reports.** Write down dates and times. Get together with them per

the date and time. If they're caught off guard, schedule the follow-ups closer together. If they're ready for you, schedule the next follow-up a little farther down the road.

5. **Work the list, know the list, and love the list.** It's a wonderful motivational leadership device.

Keep in Mind Who Is Ultimately Responsible

As a lieutenant in the U.S. Army, I remember being told by my commander to pull a few of my soldiers out of jail. They had been arrested for drinking too much and getting into trouble. "Uh, sir," I asked, "all of the men involved have families. Why can't their wives go get them?"

"Because," he stated matter-of-factly, "their behavior is a reflection on this unit and on their platoon leader—you. They should know that, and you should be the first person they see when they're released."

Yikes! *Me* responsible for what a couple of grown men did in their spare time? How was I to control the social habits of a couple of crazy GIs? But at some point, I got the message: I was ultimately answerable for everything that happened to every one of my soldiers, before, during, and after duty. And if one of them screwed up, it was my responsibility to clean up the mess. If one of them got lost—literally or figuratively— it was my responsibility to find them like a lost lamb and show them the way back.

Of course, in the civilian business world, people aren't asked to keep an eye on people 24-7. But sometimes, even things that you don't feel you should be held accountable for will still fall at least partially under your shadow. And at some point, that condition will probably result in your making tough and unpopular decisions. When an organization suffers any sort of setback for any type of reason, it's important to keep in mind who is ultimately accountable.

Yes, it's you. And sometimes it's not pretty. Leadership can be a lonely ship, indeed. I mentioned Harry Truman earlier. Although he is generally considered one of the best presidents ever in the United States, Truman's candor and ownership did not win him lots of popularity contests at the time. After losing a primary and giving up his bid for reelection in 1952, Truman returned to his hometown of Independence, Missouri, arriving with little fanfare as a widely unpopular ex-president. It wasn't until years later that historians and the public came to appreciate the value of his frankness and willingness to make tough decisions.

Do like Truman did. Don't pass the buck. Instead, free yourself from the preoccupation of self-preservation and responsibility avoidance. Celebrate ownership and accountability, and let that celebration spread.

Repeated Excellence

It's not in the nature of politicians to admit mistakes. For example, you could probably count on one hand the total number of times, throughout history, that a United States president has blatantly acknowledged an error. One of those times was during the presidency of Ronald Reagan, a consummate motivational leader in my humble opinion. In 1987, after it became apparent that diplomatic overtures to Iran had degraded into arms-for-hostages deals, Reagan addressed the nation and admitted the misstep. "I take full responsibility for my own actions and for those of my administration," he said. "I'm still the one who must answer to the American people for this behavior. And as personally distasteful as I find secret bank accounts and diverted funds—well, as the Navy would say, this happened on my watch." Reagan's popularity, which had faltered during the investigation, returned to earlier high levels following that speech.

The Least You Need to Know

◆ The motivational leader stands out as one who accepts blame, seeks new areas of dependability, and encourages others to do the same.

◆ By assuming accountability instead of passing the buck, you display yourself as someone in charge, and you free yourself from the worry of constantly trying to protect yourself.

◆ Offering ownership of situations as a leadership tool involves identifying volunteers, providing as much autonomy as possible, addressing mistakes as learning experiences, and keeping documented track of assignments.

◆ Offering ownership of situations as a reward involves giving accolades to volunteers, offering independence and self-rule, portraying the experience as pleasurable, presenting the experience as a learning one, and providing monetary and other employment-related incentives.

◆ Keeping track of and following up on the ownership and accountability you give others helps you to document their responsibilities, prioritize them, modify them, schedule their follow-up, and love the schedule.

◆ Owning a situation and being accountable as a motivational leader means that you'll be held ultimately responsible, even for things that you're only somewhat connected to.

Chapter 8

Utilize Rewards and Discipline

In This Chapter

- ◆ Looking at a brief overview of the business school theories of motivation
- ◆ Drawing from the theories, a basic look at what motivates people
- ◆ Combating resentment among employees
- ◆ Finding the right mix of rewards and discipline
- ◆ Addressing poor performance with counseling and verbal or written warnings
- ◆ Addressing poor performance with discipline

Motivational leaders appreciate the academic models that explain human behavior and how this behavior is changed and channeled.

They're able to tie in these theories with real-world motivators—those things that really point people in the right direction.

Motivational leaders know how to create extrinsic rewards, emphasize intrinsic rewards, and enforce discipline when necessary. They know how to address poor performance, how to counsel, and, unfortunately, how to sometimes punish, and how to do so in ways that help a team member if the team member wants to be helped. In this chapter, we'll learn why leading with only threats and punishments is a formula for disaster and how rewards, even very small ones, can be used effectively.

Learn the Theories of Motivation

Yes, there are some people in charge in this world who administer rewards and punishments just for the sake of amusing themselves. In fact, I think many of my high school teachers fell into that category. And certainly my drill sergeant did (punishments only). But the vast majority of managers and superiors find no joy in rewarding or disciplining people. Quite the reverse—most of them find dishing out *attaboys* or *shame-shamies* a real hassle. There's too little gratitude when rewards are given, and there's too much paperwork when punishments are doled out.

However, you can't be a motivational leader without understanding what motivation is. And you can't motivate people without, at some point, making use of rewards and punishments.

Just as it was important to consider power and organizational behavior from an academic perspective, let's look at some of the theories behind the word *motivation*—a term that's given a lot of lip service but is often presupposed or discounted when it comes to actually stimulating a team.

What Turns People On?

In 1985, business professors James L. Bowditch and Anthony F. Buono offered *A Primer on Organizational Behavior*, which, among other great feats, sorted motivational factors into three categories. Their first category dealt with theories of motivation that answered the question, "What is it that prompts a particular human activity?" These theories were also called *static-content models*, because they looked at what was going on in someone's mind at any given moment, as opposed to what motivated a person over time.

The most prominent theory that answers the "what prompts activity" question is psychologist Abraham Maslow's "Hierarchy of Needs," mentioned briefly in Chapter 1. During the middle of the twentieth century, Maslow suggested that people tend to go from more primitive, basic needs and then, as each need is met, to more enlightened needs. For example, Maslow said that we are motivated, first, by thirst, hunger, and the desire to reproduce. Once these needs are met, we go on to security needs, such as safety and shelter. From there, we are motivated by our innate desire to belong to and be accepted by groups. Again, peer pressure is a powerful motivator. And once belongingness needs are met, we go on to developmental needs, such as the desire for status and inner advancement—what Maslow called *self-actualization*. Maslow suggested that we tend not to move up this ladder of needs until the rung we're on is taken care of, and if a lower-rung need becomes unmet yet again, we move back to that prior rung to address that more basic need again.

Best Voices Forward

Famous, a pioneer, and ever controversial, Harvard psychologist B.F. Skinner was, in many ways, the face of behavioral psychology and the study of motivation. By experimenting with animals, Skinner developed notions on positive reinforcement, where animals performed tasks after figuring out there was a positive effect from doing so (such as a food treat). He also looked at negative reinforcement—bad conditions, such as constant noise, that animals could make go away by performing a similar task. Skinner observed the positive and negative reinforcements that prompted children to behave in certain ways. Controversy over Skinner brewed when he suggested that societies could be shaped certain ways by channeling the collective behavior of citizens. (I'm oversimplifying the argument.) He remains important 70 years after his ideas were first introduced, because he noted that people's behaviors were motivated by their surroundings and by their experiences. "In the behavioristic view," wrote Skinner, "man can now control his own destiny because he knows what must be done and how to do it."

David McClelland's "Achievement-Power-Affiliation Theory," mentioned in Chapter 7, also falls under this category of motivation models. In the 1960s, this behavioral psychologist suggested that each of us is motivated by one or all of three things: the need for accomplishment, the need for control, or the need for bonding with others. Interestingly, McClelland argued that we are each motivated by these three things differently and in different doses, based on our individual life experiences. Importantly, his theory not only proposed that people are drawn toward different things, but he argued that their motivations change throughout their lives as their life stories progress.

What Points People in a Certain Direction?

Whereas "static-content" theoretical models take a snapshot of people and what fires them up at any given time, a group of models called "process theories" consider the before-and-after effect of specific motivators. Bowditch and Buono suggested that theories belonged in this category because they dealt with processes that could channel people's behavior in a particular direction.

Among these process models is the "Expectancy Theory," initially suggested in the 1960s by Victor Vroom. (With a revved-up last name like "Vroom," it's no wonder he investigated concepts in motivation!) Vroom argued that for a reward to work, you must convince your team members that their extra effort will lead to better accomplishment, that the better accomplishment will lead to the promised reward, and that the promised reward is something worthwhile. If the team members don't believe in their ability, the promise, or the reward's worth, then the extra effort won't happen.

Similarly, in the 1970s, British professors Martin Evans and Robert House offered the "Path-Goal Theory of Motivation," suggesting that your team members will travel down paths that lead to rewards, and that, as their boss, you should point out those paths and lead your team down them.

What Keeps People Charged Up?

Once people are motivated toward a certain behavior and pointed in a particular direction, what keeps them doing it? Bowditch and Buono answered this question within their third category of motivational factors, called *environmentally-based theories.*

Two environmentally-based models stand out. One is the "Social Comparison Theory," proposed by social psychologist Leon Festinger in the 1950s. Festinger suggested that people are motivated by comparing their situation to that of other people. This theory explains, in part, how people are prompted to act in a particular way based on what their heroes are doing or perhaps what celebrities are doing. On another level, Festinger argued that people in very bad work environments can rationalize their situation based on how others around them are handling the same environment. In some cases, workers can perceive very tough work as enjoyable if they think others around them are enjoying it as well.

Another, similar model is the "Equity Theory," proposed by J. Stacy Adams in the 1960s. Adams suggested that people are motivated when they perceive fairness within the workplace. That is, if they believe their reward/effort ratio is the same as (or better than) the reward/effort ratio of others, they will continue to work hard. If, on the other hand, they believe that someone is getting the same rewards for less effort, or that someone is getting a bigger reward for the same effort, then they will rebel by working less, calling in sick, and so on.

def•i•ni•tion

The **environmentally-based theories** of motivation are perhaps the most interesting because they are the social psychological theories that deal directly with rewards, punishments, and expected outcomes for work.

Understand What Motivates the Individual

Although some of the above theories don't necessarily mesh with one another, most motivational theorists over the years have agreed on one thing: people are complex creatures. Attempting to apply any of the above models into a cookie-cutter type of leadership application will likely fail. The key is to understand the academic theories, to appreciate what they bring (and what they don't bring) to the table, and to attempt to influence your team in a way that lends a respectful, knowing nod to these teachings.

Let's consider a short list of human motivators that incorporates the above theories in a realistic way.

The Human Motivators

As mentioned earlier, people are motivated, in a big way, by what other people are doing around them. The attraction toward conformity, agreement, and obedience is strong, as is the effect of peer pressure. Don't think for a second that you're above it all—you are drawn toward acceptance by others a lot more than you might know or care to admit.

Another great motivator, of course, is economic reward. It is often thought to be the *only* motivator, which it is not. But good pay, appropriate bonuses, benefits, health care—they all mean something, lots, in keeping good people around and pointed in the right direction. More on such rewards in a moment.

Another fine motivator—or, perhaps, the symptom of a fine motivator—is utility. People tend to be driven by things that are particularly useful to them. If someone promises you a lifetime supply of peanut butter for painting his house, but you're allergic to peanuts, the house will go unpainted. Frequently, managers have trouble offering and adjusting motivators that pertain to the entire team.

It might seem obvious enough, but lots of research has been done to prove the notion that people are very likely to complete a task if they perceive a straightforward connection between the task and the reward. If the path from one to the other is poorly mapped out, defined, or explained, the existence of a reward might not matter at all and, in fact, might have a negative effect if its apparent inaccessibility triggers frustration. But if, as a motivational leader, you are able to demonstrate a very real link between the performance and the prize, you are likely to generate your desired effect.

Along with path attainability is goal attainability. That is, if the way to get to a goal is clear enough, but the goal itself is unachievable, then you might have difficulty getting your team to do the work. Goals must be clearly defined and fairly possible to complete.

A Word About Punishment

What about *punishments*? Yes, people are, indeed, motivated to conduct themselves in ways that avoid reprimand, and it would be silly to write a book on motivational leadership without addressing the process of carrying out disciplinary action. However, you may have noticed that I have placed it at the bottom of this list, and, I suggest, rightfully so. When you administer punishment, you're essentially conditioning people to avoid future punishment—not necessarily to do the right thing. Avoiding punishment might simply mean not getting caught, and the more someone gets caught, the more likely she's going to get better at *not* getting caught. Hopefully, as a motivational leader, you want a team run by people who are concentrating on things other than simply not getting caught.

def•i•ni•tion

A **punishment**, from a psychological perspective, is anything unlikable enough that it prompts someone to reduce the behavior connected to it. Threatening punishment is generally considered the least desirable way for a motivational leader to get people moving in a particular direction, because it directs people away from unwelcome behavior, rather than directing them toward preferred behavior. It also tends to make people clever at avoiding punishment, rather than making them inclined to do good work.

If rewarding is the best way to motivate someone, then let's look at some more rewards.

The Limitations of Pizza and Soda

I have worked at several locations where pizza and soda were offered as rewards to the organization. If a department went so many days without a work-related injury, or if a department reached its production goal or quality goal for the month, pizza and soda (or, at times, a nice catered meal) was offered as a reward and a thank-you to the people who made it happen.

The reaction?

Interestingly, no one—and I mean no one—seemed to appreciate the gesture. They either complained about the meal being cold or second-rate, or they complained that there wasn't enough. Sometimes, they complained about being manipulated, like rats, as if the meal were being offered in a condescending or disdainful manner from the management to its workers. So the workers grumbled, the managers smiled and pretended they didn't hear anything, and everyone ate pizza and drank soda.

Doesn't sound like much of a reward, does it? Why were the workers bitter? And, sensing the resentment, why didn't the managers simply stop the routine? The answer is that both sides failed to grasp the true nature of a reward. A reward, by definition, is a gratifying result or something offered for a special accomplishment. That doesn't have much to do with a slice of pizza held in front of someone's face as a promise for meeting some sort of objective or going without getting hurt for a period of time. If such were the case, then every time a walrus rolled at a theme park for a sardine, we would call it a reward. That sardine may be a work-for-food arrangement, or it may be an automatic positive reinforcement. But it *ain't* no reward.

The fact is that when the same reward (even a somewhat expensive one) is offered repeatedly, hoping to bring about the same response among workers, it results in minimum obedience—but it falls extremely short of the type of loyalty, buy-in support, and performance that today's dynamic organizations call for. Such rewards are called *extrinsic rewards*, and while they serve their purpose to draw people to complete tasks, it is important to remember that they have their limitations and can ultimately produce resentment.

The better type of reward to cultivate performance among team members is called the *intrinsic reward*. Intrinsic rewards essentially are feelings of satisfaction produced by a job well done. For example, playing sports, volunteering for a charity, writing a book, or offering advice are all tasks that people undertake simply for the sake of completing them. The good feelings that these tasks produce are their intrinsic rewards. It is possible, depending on the nature of your work and your organization, to motivate people through the intrinsic nature of what is expected of them, especially when combined with the more meat-and-potatoes nature of well-planned and desired extrinsic rewards.

Carrots vs. Sticks

I mentioned mixing intrinsic rewards with extrinsic rewards. What about mixing all types of rewards with punishments? That is, what's the right cocktail of rewards and discipline? When do you tie a carrot on the end of a stick to lure the mule, and when do you simply use the stick to prod the mule into moving?

Although I've worked for my share of bosses who emphasized the "do this or else" philosophy, the reality is that the most motivational way of managing involves a positive/negative reinforcement mix that dramatically emphasizes rewards over punishment.

One Step Back

Sometimes, you have to embrace the unpleasant nature of power, as well as the rewards and punishments that generate it. Frankly, you will likely upset some people. Don't be so afraid of reward power and punishment power that you avoid it altogether and lose the power. In his great book *Managing with Power*, Jeffrey Pfeffer writes, "In many domains of activity we have become so obsessed with not upsetting anybody, and with not making mistakes, that we settle for doing nothing … This is why power and influence are not the organization's last dirty little secret, but the secret of success for both individuals and their organization."

Recognizing the relatively unconstructive nature of punishments, even policies that would otherwise clearly serve as negative reinforcement, such as worker attendance policies, are often tinkered to accentuate the positive. For example, many attendance policies today reward workers for good attendance rather than threatening disciplinary action for a host of absence reasons. By considering the frequency of absences rather than the types of absences, these policies attempt to provide positive reinforcement for showing up. (As an aside, there is some debate these days about whether such policies bring too many sick people into the workplace, possibly causing even less overall productivity as many other people catch the illness.)

Depending on the training and skills of the workforce, the nature of the work, and the turnover of your workforce, you should strike a mix that emphasizes extrinsic rewards, points out (and, if possible, creates) intrinsic rewards, emphasizes counseling and encouragement over discipline, and uses punishment as a last, but important, resort.

Counsel Before Disciplining

Before digging into the uncomfortable duty of counseling or disciplining, you should check your organization's policies and procedures, and perhaps you should consult with your human resources department. What you'll probably find is that there's no need to reinvent the wheel: your organization should have a set process for tracking and addressing undesired behavior or job performance. Don't be a cowboy: find out how such discipline has been used in the past and follow the procedure.

By most accounts, it is best to counsel someone before punishing him. The counseling should be offered calmly and a bit detached, when passions aren't high. The counseling should be held in private, away from the rest of the team and out of the earshot and eyeshot of others. As quickly as possible, you should let the person know that this get-together has more to do with "making something wrong go right" than with anger, disappointment, or getting him in trouble.

The Verbal Warning

Many organizations, depending on the behavior, start the counseling process with a private conversation or a verbal warning, if bad behavior is involved. Although the comfort of a one-on-one conference might lead you in that direction, if someone's job is on the line you should consider having another administrator in the room. In fact, many organizations require it. If lawyers get involved later, a "he-said-he-said" or "he-said-she-said" dispute will completely overshadow your good intentions and will make things legally difficult for you and your organization.

Let the person being counseled talk, and don't allow the conversation to escalate. When criticized, it is common for people to become very defensive and highly confrontational. Allowing the person to vent, as well as sincerely taking into account what he says, lowers the defensive walls and makes for a more productive get-together. Remember, your initial goal is to change or channel behavior—not to win an argument.

Some organizations require written documentation of an oral warning. Doesn't that make it a written warning? No. The written documentation of a conversation is simply a signed agreement between the two parties that the discussion took place, without the specific items or agreements spelled out. A written warning, on the other hand, details in writing what the person has done or is doing wrong, and it makes plain what the person needs to do to turn things around. It's not a pleasant thing to do, but the fact is, if this person doesn't improve and, at some point, it is necessary to let him go, documentation of his poor performance and your attempts to address it will be your legal armament.

Allow the person being counseled to take part in the solution. He's more likely to sign and buy into the written warning if he's helping to write it. Quite often, people know what they need to do. Sometimes they are simply looking for a little structure to get themselves moving in the right direction. If possible, have the person provide his own brick or two to that structure.

Repeated Excellence

Do you want to end an uncomfortable counseling session on a positive note? Try this short sentence: "I'm counting on you." When you discuss with a team member some type of inadequate performance, let that person know that he is critical to the team and that you need him and his skills. "You're an important part of this team. When you're on your game, no one does it better. I'm counting on you." If you mean it (and you should), you're likely to see things turn around.

Make sure the person knows that this counseling is not the end of his career—far from it. I don't think I have ever worked a job where I wasn't counseled by my boss at some point for some sort of performance he or she wasn't happy with or wanted done differently. At several of those jobs, the counseling was followed (sometimes in the same year) by good or excellent job reviews and raises and promotions. Was I overly defensive at a few of those meetings or verbal warnings? Sure. But I learned, over time, that the counseling process was more about making me a better employee than in sending me up the river career-wise.

Carry Out Appropriate Discipline

Again, check with your human resources department before administering verbal or written warnings or any type of punishment. There's a good chance that they have a step-by-step course of action, and they may even offer to help you through the sequence.

People often have a difficult time learning how to do things right. But they have no trouble whatsoever learning how to do things wrong. And if they sense, very early on, that they can do things the wrong way and get away with it, at least a few of them will do so with relish. With rewards and support and reinforcement, you can usually prompt 90 percent of your team to stay pointed in the right direction. For that other 10 percent, it's important that they understand that certain actions carry certain consequences. For them, it's kind of a "Bizarro-Vroom Expectancy Theory:" "If you screw up badly enough, you can *expect* to be disciplined." If you are to use punishment properly, your reliability as a firm-but-fair disciplinarian must stay constant.

The Motivational Traits of Discipline

If discipline is to work as a motivator—both for the person being disciplined and as a misbehavior deterrent for the other team members—then it should be carried out in a certain manner.

For example, when you begin a disciplinary process, make sure to scrutinize the situation thoroughly, properly, and impartially before administering the punishment. If possible and appropriate, appoint someone to conduct the investigation. Don't be too hasty to punish. Knee-jerk discipline can turn a team again you—fast.

If discipline is warranted, it should be done as promptly as possible. The nearer in time a punishment is to the offense, the more impact it has on the person being corrected. If the organization deems it appropriate and legally okay, the punishment should have some sort of visibility to it, so that others might know that the organization is serious about not allowing certain things to keep happening.

I mentioned before that counseling should come before punishment. I should mention now that counseling should also follow punishment.

If the person is not being fired, she is still in need of structure and guidance and support. Let's face it: you, as a manager, still have to deal with this person. Follow up your punishment with a meeting similar to the one that preceded the discipline.

Again, remember that the paramount goal of rewards and punishment is to regulate and channel behavior in a way that achieves team goals. If making people feel bad about themselves or running people out makes you feel good, there are undoubtedly certain places in this world where you will go far. But you will never be an authentic motivational leader.

The Least You Need to Know

◆ Motivational theories are best grouped into three categories: academic models that explain what prompts behavior, academic models that suggest how behavior is channeled in a certain direction, and academic models that indicate how desired behavior is maintained.

◆ Drawing from the academic models, the most tangible human motivators are the desire to conform, peer pressure, money, rewards that are useful, rewards that are accessible, rewards that are attainable, and, lastly, the desire not be punished.

◆ The same rewards offered repeatedly for the same performance are ultimately resented and result only in minimal compliance.

◆ Even policies that clearly are intended to stop undesired behavior should attempt to encourage positive performance over punishment for bad performance.

◆ Find out your organization's process for addressing poor performance or bad behavior. In all likelihood, the process will include some form of counseling or verbal or written warnings before disciplinary action.

◆ When you absolutely must dispense punishment, make certain that you administer it impartially, consistently, as quickly as possible, and—depending upon the circumstances—in a way that's visible for others to get the message.

3

Offer a Vision, Manage Communication

By stirring the imaginations of others, a successful motivational leader often can prompt people to do extraordinary things—sometimes for no other reason than to seek his approval and praise. The visionary leader isn't interested in being larger than life, but instead wants to embrace life and all its vibrancy as he directs the group toward new goals.

This leader creates a vision for the team—characterizing success for team members in ways they can picture and join forces to create. Great leaders enjoy fashioning, celebrating, and championing that vision.

9

Develop a Vision That Serves as a Beacon

In This Chapter

- ◆ Finding a sense of vision
- ◆ Setting goals and a direction
- ◆ Selling vision with hope and encouragement
- ◆ Putting vision into words
- ◆ Transforming the vision into a mission
- ◆ Breaking the mission down into objectives

Motivational leaders appreciate the need to create a *vision* with their team, one that inspires and encourages them. They understand the importance of promoting that vision and cheering their team on. They understand the techniques for writing a motivational vision statement (offering an ideal) and a practical mission statement (offering a brief strategy for reaching the vision). They realize the value of agreeing with team members on measurable objectives and timelines for completing the mission and striving for the vision. In this chapter, we'll look at specific steps for crafting a vision and team goals that motivate.

Get on Board with "the Vision Thing"

In 1988, at a campaign press conference, presidential candidate George H. W. Bush (then vice president) was asked about his long-term goals, as opposed to his short-term, election goals. "Oh," Bush answered mockingly, "the *vision* thing." His indifference was telling: during Bush's presidential years, his abrasive chief of staff, John H. Sununu, more than once aloofly proclaimed that the White House would not be offering any major legislative innovations. We're basically done, Sununu said in one way or another.

def·i·ni·tion

From a motivational leadership perspective, the term **vision** means a couple of different things, all of them important. When a leader is mentioned as having farsighted vision, it means that she has a keen intuition into the future of her business and the marketplace where it thrives. When a leader is mentioned as being visionary or a leader of vision, it means that she is imaginative and strategically creative to the point where her inventiveness will one day intersect with some future customer need—resulting in great success. If a leader has offered a vision to her team, it means that she has created a mental picture for them of a prosperous future, generating feelings of inspiration and hope among the team members and motivating them to work toward this vision's realization.

Bush *was* done. He lost his bid for reelection to Bill Clinton in 1992—a relatively unusual happening for an incumbent president over the last 75 years. The feeling in some circles was that Bush had served as a minimalist president and had essentially phoned in his reelection campaign. His lack of a bold vision for the country—and his seeming apathy over it—didn't do much to counter this perception.

Your invitation to be a motivational leader doesn't say, "Vision for the future optional." Providing an image of what the future might look like isn't just a convenience or a cute alternative. Offering your team a vision that they can embrace and get excited about is a necessity. It is the difference between getting your team members to act and simply getting them to go through the motions. Which would you prefer?

Sometimes, visionary leadership is associated with prophesy, sometimes with imagination, and sometimes simply with good planning. ("Where do I want to go, and what logistical steps do I need to get there?") Having a leader's sense of vision means possessing a little of all those things. The common attribute of all these loose characterizations is that they involve a boss who is focused on the future, rather than obsessing over the present or nitpicking about the past. The truly motivational leader keeps people pointed forward in spirited fashion.

In the book *A Christmas Carol* by Charles Dickens, Ebenezer Scrooge asks the Spirit of Christmas Yet to Come, "Are these the shadows of things that *will* be, or are they the shadows of things that *may* be, only?" The question answers itself, doesn't it? When we can't see the future, we play victim to it. But by looking into the future, in a bad way like Scrooge did or in a good way like the motivational leader and her team do, we are instantly able to choose *that* future or a *different* future. The visionary leader does not simply offer a look into the present or imminent future, but she provides a much-needed glimpse of how things *could* be, if only the team accomplishes a, b, and c.

Perennial leadership authority Brian Tracy says that, throughout the 3,000 or so studies he has read, vision, as a management attribute, shows up more than does any other trait. He places it at the top of his list of common leadership qualities. A vision, suggests Tracy, generates hope, and hope is one *powerful* motivator.

A vision has an uncanny way of getting an organization moving in a positive direction. It provides an agreeable mental image that keeps people in "big picture" mode. Motivational leaders know how to create that vision, how to sell it to the team, how to add some authenticity to it, and how to help the team work toward it. Motivational leaders also understand that, once a vision becomes reality, the first thing they need to do is get the team excited about and working toward yet another vision.

Set a Vision for the Team

An interesting thing about vision: it's probably the one thing you can *never* subcontract. Certainly some major corporations hire consulting firms to form and fashion interesting vision statements and mission statements. But they surely don't stick around to publicize and promote it. And even if they did, who would listen? A truly rousing vision has to come from the leader's heart—from his gut. He has to be on the verge of passionate tears (real ones, not crocodile ones) when he describes what he sees in the future for his team.

> **Best Voices Forward**
>
> King Solomon is considered by many to be the author of the Bible's "Book of Proverbs." Perhaps that makes Solomon the first leadership consultant! After all, it is in Proverbs where we are first approached with the notion that people with no structure in their lives or hope for the future are doomed. The verse is Proverbs 29:18—"Where there is no vision, the people perish."

If people are prompted to act by the divergence between reality as they perceive it and reality as they would like it to be, then they are likely to do so more enthusiastically when the future's canvas is colored brightly and vividly. As the motivational leader, you're responsible for painting that picture. When you're finished, you should reek (figuratively) of the oils and the pigments and the mixing agents. The picture should be a part of you, and you should embrace it fully. Frankly, if you don't feel that way about your vision for the team (or, for that matter, the personal vision you see for yourself and your career), it's probably time to move on. A passionless vision is like a paint-by-numbers kit. It covers the wall when you're finished, but people can sense that you simply went through a routine, and therefore it neither impresses them nor moves them.

As a young man, I remember once being quite lost in the woods with a group of other young men. (No jokes about men being too stubborn to ask for directions, please. There were only snakes and birds to talk to!) Once we realized that we were not where we thought we were and didn't know how to get back to camp, we got into a pretty heated discussion about what to do. Finally, after considering the map and debating some more and, in fact, voting on a course of action, we all became friends again and started on our way. I remember asking one of my buddies quietly, "Why are you in such a cheery mood? We're doing just about the exact opposite of what you suggested?"

"Yeah," he replied. "But at least we're not wandering aimlessly. There's a plan, there's some hope, and that's okay by me."

Well, we found our way back to camp eventually. That's what a vision does. It creates a sense of hope and a sense of optimism where such sentiments might not otherwise exist. Sometimes a vision is important, not because it's the perfect ambition or even the best ambition, but simply because it *is* an ambition. Most people would gladly follow such a vision rather than wander aimlessly in the woods.

Best Voices Forward

If there were ever a truly inspiring vision created by a leader, it was the ideal portrayed by civil rights leader Martin Luther King Jr. in 1963, in front of the Lincoln Memorial in Washington, D.C. King painted a picture of racial harmony, where one day "the sons of former slaves and the sons of former slave owners will be able to sit down together at the table of brotherhood." In this great speech, King suggested that such a day could happen in the lifetimes of those present. "I have a dream," he said, "that my four little children will one day live in a nation where they will not be judged by the color of their skin but by the content of their character." King's vision had a huge impact on the passing of the Civil Rights Act of 1964, the Voting Rights Act of 1965, and other civil rights legislation.

Don't set a vision for your team in a vacuum. You shouldn't lock yourself in a room with basic supplies, only to emerge a week later unshaven and unwashed with a grand vision. Setting a vision should involve input from your team members, your bosses, your peers, and your customers. The more contributions you get from others and the more involved they feel in the process, the more likely they are to buy in to the ultimate vision you offer them. That's your objective, really: you want to offer a light that looks so compelling from a distance that people want to follow you through the woods to see what that light is all about.

Get People to Buy What You're Selling

The motivational leader boldly and confidently offers her vision. "Follow me," she decrees, "and let's go for an exciting ride together." When people follow her, they do so because she's selling them a vision, and they're just hopeful enough to buy what she's selling.

The Role of Hope

Alfred Adler was an Austrian doctor who founded individual psychology, the study of why individuals are psychologically different from one another, during the turn of the last century. Adler was a strong believer in people's innate ability to break free from the demons in their heads and to start their lives in a bold, new, improved direction. Adler believed that the beginning of this change started with hope, and that, as long as people hold hope, they will be inclined to push forward toward positive change. In fact, Adler suggested that most positive changes originated with the anticipation and optimism that such change was possible.

And so, the sale of a vision begins with the expectation that such a wonderful prophecy is possible. *It CAN be done!* was the sign on President Ronald Reagan's desk, and it was the motto his passionate administration lived by and espoused. His vision included a country with a strong military, with free-market regulatory settings that allowed an entrepreneur to grow a successful business, and with a collective return to pro-democracy, ethical values that people could rally around. Such a belief was contagious: the country quickly bought into Reagan's optimism and vision for a return to an America that many thought had long gone. It was a vision, to be sure, that suffered through failures and scandals. But, a couple of decades later, it is the thing people remember most and consider most successful about the Reagan years.

The thing that kept Reagan's vision going was the constant encouragement he brought with it. Whenever the vision seemed to be fading, the Great Communicator sought a national audience, reaffirmed his vision, congratulated those who had made some strides in that direction, and sold the country on continuing forward. Constant encouragement—it was the key then, and it's the key now as you move toward being a truly motivational leader.

> ### Best Voices Forward
>
> If you look up the term *motivational speaker* in the dictionary, you just might see Zig Ziglar's picture there! Still working hard in his eighties, Ziglar continues to inspire audiences with his blending of preacher's passion and leadership-psychology pragmatism. Ziglar (Ziglar.com) has been in the business of helping people and companies create visions for over 30 years, and he has written over a dozen books (including the bestselling *See You at the Top*) on the topics of success and self-improvement. Ziglar says that a clear vision creates hope for your team, and that encouraging your team along the way is how you keep that vision fresh and meaningful. "Encouragement," notes Ziglar, "is the fuel on which hope runs."

Incidentally, I've used the words *sell* and *encourage* several times in this discussion about vision. Why is it that some of today's best motivational speakers (like Zig Ziglar, mentioned in the *Best Voices Forward* sidebar on this page, or Brian Tracy, or Anthony Robbins) serve almost interchangeably as sales experts and leadership experts? I suggest it's because selling a product to a prospective customer is essentially the same as selling a vision to a team that might or might not be inclined to buy into it. Here are some thoughts on how to promote your vision and persuade your team that they should be excited about subscribing to it.

Steps to Selling Your Vision

First, remember that the more your team provides input toward the vision, the more energized they're going to be from it. Make sure that you don't put this vision together by yourself—discuss it freely and frequently as you begin formulating it. Make sure that you genuinely and passionately listen to your team members as you gather their input. It's been said before: no one ever listened himself out of a sale or out of someone else's loyalty.

Second, make sure that your vision meets both the needs of your customers and the needs of your team. On either side of the vision, no perceived need means no perceived interest. If the need is real, make sure the vision, though idealistic, isn't so far in the clouds that it fails to address that very real need.

Third, make sure that the vision carries with it the air of authority. As mentioned earlier, people generally don't mind following the lead of someone who seems competent and in charge. Make sure that the vision portrays that competence and clout.

And finally, remember that, just as successful salespeople are often bold and courageous, so, too, must your vision be bold and courageous. And so must you be, as you serve as its constant, fervent cheerleader.

Define Your Winning Motivational Vision

Let's see. If you were to put your vision down in writing, what would you call it? Eureka! How's about calling it a *vision statement*? Okay, I'll admit it—I didn't just come up with that one. In fact, organizational vision statements have been around for decades. Their origin is not easily traced, but the best bet is that leadership guru Warren Bennis, if not its creator, was probably the one who made the practice popular by the mid-1980s.

Various methods exist when it comes to putting together a winning vision statement, most likely because the jury is still out on what constitutes the ideal vision statement. The following steps are one possible technique for putting an inspiring vision into words.

def•i•ni•tion

A **vision statement** is a team's written description of what it wants to be in the short-term or long-term future. The statement serves to point a team in a particular direction by providing an idealized mental picture of what good things could happen and by attaching big-picture goals to that picture. A vision statement typically is optimistic and as inspiring as possible. Its reference to the future can vary. It might set a time goal for completion, such as five or ten years out. Or it might offer this positive, future depiction by bringing it into the present. That is, instead of saying, "We'll be a world-class accounting firm in five years," the declaration might say, "We are a world-class accounting firm." The idea is to say it first and then to bring the reality to the proclamation.

How to Create a Vision Statement for Your Team

The first step is a *don't*. That is, *don't* form a vision committee or hold meetings. The world has way too many committees and way too many meetings, and the necessity of any of them is questionable. Instead, draw your input, one-on-one, from your supervisor and from your team members, especially those members who have been around a while and quietly maintain the admiration of others. Tell each of them what impassions you, where you see the world headed, and how you see this team fitting into that future world. If it's a grand vision, portray it as such. Don't be afraid to sound corny.

Second, after listening to their feedback, ask yourself, "Just how good could it get for us?" In writing, describe that ideal world and your team's ideal place there. Describe how your team has possibly made that world better, and how it has addressed a need, or several needs, over time.

Third, get vivid, and get quixotic. Add to your vision majestic descriptions and romantically bold mountains that one day will be climbed. Describe the future success and status of the people on your team, having been integral parts of this triumphant story. Be plucky. Let it go over the top, at least a little. If it's too silly, the next round of reviewers will tell you so. Read it to yourself and see if it fires you up.

Fourth, add your team's core values to the vision. Include your passion for what you do and what your team does, plus your commitment to integrity, excellence, and customer satisfaction. Describe what it is about that passion that will one day soon put your team at the forefront of your field.

Fifth, add a brief statement about your team's expertise, strengths, and authority in the field.

Finally, go to that original group of people and ask them again individually for their feedback. Look for more than simply a thumbs up or thumbs down. Have each of them offer changes in the wording, in the priorities, in the passion, and in the future world portrayed in the statement. Let them tell you if it's too gooey, and how it might be reeled in a bit. Let them tell you if it's wildly unrealistic, and how it can be made to sound a bit more attainable.

Once your vision statement is completed, make it your mantra. Post it on your website, at your workplace, in your conference room, and in your office. Talk about it enthusiastically. Get people excited. Let them know that they are on a ride to great places with great things!

A Model Vision Statement

Covered Bridge Produce is an organic farmstead in Oley Township, Pennsylvania. Their vision statement, excerpted below and one of the best I've ever read, encompasses all the goals, passion, and core values of an ideal vision.

> Covered Bridge Produce is a small, certified organic market garden specializing in heirloom vegetable varieties. It was established by its proprietor so that he might find spiritual refreshment and occasion for honest labor. Although the operation must become profitable in order to remain in existence, its real purpose is not economic …
>
> Covered Bridge Produce will strive to be respectful of all living beings on the farm, the land upon which it operates, its customers and those who labor in its fields. Accordingly, no animals will be raised for slaughter and the use of poisons and other lethal pest controls will be kept to a minimum. Care will be taken to replenish that which is removed from the soil and the local environment will not be harmed by inconsiderate farming practices. Customers will be offered the highest quality vegetables we are capable of growing at fair prices. Workers at the farm will be well compensated and provided with good working conditions …
>
> Covered Bridge Produce will be an educational enterprise. Interns and other workers will find an unusually rich learning environment at the farm. Processes will be explained, reading materials and time to study them will be made available, field experiences off the farm will be arranged, and an attitude of inquiry will be encouraged. The farm will welcome visitors from all walks of life and workers will engage them in an attempt to convey a good sense of the motivations, spirit, and techniques of sustainable agriculture …
>
> Covered Bridge Produce will be of service to society as well as to its customers and workers. The farm will contribute at least 10 percent of the food it produces to food banks or other charities

which feed those in need. It will welcome opportunities to educate or encourage those seeking a more positive vision of life by participating in training or work experience programs for the disadvantaged or disabled. With appropriate modesty, the farm will offer itself as an example of how people can function sanely in the twenty-first century.

A model vision statement, like the one above, offers wonderful, bold descriptions of the future. It tells customers how their need will be met and, specifically, what they will attain by doing business with this organization. This vision also includes the organization's core values and areas of expertise.

Turn Your Vision into Priorities

I know many dreamers. They're great people and wonderful to be around. They have many life passions, they are full of brilliant ideas, and at any given time, they each have about 100 different projects going on. The trouble is that they seldom finish any of them. The motivational leader not only promotes the vision, but he also makes the vision functional by turning it into measurable goals and, later on, into more specific, daily objectives.

The first measure toward transforming vision into reality is taking your vision statement and using it to create a *mission statement.* As I found out in those lost woods many years ago, if you don't know where you're at, it's tough to know where you're headed or where you've been. The mission statement is something of a compass for your team members. It reminds them of their purpose and their aims. It also tells them what they're good at and what that's going to do for them.

def•i•ni•tion

A **mission statement** is a team's written description of how it strategically plans to meet the ideal portrayed by its vision statement. A mission statement defines a team's calling and its current undertakings. It typically includes descriptions of team strengths, customer communities, and specific goals and objectives related to both. Whereas a vision statement is wordy and idealistic, a mission statement tends to be shorter and more matter-of-fact.

Your mission statement typically explains, through a brief declaration, how your team plans to reach its vision. It states matter-of-factly what your team does and what it sees as its core passion. It itemizes which strong points it brings to the table of free-market competition, and who might be interested in purchasing and benefiting from those talents. It lists concrete targets for achieving its vision.

As with the vision statement, writing a mission statement can be accomplished in several different ways. The following steps are one possible method for turning your vision into a written mission.

How to Write a Mission Statement with Your Team

Much the same as with writing a vision statement, don't form a committee or hold meetings to develop your mission statement. Again, go to your key players and, with them, take a thorough look at your team's strengths and capabilities.

Zero in on those strengths and capabilities currently serving as the crux of expertise that's bringing results to your team. See if you can summarize this core talent in one or two sentences.

Next, determine who your important customers are. Call your primary clients and ask them what it is about your service that keeps them coming back. List the types of clients your team serves and why these clients chose you. Reduce it to one or two sentences.

Considering all these factors, catch a glimpse of how you see your team leveraging these strengths, capabilities, key players, and core customers toward your vision. See if you can reduce it to one sentence.

Combine these three to five sentences. See if you can create a compound sentence or two (using *and*, *because*, or *while*), reducing the mission statement down to two or three longer sentences. Check out the flow and the punch of the statement. Does it sound like the plan of attack it's meant to be? Will it look good when it's posted everywhere?

Run the statement another time by your key players and your customers. See if your key players want to support such a mission and if your customers believe they'll benefit from it. Respond to their suggestions.

Once your mission statement is done, post it alongside your vision statement—again, on your website, where your team works, and where you personally can view it as often as possible. While your vision statement is your rallying call, your mission statement quietly, succinctly, and pointedly reminds your team how you're someday going to get there.

A Model Mission Statement

My good friend John Schwab is the president of JPS Engineering (jpsengr.com), based in Colorado Springs, Colorado. JPS Engineering's mission statement, shown below, does a nice job of expressing what the firm does (engineering services), who it serves (civil engineering and infrastructure projects), what its strengths are (technical excellence, innovation, and personalized service), and what its goals are (establishing a reputation for quality, receptiveness, unparalleled service, and cost effectiveness), without being wordy. Notice how many times *service* appears in this statement? There's little doubt what Schwab considers important.

> Our mission is to provide the highest quality professional civil engineering services while establishing a reputation for technical excellence, innovation, and personalized service. We are committed to providing unparalleled client service with a focus on quality civil design and cost-effective, responsive solutions to civil engineering and infrastructure challenges.

A perfect mission statement. It includes the team's core talents and core clientele. It states how its forte will be leveraged to achieve a long-term vision. And it states all these things in two crisp, well-structured sentences.

Manage by Objectives

After your team's vision and mission have been established, you should consider breaking the mission down into objectives and leading your team in attaining these objectives.

The phrase "management by objectives" was introduced by Peter Drucker (mentioned in Chapter 6) in the 1950s. The idea was, and still is, to have team leadership and team members agree to measurable aims within specific time periods. The progress toward meeting these objectives is charted along the way by using key performance indicators.

Such objectives need to be relatively flexible to allow for a team's occasional failures and lessons along the way and to accommodate a very fluid business and enterprise environment. A 100 percent unyielding objective might lend itself to the temptation to report untruths, as your team members feel pressured to reach arbitrary benchmarks at all costs.

The Management By Objectives (MBO) process is, really, a book in itself, and many of its methods are quantitative, as opposed to the qualitative (but every bit as scientific) nature of motivational leadership. However, it is important to note here that getting the team to help create and buy into its vision, mission, and objectives is nothing new. It just keeps getting forgotten or ignored by really bad managers over generations. The good news is that it keeps getting rediscovered and relearned over generations by new motivational leaders.

The idea is to help create an ideal that fires people up and makes them want to stick around to see where it all will lead. Additionally, the MBO process is meant to help people live by a crisp, well-stated mission that keeps them on track and gives them a more detailed set of objectives that can be measured along the way.

The Least You Need to Know

◆ Creating a vision for your team instills a mental picture of the future that inspires and motivates them. A leader with vision enjoys a combination of foresight, imagination, and even preparedness.

◆ If a leader offers a vision to the team, it means that she has created an inspiring, energizing mental picture of a better future.

◆ Make sure that the vision addresses a need; is connected to the expertise and clout of you and your organization; and is bold, courageous, and as far-reaching as it can be without seeming unrealistic.

◆ A written vision statement serves as your mantra. Write down the ideal future for your team and share it, one-on-one, with your most respected team members, as well as with your supervisor.

◆ A written mission statement serves as a brief but pointed description of how your team will reach its vision.

◆ Management by Objectives (MBO) is one process in which the mission is broken down into objectives. The team leaders and members agree on measurable aims and the amount of time needed to accomplish them. Progress along the way is tracked by key performance indicators.

Chapter 10

Serve as Cheerleader for Your Team

In This Chapter

- ◆ Feigning zeal can fool even you
- ◆ Making corny sayings work for you and your team
- ◆ Leading "your troops" from the trenches
- ◆ Using cheerleading without becoming one of the gang
- ◆ Becoming a one-on-one manager
- ◆ Finding heartwarming stories about team cheerleading

Motivational leaders are comfortable serving as cheerleaders for their teams and for their organizations. They recognize the importance of being on hand and available. They also understand the value of one-on-one support and feedback. In this chapter, we'll take a serious look at what some might mistakenly believe to be a not-so-serious aspect of leadership—heartfelt cheering on and encouraging.

Act Enthusiastic and ...

One of the best writing teachers I ever had—and certainly the most down-to-earth—was John Jeppi, the president of the Broadcasting Institute of Maryland. In the early 1980s, I took a six-month course with Jeppi, where I learned how to crank out a comprehensive news story pretty quickly. In fact, he got me my first real job out of high school—writing news copy for a small, all-news radio station in Wilmington, Delaware. Although I stepped away from professional writing for about 20 years after that, I'd say his functional methods for breaking down a story and relating it lucidly on paper have stayed with me all this time.

Jeppi was a huge fan of the Dale Carnegie maxim "If you act enthusiastic, you'll *be* enthusiastic!" He would repeat it over and over again, driving home the point that if you were having a bad or wearisome day, you could turn it around simply by pretending you were having a good time. According to Jeppi, at some point during the façade, you would, in fact, discover that the show was getting to you, getting *inside* you. He suggested that you would eventually wind up buying into your own performance! And the day wouldn't be so bad after all.

Well, it may have seemed silly at the time, but it has worked for me over the years. And if it has worked reasonably well for me as a team member, it has worked big-time for me as a team leader. Motivational leaders get it. Staying fired up and walking around with a sincere smile and an encouraging word makes all the difference. It sets the entire tone for the workplace first thing in the morning, and it's infectious as the day progresses. Some things at work are a constant—too much to do, too many deadlines, too many interruptions. So why not change the one variable you have total control over—how you approach them and what sort of attitude you display for others as you handle these same things day in and day out?

Jeppi (as well as Carnegie) was right. Behaving in a fired-up manner not only keeps others motivated, but it also tends to have a self-charging effect. That is, if we render motivation in front of others, we tend to find ourselves motivated by the performance.

> **Best Voices Forward**
>
> Dale Carnegie was perhaps the original corporate team cheer-leader. A hugely successful corporate trainer in the 1930s and 1940s, his name, products, and franchised self-improvement seminars continue to this day. Carnegie's best-selling book, *How to Win Friends and Influence People*, still sells very well in paperback and on CD.
>
> Carnegie believed that a team's behavior could be changed and improved by how the leader responded to their behavior. His thoughts on positive control, cheerleading, and encouragement came at a time when corporate America was struggling with high employee turnover and an increasingly negative reaction to tough, assembly-line conditions. His suggestion: get the teams involved, make jobs more worker-friendly, and listen, give confidence to, and cheer on team members every step of the way.
>
> Carnegie was a big believer in a motivational leader's need to maintain a constant, high level of enthusiasm. "Flaming enthusiasm," said Carnegie, "backed up by horse sense and persistence, is the quality that most frequently makes for success."

Is it *really* that easy to kid ourselves? Sure. People lie to themselves all the time. As leadership trainer Chris Widener notes, people generally make decisions with emotions: they simply use logic to justify them. If we can kid ourselves about the front lawn not *really* needing mowing or that there's nothing *really* wrong with having one more piece of chocolate cake, then why shouldn't we be able to trick ourselves at work that there's nothing *really* stopping us from being happy and maintaining a smile? And, unlike the grass-cutting procrastination or the chocolate-fueled expanding waistline, hoodwinking ourselves into being enthusiastic carries no adverse consequences. Just the opposite: it keeps us energetic, full of life, and inclined to make our team feel better and work better. *Act enthusiastic, and you'll be enthusiastic!*

Know That Corny Often Works

I once had a boss who oozed phony flattery. "My, you're looking especially lovely today," he'd say nearly every day to his secretary.

Of course, she had heard it all before, time and time again. "You're so full of bull stuff," she'd say. (I may have gotten a word or two wrong.)

"Yes, I am," he'd reply. "But it's *sincere* bull stuff!"

Everyone would laugh and go about their day, recognizing that, once again, the corny sweet talk of this old man had managed to cheer them up.

Depending on the workplace climate, I'm guessing that daily complimenting on the appearance of your administrators might be considered more harassment these days than motivation. But if constantly complimenting, say, good work or good decision-making is corny, then the question is important. Does corny still work?

Examples of Corniness That Worked

President Ronald Reagan, whom I've mentioned before, used to say things that must have made his speechwriters gag as they helped write them. "He's not really going to say this?" they probably asked behind closed doors. But Reagan, known for being a very prolific writer and an avid proofreader of the speeches he was handed, would tailor those corny lines and jump into them with both feet.

When pushing for a new tax code, Reagan invoked Ralph Waldo Emerson by saying that, for the future businessperson, the new code would help you "hitch your wagon to a star." When (accurately) predicting an eventual end to the Soviet Union, Reagan spoke of America's fight against "the aggressive impulses of an evil empire." In a speech in front of the Berlin Wall in 1987, Reagan suggested that Soviet General Secretary Mikhail Gorbachev exert his influence over the East German government and remove the wall separating East and West Berlin. "Mr. Gorbachev, tear down this wall," Reagan insisted. In many speeches, he referred to America as "a shining city on a hill."

Regardless of where you stand politically, it's difficult to argue the notion that Reagan—in part, through the corniness of his rhetoric—brought about a renewed optimism in America, following very tough decades of war, recession, and high-level political corruption.

Although I hate to mix examples of real motivational leaders with fictional ones (and yet continue to do so throughout this book!), I have to mention one of my favorite movies, *Master and Commander:*

The Far Side of the World, with Russell Crowe playing British Royal Navy captain Jack Aubrey (who never really existed) during the time of Napoleon. In one scene, during a ship officers' dinner, Crowe's character recalls Admiral Lord Nelson (who really did exist) on deck during a cold evening, being offered an overcoat. No need for that coat, as Crowe quotes Lord Nelson saying, "his love of king and country kept him warm." Corny, yes, confesses Crowe's character, but a statement forever cherished by a leader hoping to be as dignified as the one who inspired him.

My argument: corny often works, because it looks a lot cornier on paper and perhaps sounds a lot cornier coming out of your mouth than it does to the inspired ear that hears it.

Expressions That Work, Even Though They Look Corny in Print

As you read the following expressions, they certainly look corny in this book—definitely too corny to ever use at your workplace or with your team members, right? Wrong. Try one or two of them out every now and then. You just might discover that corny often works.

- ◆ "I'm counting on you."
- ◆ "I have faith in you."
- ◆ "Great job! Keep up the good work."
- ◆ "We really appreciate what you do around here."
- ◆ "Be all that you can be."
- ◆ "I stand corrected. Thank you for fixing my mistake."
- ◆ "What a great presentation—it looks like something in a catalogue!"
- ◆ "What a wonderful idea! How'd you come up with it?"
- ◆ "You're smart—what do *you* think of that proposal?"
- ◆ "I'm so proud to be a part of this team."

Get Dirty

Football team cheerleaders don't cheer from the stands or the food line. They cheer down on the field. The same should go for you as the motivational leader. You can't cheer on your team members from your office or the executive lounge. You need to be where they are, getting dirty with them, day in and day out. When they're feeling the heat (literally or figuratively), you need to be feeling the heat. When they're fatigued, you need to be fatigued alongside them. And when they're lying on the field, wet, muddy, and victorious, you need to be there with them, celebrating the win!

During my years as a manufacturing manager, people used to tease me for being, literally, the filthiest boss at the mill. I'd show up for work each day just as clean as the next foreman. But by the end of the shift, I was covered head-to-toe with blending chemicals, starches, gear grease, sweat, dust, packaging ink, and dirt. I got blissfully filthy for two reasons. First, I wanted to learn as much about the job as possible, and although jumping into a lake isn't the smart way to learn how to swim, it certainly is the wettest! Second, keeping tabs on a team that was spread far and wide throughout a mill was a lot easier if I didn't mind getting dirty in the process.

Repeated Excellence

Although General Douglas MacArthur is far more famous for his World War II successes, my favorite MacArthur story is of a very young, one-star General MacArthur, living in the trenches of no-man's land during World War I. When other senior officers were calling the shots from well behind enemy lines, MacArthur stayed for long periods with his soldiers in those trenches, at one point breathing in enough enemy mustard gas to nearly kill him. His encouragement from within those ditches won him the fierce loyalty of his soldiers and the admiration of his superiors. His commanding officer, Charles T. Menoher, said that there was nothing a soldier was asked to do in that war "that he is not liable to look up and see MacArthur at his side." That's where you'll find most motivational leaders—in the trenches with their people.

Safety note: if you're going to "get dirty" with your team, and your team engages in genuinely tough manual labor, make sure that you dress properly and go through the required safety training before plunging into where they do their thing. If you're around machinery, the last thing you need is to get your necktie caught in the ingoing nip of large press rollers! The tie will get a nice press, but you won't fare too well at all.

If your job is strictly administrative, "getting dirty" becomes a more figurative term, but is every bit as important. As a team leader, you might find yourself cheering on your team as you join them in the bureaucratic trenches. An example might be helping your team conduct an office inventory or preparing for an inspection or a visit from a corporate bigwig. The work might be tedious, and the objectives might be mundane, and, frankly, you might not be able to offer all that much help! But your presence will be duly noted and, down the road, appreciated when it's recognized as sincere and not a scam.

One more thought on getting dirty and leading from the trenches with your people: don't be rolling in the mud with them eight hours a day. Make sure that you give them some space—or you'll undermine your confidence and stifle their innovation. In his brilliant leadership novel *Starship Troopers*, sci-fi writer Robert A. Heinlein (a U.S. Naval Academy graduate) suggests—through his main character Juan Rico—that a team leader who never leaves his team members' sight, even if he's contributing to their work, tends to make them very nervous. "You are stirring them like a nest of wild bees (by hanging around them too much)," says Captain Blackstone to Rico, who is assigned to Blackstone as a third lieutenant. "Why the deuce do you think I turned over to you the best sergeant in the Fleet? If you will go to your stateroom, hang yourself on a hook, and *stay* there … he'll hand that platoon over to you tuned like a violin."

Make sure that you balance your encouragement from the trenches with enough breathing space and time away from your team members to let them do their jobs without feeling beleaguered.

Know When Some Things Are Beneath You

This might be a good point to mention that just because you're a cheerleader for the team doesn't mean you get to date the star quarterback. Huh? What I'm trying to say is that there's a difference between cheering on your team and encouraging your team members as their leader and simply becoming "one of the guys." As you express enthusiasm, and as you root for your team and their cause while you work in the trenches, make sure that you maintain an air of authority.

One of the keys to being a motivational leader is to be very hands-on without losing the position power that comes with your title. You don't need to wave your title in people's faces, but they should recognize at any given time that you're the boss—a boss who looks out for them, who supports them, who listens to them, who inspires them. But, still, the boss.

The truth is that some things, frankly, need to be beneath you. You're no better than anyone else, of course, but sometimes being in charge of folks means making tough decisions and taking stands that aren't very popular. Your manner of authority helps you enforce those tough decisions. So don't put yourself in a highly visible position that compromises that aura.

For example, if everyone on your team is, say, mopping a floor and you, as team leader, are scraping the gum off that same floor, well, it's tough to retain people's respect after a scene like that. Can you occasionally pick up a mop, especially if time is of the essence? Sure, if union rules say you can. But don't be on your knees scraping gum while other people are only mopping. Be a part of the team—but don't be its whipping boy, hoping to gain favor. Bring yourself "down," but not "beneath."

When noting that some things need to be beneath you, perhaps "beneath" is the wrong word. The better way to put it is don't put yourself in a situation where you may not receive a certain level of respect. For example, going out at the end of the workweek, with your team, and drinking to the point where you are more touched by the alcohol than those around you are, tips the balance too far toward "one of the guys" and away from "team leader who has earned respect." In fact, for all sorts of reasons, it's probably a good idea never to go boozing with your team. Are you there as a buddy, as a boss, as a representative of the company? Are you condoning someone's drinking and leaving with his or her car keys? If you've switched off the "boss" light, what conditions merit turning it back on? Who needs it? Again, stay away from situations where you might lose your air of authority as you attempt to be one of the gang.

One Step Back

Remember that there's a line that should never be crossed. It's the line that keeps you as the team leader who can ask your team members for results and responsibility. If, in the interest of socializing and trying to be "one of the guys," you cross that line and lose accountability of even one team member, it is very, very difficult to find your way to the correct side of that line again. It is much easier to maintain lots of distance initially—especially in regard to after-work get-togethers—and allow yourself to ease up a little over a long period of time rather than to start from a too-friendly position and try to backtrack into a more distant posture of authority.

It has been mentioned already, but it's worth reemphasizing that motivational leadership doesn't mean getting your team to do things because they think you're their buddy. It means motivating and encouraging them to the point where they *want* to do those things as they seek your respect and approval.

Consider One-on-One Management

I consider one-on-one management, much like listening, to be a lost art. Are we convinced that it's more time-efficient to pack people into a conference room, or are we simply afraid to approach people individually? I'm guessing it's a little of both.

Time Efficiency

Let's consider the time-efficiency argument. Assume that you're in charge of a team of 1,000 people. Assume that there are two levels of management under you, and assume that the first, or base, level managers are each in charge of a ten-person team. Okay, that's 100 managers.

Now, assume that 10 second-level managers, your key players, are each in charge of 10 of those base-level managers. Even if you met with each of your key players for 20 minutes each day, met with your administrator for 20 minutes in the morning and 20 minutes in the afternoon each day, met with one base-level manager for 20 minutes each day for mentoring, went to lunch for an hour, and spent the next four hours reporting to your bosses, walking and visiting the different departments, putting out fires, tending to legal issues, writing up reports, and scheduling your next workday, you'd still be at work only nine hours that day. That's probably less than most people in charge of 1,000 people work on any given day. And imagine how many lives you could touch, meeting one-on-one with your key players, walking around, mentoring, and being visible during that day.

One-on-one management doesn't cause time problems. It *solves* time problems by vacating the conference room and affecting people, personally and up-close, a third of an hour at a time.

What about confronting people individually? Hey, it's understandable. It's easy to say to a group of people, "It has been decided that ..." Aside from using the weak passive voice (a minor sin for writers like me), announcing new policies that way takes the heat off you as the team leader. Once you get in front of individuals, well, things get a little hotter, don't they? Instead of "It has been decided that," when you're in front of someone, one-on-one, you're forced to say something like, "Uh, there's a new way I need you to do this." Not an easy thing to say, even for experienced leaders. And so we shy away from walking around, approaching people as individuals, and exposing ourselves to their up-close reactions, rebuttals, tantrums, and anxieties. The problem is, once you push past all reactions, as well as your own hang-ups with facing people, you find that the *real* power and control over people—the things that differentiate the good leaders from the great ones—all happen up-close and personal.

The most wonderful thing about one-on-one management is that, aside from conveying your enthusiasm and pride and priorities over and over again in a very personal way, you also get to encounter that very rare experience of conveying a single thought—completely and fully understood—to another person's mind. That is very uncommon in today's workplace, unless you're the consummate one-on-one boss.

Here are some measures toward becoming a better one-on-one manager.

Steps Toward Becoming a One-on-One Manager

First, as you walk around, get people to internalize the priorities of the team. Explain to each person what he or she stands to gain if the team succeeds in completing its mission. Give details on why the mission is important to the team and to the organization. You can be the toughest boss in the world, but if you don't convince people, as individuals, that something is important, you'll only get the minimum out of them.

Second, set specific goals with specific people. The nice thing about walking around, with planner in hand, is that you can ask individual team members for precise tasks that support the larger mission. Let each person know that you plan on following up. Give an exact time. (No need to round to the nearest half hour.)

Third, follow up, follow up, follow up. Follow up when a team member asks you for something that you can deliver, and follow up at the specific time you said you'd be by to track the progress of an individual team member's request.

Finally, continue to establish rapport (mentioned in Chapter 11), hone your listening skills (mentioned in Chapter 11), and avoid unnecessary meetings (mentioned in Chapter 12—and by the way, they're *all* unnecessary).

Read These Cheerleading Stories

Here are a few stories about motivational leaders who transformed their teams and their environments by passionately cheering them on.

First, there's the story of General George S. Patton Jr., who advised young officers that the best way to lead their soldiers was at the very front of their units, charging forward. "You young lieutenants have to realize that your platoon is like a piece of spaghetti. You can't push it.

You've got to get out in front and pull it!" Patton insisted that each officer under his command spend part of his day in the field, away from his desk. I had the pleasure of meeting Patton's son, George III, who also served in the U.S. Army as a general. He related another food-related story—of making a mess officer eat the spoiled food he had tried to serve his soldiers, until he got deathly sick and learned his lesson. Okay, so not *all* of these stories transfer to feel-good, all-for-one corporate work and efficiency. But I'll bet that mess officer sure was motivated!

> **Best Voices Forward**
>
> Corporate trainer Dale Carnegie believed that a positive word spreads like a pebble in a lake, rippling for a very long time. "You have it easily in your power to increase the sum total of this world's happiness now," he said. "How? By giving a few words of sincere appreciation to someone who is lonely or discouraged. Perhaps you will forget tomorrow the kind words you say today, but the recipient may cherish them over a lifetime."

Next, I like the story of Queen Elizabeth I, the great monarch who ruled England nearly 500 years ago, who spent every summer on "progresses," as she led thousands of attendants and soldiers on these overland journeys across England. Her expeditions were considered arduous and dangerous, and yet she went on them unfailingly. Her objective, quite simply, was to get out and meet the people, convinced that encountering them, hearing their concerns, and wishing them well would solidify their loyalty. "We come for the hearts and allegiance of our subjects," she said.

And finally, there's the story of John McCain, the young Navy pilot in the late 1960s who was offered release from a Vietnamese prison camp when his captors discovered his father was commander-in-chief of the U.S. Pacific Command. McCain refused, choosing to stay behind, support, and give confidence to his comrades also imprisoned. His decision resulted in an extended five-and-a-half year stay. Today, United States Senator McCain says that that comradeship defined who he would become. "Nothing in life is more liberating," he has written, "than to fight for a cause larger than yourself, something that encompasses you but is not defined by your existence alone." That's what motivational leadership is all about—defining yourself by your undertakings and the people around you that you continue to cheer on.

The Least You Need to Know

- If you ham up your gusto on any particular day, you'll invariably convince even *yourself* that you're motivated, and then you *will* be! Such enthusiasm is highly contagious.

- Sometimes, being a truly motivational leader means saying things that look corny on paper and might even sound corny as you're saying them but register in a positive way with your team members—and resonate with those members in a wonderful way long after you've said them.

- Leading your team "from the trenches," rather than hiding in your office, helps you gain their admiration and adds to your influence as a cheerleader and a motivator.

- Being "in the trenches" with your team doesn't mean putting yourself in a position where you compromise your air of authority and responsibility.

- One-on-one management counter-intuitively opens up the work-day, rather than taking up more time. It allows for very personal, persuasive management, and effective communication of important concerns.

- History is filled with figures who transformed their surroundings and history itself by cheering on, encouraging, and inspiring their teams on personal levels.

Chapter 11

Establish Relationships

In This Chapter

- ◆ Harvesting the curious relationship known as rapport
- ◆ Showing more than a cursory interest in the personal goals and aspirations of others
- ◆ Fostering teamwork as something more than just a cliché
- ◆ Selling a team on synergy
- ◆ Developing a fresh (and savvy) appreciation for the opinions of others
- ◆ Using communication as the fuel that feeds good work relationships

Motivational leaders understand that while it's not easy to clearly define rapport, it's very easy to see its merits. They know how to develop it and how to demonstrate genuine interest in the individual talents, opinions, and interests of their team members. On the other hand, they know how to look past those individual identities and to foster a team identity and encourage a spirit of collaboration. They know how to plainly portray to others that the lines of communication are open and how to listen for the nuggets of useful information that are always available for mining. In this chapter, we'll learn why the most motivated teams are often the most hospitable, gracious teams.

Know What Rapport Means

Your job, even as a motivational leader, is not to get people to love you or even to like you. Many well-liked bosses never get anything out of their teams. It's not even to get them to respect or admire you. After all, forced respect isn't really respect at all. In fact, as a team leader, who is forced to make tough decisions sometimes, you're often going to be anything but cherished. Your job is to build the type of relationship that will continue to generate some kind of loyalty and good work results, even as you go forward with the occasionally unpopular policy or course of action.

That relationship is what is known as *rapport*. It is a bond that's created through openness, trust, appreciation for information and support, and a displayed sense of what someone else is going through at any given time. The funny thing about rapport is that, when it's generated, it *does* bring about feelings of fondness and respect and admiration (even though that's not what it's there for). This common sincerity among team members starts as nothing more than mutual deference and openness, but it eventually builds into the kinships that make good teams great. In other words, you don't *have* to love your teammates, but on a great team, you probably will.

def•i•ni•tion

Rapport (pronounced "rah-POOR") is a working or business relationship steeped in mutual trust, empathy, a sense of kinship, and warm personal regard. While it is not a necessary component of workplace life, it tends to make people more productive, more likely to share ideas and solutions, and more likely to collaborate. It fits nicely into a list of attributes that workers use to describe the ideal workplace.

Know Why Rapport Matters

There are bosses and leaders who consistently get things done without an ounce of rapport between them and their teams. It's not a necessity.

But it absolutely matters. Without rapport, there's no sense of teamwork or of collaboration or of generally good feelings among team members. I once worked with someone who felt nothing but disdain for the people who were in charge of him. His mantra? "Eight hours is eight hours," he used to say regularly and loudly. In other words, "You're getting the bare minimum out of me, and not a minute more and not an ounce of energy more." He did his job, and, people begrudgingly admitted, he did it well, and he was generally untouchable because of it. But he never reached his potential as a team member or even as a prospective supervisor. The team suffered, too.

Without rapport, you might always get the minimum required from people, but you'll never get anything more, and you'll never take the team to new, important heights. Without it, you'll never be a true motivational leader.

> ### Best Voices Forward
>
> Famous leadership expert and consultant Chris Widener (MadeForSuccess.com) says that his chats with young, aspiring managers suggest that character traits, such as rapport and thoughtfulness, make up 90 percent of the qualities people expect in a motivational leader, with talent and skill making up the other 10 percent. "How curious it is," notes Widener, "that we spend so much time in school learning skills, but so little time, if any, learning character!"

Get Out the Word

Get out the word that you're interested in your team. That is, you're interested in their professional development, and you're interested in their career progression—even if such progression means they're going to leave at some point. If you show you're concerned with them, it will come back to you in a variety of ways as the team leader. One of these days, meet with your team members individually and see what each one of them is all about. What makes her tick? What makes her important to the team? What skills does she bring? What are her concerns about the team as it's currently set up? What are her apprehensions about the organization? What are her personal aspirations? What are her current career goals?

Repeated Excellence

Establishing constructive relationships with your team first requires that you get their guard down. Karen Barry, a district manager for Verizon Wireless, says that nothing good can happen when you take on a team until they get the notion that you're with them and not against them. "Very often, the team you take charge of will include very smart, very experienced people," she says. "It is important that they know you're not arriving to immediately stir things up." Barry suggests early get-togethers, one-on-one if possible, with the team members you're newly responsible for, finding out what team members are hoping for, and encouraging new, innovative approaches. "Tell them, 'these are the facts,'" she says, "'but let's see what sort of new ways *you* can interpret these facts.'"

Keep in mind that you're not saying, "I want to be your friend." Again, there will be times and hard decisions that identify you as a boss and not a buddy. Instead, what you're trying to say is, "I want to support you in all you do, and I want the people on this team to support each other." That's how to get out the word that you're hoping for helpful relationships up, down, and across.

Okay, you say, but talk is cheap. You're right—it is. At some point, you're going to have to put your money where your mouth is. As early as possible, check your planner for an item that one of your team members thought important and maybe personally pertinent. Take action on it, or at least follow up on it with some time, energy, and information. Let that person know you're on it. Try as quickly as possible to follow it through to some resolution. *Then* you're getting out the word.

From the perspective of professional advancement, your superiors might initially balk at your encouraging someone's career progression to the point of losing that person. Ultimately, you must do what your bosses tell you to do. But hopefully, you can persuade them that creating a crackerjack team is going to mean that some people will have to spread their wings. Remind your bosses that if you're not developing people to move on at some point, then your people are not going to be at their best during the time they work for you. Besides, the loyalty you'll generate from showing personal concern in people's futures will easily offset the occasional loss of talent.

Develop Teamwork

As mentioned earlier, people want to belong and inherently yearn to identify with a group. Why not tap into that inborn human trait and encourage team pride and identification? Hey, I'm not talking about company T-shirts. Er, well, maybe I am, but not *just* that! I'm talking about the feeling you get when you think you're a part of something bigger than just you. It's a wonderful emotion—that sentiment you get from contributing to an important cause and believing that you're an integral part of the effort.

After team identity is established and solidified, a healthy competition between your team and others is another way to keep this team's identity and pride going. When your team stands out over others, point out this achievement whenever possible, and loudly proclaim your gratification at being a part of such a fine lineup. It may seem corny, but it often works to make people feel good about themselves and the team they're a part of.

Having said that, teamwork needs to be more than just a cliché. Psychologists have pointed out for years that the dynamics of a team—groupthink notwithstanding—can contribute to its own success through a turmoil-and-creativity period that eventually settles into a productive and positive relationship.

> **Best Voices Forward**
>
> U.S. Steel founder and famous philanthropist Andrew Carnegie had this to say about teamwork: "Teamwork is the ability to work together toward a common vision—the ability to direct individual accomplishments toward organizational objectives. It is the fuel that allows common people to attain uncommon results." Perceptive words from one of the most singularly powerful American businesspeople ever.

For example, in 1965, educational psychologist Bruce Tuckman (who, at this writing, teaches at Ohio State University) wrote an article titled "Development Sequence in Small Groups," which appeared in the academic journal *Psychological Bulletin*. Sound like a yawner? No way! In that article, Tuckman came up with the ultimate mnemonic (memory aid) for characterizing the progression of the most effective teams: *forming, storming, norming, and performing*!

Tuckman said that teams begin their process by *forming*, where team members learn about one another while staying focused primarily on themselves. The *storming* phase occurs when differing personalities and priorities start banging against one another in conflict, sometimes creative and professional, sometimes not. Assuming a collective maturity among the group prevails, it moves to the *norming* phase. This is the phase in which much of the norm setting, peer pressure, and conformity (mentioned earlier) takes place. It all serves a purpose, but if it is allowed to take over without the occasional devil's advocate, it might become paralyzing as groupthink and unreasonable calls for obedience conquer everything else. If things continue to move nicely for this team, it moves to the *performing* stage, where teams function with minimal supervision while staying innovative and dynamic. (Tuckman later added two other stages: *adjourning* and *transforming*.)

It's important, in establishing relationships, that teams learn to identify themselves as such—proud, self-motivated, energetic teams—as they work toward common goals.

Encourage Collaboration

As a motivational leader, you must work to foster an environment where people are likely to pool their individual skills and resources to accomplish something for the team. This ideal runs opposite to the situation where people prefer to stay segmented, isolated, and self-focused.

The key to good collaboration is not simply to bring the best people forward in some crazy gifted mind merge. It would be an odd forest, indeed, if only the most beautiful-sounding birds were allowed to sing. We all bring something different to the workplace, some skill or knowledge or work preference. And what we might not have in talent, we might make up for in passion. As all those gifts come together, they merge in a manner that has a funny way of getting things accomplished. It boils down to the somewhat hackneyed but forever real notion of synergy, where the whole is greater than the sum of the parts.

Know the Ways to Encourage Collaboration

There are some quick and easy ways to promote an atmosphere of collaboration within your team. First, take a laissez-faire approach. Allow the free market of ideas, skills, passions, and needs to merge and interlock. Forced collaboration, just like a command economy, won't get the job done the way a free-market merging of talents, like a free-market economy, does.

Second, emphasize combined performance as much as you do individual performance. If a collaborative effort takes place, identify its results and make a fuss over the two, three, or more people who made it happen. If things go famously, make certain that, when it's time for each person's annual evaluation, the collaborative effort is mentioned on each person's review.

Third, for special, shared projects, reward people as groups. That is, identify them as the small subteam that put together their efforts and made it happen. Take them all out for lunch. Give them all time off (if you're allowed to as team leader).

Fourth (and this is a recurring theme), sell people on the team's mission as much as possible. Remind them that what's good for the organization is good for the team, and what's good for the team is good for each of them. At some point, hopefully, they'll put aside their more self-serving efforts and interests in order to get the collaboration going.

Fifth, hold training sessions. Share ideas and debate different styles and techniques for doing things. Allow people to share, aloud, what they're good at and where their passions lie. If, at a later meeting, a collaborative effort has resulted in some type of new best practice, have that subteam brief the rest of the group on what they're doing new and right.

Conversely, if you want to encourage the pooling of resources, avoid holding standard workplace meetings whenever possible. Ironically, time in a meeting (as opposed to time in training) is time away from having people collaborate, innovate, and blossom. (More on that in Chapter 12.)

Know that Good Communication Goes Two Ways

As mentioned in Chapter 2, one of the main attributes of a motivational leader is an exceptional talent for listening. Listening isn't just for show. That is, when you look at someone and nod your head as if you're interested, you shouldn't be thinking about what you're going to make for dinner that night. You should really *be* interested in what that person has to say. When you decide to merrily absorb what your team members have to offer, you just might be surprised by what you've been missing.

Listening involves walking around, saying hello, and not hiding in an office or behind your desk or even behind your folded arms. It involves reflecting phrases back at people who are talking and asking them short, open-ended, clarifying questions. It entails writing things down so that people think you're taking them seriously. And, yes, it *does* mean occasionally nodding your head (without thinking of dinner), as you suggest to them that you understand. More importantly, it involves allowing them to finish a sentence before you begin to talk and without finishing it for them.

Unfortunately, good listening is not the norm in today's place of business. I respectfully argue that most managers like to hear themselves talk and consider it their duty to talk as much as possible.

I once had a supervisor who would ask a question and then get very angry every time someone answered it. Finally, one day, someone got up the courage to ask him what he was so upset about. "I wasn't asking the question hoping for an answer," he said, fuming. "I was asking it hoping you might all *think* about it!" Yikes! There wasn't much two-way communication going on there, was there? I remember the collective sigh of relief everyone felt when he left for bigger and better things.

In a way, I understood where he was coming from. After we assume responsibility for a team, we all get to a point where we begin to feel very sure of who we are and what we expect. And we become very certain about how we like things done. Asking a question without really caring about the answer is conveying a message: "Look into yourselves for the solution, but *my* mind is made up, so please don't confuse me with an answer."

The trouble with this all-too-common supervisory attitude is that we often tend to forget that the very best ideas come from our team members and not from us. By avoiding great ideas and important input in our daily info-gathering, due to our cavalier attitudes, we set ourselves up for eventual failure. Others will watch gleefully, recalling how we asked questions but never wanted an answer.

Keep the Lines of Communication Open

It's easy to spot a team or an organization where exchanges of ideas are rare and where secrecy and pettiness are the rule of the day. When people feel as if they're supposed to keep to themselves, or if they feel they'll survive best by keeping to themselves, it creates an ugly coating on the entire operation—a dark, sticky gum on what should be a shiny, humming machine. The secrecy and pettiness turn into paranoia. Everyone's preoccupied. Nothing gets done well.

Furthermore, in this type of dysfunctional organization, communication works in a different way—to serve the evil existence of maliciousness and rumor mongering. It's a tough way to live, and it's almost impossible to be creative and productive.

The difference begins with you, the motivational leader. At any given time, you need to be approachable. People should *want* to bring you information, even if it's occasionally bad news. Your tendency to walk around, visit people at their workstations or offices, maintain a sincere smile—it all portrays a message: "There is no wall between me and you."

Let people know you value their input. The words "I appreciate this information" will mean a lot to people, no matter how many times you say it. And you'll notice that the desire for open transmissions turns contagious. Hey, it's nice to belong to a team that freely conveys ideas and important information. It's very gratifying, and it's very self-sustaining.

One Step Back

By all accounts (even his own), James Cameron, who wrote, produced, and directed the movie *Titanic*, was very unapproachable during the filming of that movie. Busy dealing with too much water, too many character extras, and too much cost overrunning, he was something of a grouch. As a result, very creative people on the set were often afraid to speak to him with their ideas. Cameron had said early on and adamantly that he didn't want singing in the movie score. And so, the composer, James Horner, almost finished the movie without seeing if Cameron might change his mind. Finally, one day, Horner decided to push past the grumpiness and see if Cameron might be up for one song with lyrics. The result? Horner's megahit, "My Heart Will Go On," recorded by Celine Dion with lyrics by Will Jennings. It was an award-winning song that amazingly almost never happened because of a leader's inapproachability.

When this type of team is formed, people will begin approaching you not only to provide you information, but to seek it as well. And your team members will come to you not only for answers, but also for you to serve as a soundboard, as they bounce *their* ideas and solutions off you. Be a sport. Let them find their own resolutions and run them by you. Be the facilitator and the encourager.

One point of caution: ensure that people are first approaching their immediate supervisors before they come to you. You want to show your team leaders that you respect their professional integrity and give them the courtesy of not allowing them to be passed over or undermined. Corporate chains of command *ain't* what they used to be, but to the extent that they still exist, they should be revered.

Open, constructive communication is the fuel that keeps good work relationships burning. It sustains the sense of trust and mutual respect that defines rapport, and it creates and maintains the teamwork needed to take a team as far as it can go.

The Least You Need to Know

◆ Rapport defines a workplace relationship that is built on mutual confidence, empathy, and a sense of personal connection and regard.

◆ Creating relationships means showing an interest in the professional and career goals of others.

◆ Encouraging collaboration brings about a synergy of expertise and talent where the whole becomes greater than the sum of the parts.

◆ A team needs to pass through a number of phases—some of them potentially dysfunctional—on its way to being an efficient, productive entity.

◆ Good body language and proactive listening open up the type of communication that makes for highly effective leadership.

◆ Unlike dysfunctional organizations where secrecy and pettiness prevail, organizations that thrive on strong working relations enjoy very open lines of communication.

Chapter 12

Understand Why Meetings Don't Work

In This Chapter

- ◆ Looking at the inherently flawed nature of business meetings
- ◆ Reflecting on the unconventional notion that a meeting isn't really necessary
- ◆ Figuring out some human-trait reasons why meetings are destined to crash even before they take off
- ◆ Finding ways to coordinate your team without meetings
- ◆ Working out an agenda for your workday and an agenda for the occasional meeting
- ◆ Conducting the rare, well-run meeting

Motivational leaders understand how *un*motivational meetings really are. They recognize that the standard workplace meeting is an inherently flawed management vehicle. They don't hold meetings just because that's what others are doing. They recognize the unfortunate human traits that surface and thrive during meetings. They use meeting alternatives to lead. And when a meeting is absolutely necessary, they know how to put together a tight agenda and some worthwhile preparation. In this chapter, we'll consider how meetings can hinder an operation, what impact a meeting-centered culture has on a team, and how the motivational leader can overcome this culture.

Avoid "A Nightmare on Meeting Street"

How would you like to do something right now that will make your team respect you three times more than they normally do and instantly motivate them for the rest of the day? Just say, "You know, let's cancel today's meeting. I'll walk around and get each person's input later." The first thing they might ask is, "What planet are you from, and where have you hidden our boss?" The second thing they might ask is, "Uh, are you serious?" When they realize it's no joke, they will be wholly energized for the rest of the day—and maybe longer!

People hate *meetings*. If you were to prompt your team, individually and anonymously, to list the five worst things about working for your organization, I suspect meetings would make most "Top Fives." And rightfully so. There's something painfully stifling and grating about the majority of meetings. They're a nightmare: "A Nightmare on Meeting Street." To the majority of people who attend them, they are worthless endeavors, pulling key players away from important tasks and eating up time that could be better used a hundred other ways.

def•i•ni•tion

Before we criticize the inner workings of a **meeting,** let's make sure we clarify what we're talking about. That is, let's spell out what constitutes a bona fide workplace meeting. A meeting is a real-time get-together among three or more people, with a moderator, an agenda, goals, and two-way communication. Events that don't exactly fit this definition (and, therefore, hold a lot more merit than most meetings) include training, safety briefings, and pep talks.

A National Pandemic

The revulsion for meetings isn't just a silly part of workplace griping or water cooler custom. Disillusionment over meetings is evidenced by how much they have taken over the work culture and how inefficient they have proven themselves to be. Year after year, business school studies delving into the nature of meetings find the same, regrettable statistics. That is, managers and administrators consistently spend between 25 and 50 percent of their workdays in meetings, and at least half of all meeting time is unproductive. With over 85 million professional workers in the United States (managers, specialists, salespeople, administrators, and technical staff), that works out to between 41 billion and 82 billion combined hours per year spent in meetings, with at least half of those hours forever wasted. From the perspective of national productivity, the flawed nature of meetings is ominous and very sobering.

Books abound on how to make meetings run better. But a small cadre of business writers (including myself) make a somewhat different argument: it's fundamentally impossible to mend a business meeting, because certain things about it are inherently flawed. That is, you can't fix the standard workplace meeting, because it never worked to begin with. Sound nutty? Consider, then, how much you see getting accomplished in a meeting, whether you're running it or whether you are an unwilling participant.

The motives for holding most meetings initially seem obvious enough. They include putting out information, asking key players for input, and participating in group problem-solving. Now ask yourself these questions. (Be honest.) Do most people who attend your team's meetings *really* absorb the information that is disseminated, or is roughly three-quarters of the info lost in translation or forgetfulness before people reach the door? Does advice at your meetings *really* come from the smartest people, or do the smartest people sit silently—waiting for the agony to end—while the showboaters, grandstanders, and whiners perform their daily exhibitions? Do tough problems *really* get solved by the group during meetings, or do unbelievably bad solutions develop lives of their own, courtesy of groupthink (discussed in Chapter 6)? Are meetings *really* doing the things you hoped they would do? And, if not, why are you still doing them? Let's consider the last question first.

Know If a Meeting Is *Really* Necessary

If anything mentioned above rings true, why were you about to hold that meeting that you were about to hold? Was it *really* necessary?

If you find yourself internally conflicted over knowing your meetings are probably useless and still feeling compelled to hold them anyway, it may be because there's a difference you haven't exactly resolved between why you hold meetings and why you *think* you hold them.

Why do you *think* you hold meetings? Jot down a few reasons. My guess is that your list will include passing along information, putting people on the same sheet of music, getting "face time" with team members, solving problems, and bridging differences.

But if few of those things are really happening, then why do you really hold meetings? Reach down deep and see what you find. My guess as to what this revelation list might divulge? You hold meetings because that's what your predecessor did. You hold them because that's what your peers are doing. You hold them because you occasionally equate running a good meeting with getting something done. (Hey, it's a self-deception that happens to all of us.) And you hold meetings because you haven't yet tapped into the ways a motivational leader gathers information and makes decisions. (Of course, purchasing this book is a wonderful commitment toward selecting a new path.)

Some Signs a Meeting Is Necessary

Having said all that, there may, admittedly, be times when a meeting is entirely unavoidable. Examples include episodes where urgent face time is needed with your team, perhaps to ease some anxiety about a looming crisis or to address a recently announced, calamitous corporate change.

Another sign a meeting might be necessary is that, in the midst of an emergency, you start getting a lot of visits to your office, and you are approached by a lot of people in the hallway. They ask a lot of questions that you have already promised to answer as soon as you know the information. Truth is, they're visiting and asking those questions more to see your reaction and to make sure that you're still at the wheel. A quick get-together to reassure the team in the middle of this predicament and to convince them that you're still in charge might not be a bad idea.

Finally, a meeting might be necessary because, in your bag of tricks, there doesn't seem to be another way of doing it. Walking around and talking to people, one-on-one get-togethers, delegating, mentoring, e-mails—if there's a situation where none of those options seem like they will work, then a meeting, for all its flaws, might be the necessary evil for that moment.

Ten Things to Ask Yourself

In an earlier book, *Stop the Meeting, I Want to Get Off!*, I suggested a list of ten things to ask yourself before you call your next potentially unnecessary meeting:

1. Are you calling this meeting because you have surrendered to its existence (or because your peers are holding the same type of meeting)?

2. Is it possible that the dynamics of your group might inherently keep this meeting from working at all?

3. Can this meeting be replaced with walking around and addressing your team members one-on-one?

4. Can this meeting be replaced with your strong leadership?

5. Can this meeting be replaced with organizational channeling (pointing people and resources in the right direction without major, meeting-centered coordination)?

6. Can this meeting be replaced with delegating?

7. Can this meeting be replaced with information or communication technology (outside of real time)?

8. Can this meeting be replaced with mentoring?

9. Is this meeting being asked for by someone else, and, if so, can you avoid that request without being disrespectful?

10. Now that you've convinced yourself this meeting is absolutely unavoidable, can you convince yourself that it is avoidable?

The necessity of a meeting should be determined from the vantage point that when people are in a meeting, they are doing nothing else.

Understand Why Most Meetings Fail

As mentioned previously, you probably have experienced the sensation that most meetings you attend are destined to fail before they even begin—for no other reason than, well, they're meetings. Your gut feelings are certainly correct. There are some psychological aspects to meetings—features that are built right in—that ensure their failure to a very high degree. We've discussed a few at length, for example the human need for belongingness and the human tendency toward conformity. There's also the spectacle of groupthink, a human quirk tailored especially for the standard workplace meeting.

Another human oddity is the *safe-and-silent slant.* That is, many very smart team members, sensing the social dysfunction of what's going on in the conference room, choose to sit silently. They might feign interest, take notes, and even nod their heads at times. They might sit silently as a very bad idea comes up and gets bought into. But these good folks have been around these spectacles enough to know that perhaps the best course is to sit quietly and wait for the suffering to end. From a self-focused perspective, there certainly doesn't seem to be much personal penalty for doing so.

But the conference-room psychology doesn't end there. If someone isn't shutting up in compliance or shutting up in disgust, there's an even-money probability that he or she is part of a quirky cast of characters who feel the uncomfortable urge to fill the silence left by others. These wacky workers include the guy who thinks the world is coming to an end with each announced change, the socialite who brings food and has a host of red-herring rumor-mill topics, and the pious team member who nervously cuts down all ideas by reciting corporate policy verbatim and ad nauseam. We've all seen these people, and we've all learned to love, er, accept them.

For good measure, throw some other, common, psychological wrenches into the broken machine we call the *workplace meeting.* They include the tendency of some people to use meetings as political battlegrounds, grandstanding, and drawing enemy lines, hoping to form alliances.

They also include the natural penchant for showing up at a meeting with some type of personal agenda. That's very understandable—very human—but it certainly isn't very facilitating.

And finally, throw poor planning into the mix. Managers and team leaders are extremely busy, often "putting out fires" and dealing with the emergency of the minute. If anything requiring time and effort is going to suffer, it is going to be meeting preparation. As a result, even very good leaders often show up for a scheduled get-together with only a broad-stroke notion about what they're going to say. It feels like an insult when we realize they're winging it. But, in deference to our leaders, we keep our mouths buttoned.

Use Alternatives to Meetings

Is there a better way of doing things? Sure. Pioneers in motivational leadership have been suggesting meeting alternatives for years. The key is to challenge a culture that doesn't seem to want to let go of this generally flawed management device.

Assuming something you've read in this chapter has touched a nerve, let's consider some different ways of putting out information, gathering input, and having team members solve problems.

Some Meeting Alternatives

Although MBWA ("Managing By Walking Around") seems to fade in and out of fashion over the years, my argument is that it never faded *into* fashion enough. Management icon Tom Peters was a big proponent of the method in the 1980s. He sold me, as have dozens of other leaders I've interviewed over the years who see MBWA as a wonderful technique for influencing others and gaining pertinent information. I suggest that the hour you spend walking around and talking holds 10 times more impact over a team than does the hour you spend addressing them in a conference room.

While you're scheduling some MBWA time, why not also schedule some one-on-one get-togethers with your team members? The walls of caution tend to come down when people aren't with their peers. And smart people, who otherwise might sit silently, tend to open up if they feel they have the ear of a caring, interested, personable boss.

Don't be fooled into thinking that meetings are more time-efficient than one-on-ones. Consider the math. If you have a team of ten, and you meet with each of them for, say, fifteen minutes, that's two and a half hours. Assuming two, one-hour meetings each eat up fifteen extra minutes by starting and ending a bit late, your one-on-ones—powerful, personal vehicles of influence—only consume the time of two very short, standard workplace meetings.

It's also worth mentioning here that delegating and maintaining a delegation list is a commendable replacement for meetings. More on delegating is discussed in Chapter 14.

A Big-Time Executive Who Limited His Meetings

It's impossible to write about the dynamics of meetings without mentioning a real pioneer in this area, retired head of logistics for Sears Roebuck & Company, Gus Pagonis.

Pagonis, a former three-star U.S. Army general known for his innovations in moving soldiers and equipment during Operation Desert Storm, brought his know-how to Sears in the 1990s and did some pretty incredible things. But just as importantly, Pagonis was big on taking the standard workplace meeting and turning it inside-out.

If Pagonis could run a staff get-together a little differently or get information to people without wasting too much of their time, he did so. For example, Pagonis helped pioneer the idea of holding brief meetings where everyone stood up. The message: don't get comfortable, because this isn't going to take long! He also executed something called the "3×5" message, which actually was written on a 3×5 index card before the advent of e-mail. The point of the message was to send a concern, all the way up the chain of command, if necessary, until it was addressed by a decision-maker and sent back down. Anyone could start a 3×5, and no meetings were necessary.

Pagonis dreaded the stereotypical, butcher-block brainstorming session. "No one has ever proven to me the benefit of having people sit together in a room and haphazardly brainstorm," he said, in typical no-nonsense fashion.

Don't Film the Movie Without a Script

This might be a good time to restate the importance of planning your workday as much as you can before you arrive each morning. If you schedule time to walk around, say hello, and gather information, you're infinitely more likely to do those things. If you schedule one-on-one get-togethers as meeting alternatives, they're more likely to work. And if your delegating list is tightly managed, you're much more likely to reap the benefits of entrusting work to others. All of these things help you reduce your desire for holding meetings—meetings that almost certainly wouldn't have had the same positive effect on your team.

And speaking of those meetings, if studies suggest that half of all meeting time is downright unproductive, then it seems the best way to tackle this inefficiency would be to program a meeting (when you feel like you absolutely *must* hold one) just as tightly. If not, it is more apt to fall prey to the human conditions already mentioned. Keep the script tight: five-minute blocks, with someone to help you stay on schedule (your favorite human attack dog).

Incidentally, here's a novel thought: start the meeting on time! If people are still strolling in with coffee and donuts ten minutes into the meeting, they either don't belong on your key-players invitation list, or they'll get the message and be on time next time around.

Don't ever extend a meeting's time with the hope of wrapping up something that wasn't resolved in the allocated amount of time. The dynamics in the conference room that kept you from an initial resolution are still there. Try it again some other time, or try one of the meeting substitutes.

Run That Rare, Successful Meeting

So now that I've made my argument that there's really no such thing as a fully functional meeting, let's consider some ways to get a meeting as close to effective as possible. If you limit meetings in the manners suggested in this chapter, those fewer, urgent get-togethers will likely progress better if you consider these measures.

The "garbage in, garbage out" philosophy unquestionably applies to meetings. If you put some preparation into your get-together, you'll get at least something out of it. If you go into a meeting with the notion, as its moderator, that you're going to wing it, you're probably going to flop it. The meeting's start time is not time to start getting ready for it.

Again, nothing rivals good meeting preparation more than setting a strict agenda. While you're at it, make a personal commitment to stick to it. Assign someone to help follow the agenda, item by item, scheduled minute by scheduled minute.

Limit what you plan to accomplish. Your itinerary and planning should be laser-focused on only two or three items at most. "Having too many meeting items is like trying to boil the ocean," offers Verizon district manager Karen Barry.

Limit the number of people you plan on inviting. It's pleasant enough (warm and fuzzy, even) to want to have everyone feel wanted and involved, but conference rooms get hot and crowded in a hurry. Besides, the larger the roster, the less work that's getting done outside the room. If your goals are limited and only a few people are concerned, limit your list to them. Hopefully, when the others find out that there was a meeting and they weren't invited, they won't feel rejected, but instead, they'll feel as if they were handed an hour or two of free life.

Best Voices Forward

When it comes to inviting too many people to a meeting, my favorite quotation comes from a good friend and former boss, planning and purchasing director John Pastor. "It's like football," he says, referring to a meeting's invitation list. "The quarterback is worried about the next play, the coach is worried about the next game, and the general manager is worried about the next season. So why should all three of them be in a room at once?"

Limit the time you plan on spending in the meeting, and be ferocious about stopping on time. Brief and mission-oriented is the key. End on time. When that second hand is sweeping around the final minute, let people know it. Get a reputation for wrapping up a meeting at all costs. There's work to be done, and the conference room isn't where it's going to happen.

Finally, ensure that, at any given moment, you're running the meeting and not the other way around. If you feel like you're losing control, grab your agenda and get back on track. Oops, you forgot to put an agenda together? Hey, no pity from me: ya reap what ya sow.

If you are truly a motivator of teams, you recognize that the last thing people really want to hear is your blathering at a meeting. Be the motivational leader. Live by the creed that the best meeting is the one not called.

The Least You Need to Know

♦ Many potentially good managers feel the need to hold meetings in spite of recognizing that these get-togethers are often unnecessary and inherently ineffective.

♦ Aside from a small list of urgent reasons to get a team together, the more likely underlying reasons for holding meetings include mimicking predecessors and peers and a fear of trying other methods for exchanging information and making decisions.

♦ Human traits that make meetings dysfunctional include the tendency toward conformity, the need to belong, the urge to remain safe and silent, the vulnerability to groupthink, the potential for playing politics, the likelihood of socializing, and the (sometimes vocal) fear of change.

♦ Some praiseworthy alternatives to meetings include Managing By Walking Around (MBWA), scheduled one-on-one get-togethers, and delegating.

♦ If you must hold a meeting, start your meeting on time, never extend the time, and aggressively follow your agenda, minute by minute, with help, if possible.

♦ If a meeting is absolutely necessary, make sure that you put some preparation into it.

Part 4

Use Inspiration over Intimidation

Negative reinforcement is easy: do your job or you'll lose it. But teams don't get very far if that's the only reason people go to work. There are several solid examples where organizations have accomplished great things because their people were inspired by grand themes, images, ideals, and goals.

Developing inspirational leadership includes becoming comfortable with delegating. Many leaders find themselves unable or unwilling to delegate, concerned that handing over tasks is akin to giving up control of the group. However, instead of relinquishing control, the leader who delegates counterintuitively gains more hands-on control when his monitoring of tasks is combined with the innovations of others. Delegating does not diminish the leader's standing as a motivational leader: delegating enhances it because the leader gains support from the group by showing confidence in individual team members.

Chapter 13

Provide Heartfelt Encouragement

In This Chapter

- Tapping into human needs
- Learning what psychologists say about the need for acceptance
- Analyzing the delicate makeup of people
- Finding constant and meaningful encouragement
- Forming a feeling of kinship
- Winning over the skeptics

Motivational leaders understand the very predicable, very common aspects of basic human needs and how they fit into organizational behavior. Motivational leaders recognize the fragile nature of self-esteem and why it's important to nurture it and constantly reinforce it among team members. Motivational leaders realize the importance of promoting a sense of community at the workplace and of winning over skeptics with caring words and common goals. In this chapter, we'll learn what makes people tick and why the encouraging word is a powerful management tool, as opposed to simply something nice to say.

Understand Human Needs

I was once hired by a manufacturing company to bring discipline into a particular department. "He's a West Pointer," the human resources director said to the department head. "He'll know how to bang some heads!" I certainly didn't promise them that I would bang some heads, but, hoping to get the job, I didn't make an issue over their presumption, either.

And so, the human resources director and the department head were surprised—and not pleasantly so—when I began my first day of work at the plant by walking around, introducing myself, listening intently to my team members, writing down their concerns, following up on as many of those concerns as possible, and trying to make their work shifts relatively pleasant. I struck up a work-related friendship with the union shop foreman, I calmed down two or three of the most unruly employees on the shift, and, if people were doing their jobs and churning out quality product, I generally left them alone after my initial round of walking around and listening. Not only did our department make a lot of good product, but we did so while enduring a couple of difficult downsizings.

The human resources director, a man who loved his confrontations, let me know in one way or another that this amity-type of managing wasn't what I was hired for. I tried to win him over by pointing out that things were working, but he wasn't convinced, and when he realized that I wasn't going to run my shift like a dictator, he moved me to another department and brought in a new hire—one of the meanest, most oppressive people I've ever met. How did things work out for this new, cruel-hearted foreman? He was fired in a few months. And a department that had, by many accounts, settled down into reasonably acceptable work habits was left in disarray.

I'm certainly not suggesting that the motivational leader is always a friend to everyone: being a pushover can be just as ineffective as being a tyrant. But I am suggesting that the leader who understands the human needs of people and tries to recognize them in dealing with his team is 100 times more likely to succeed in the long term.

We've discussed those human needs throughout this text. They include people's desire to feel healthy and secure, to feel like they fit into the group, to feel admired and occasionally important, and, sometimes, to feel like they have accomplished something creative or significant.

Consider What Else the Experts Say

When you understand human needs and how most people are psychologically inclined, it's much easier to deal with them and to provide them with sincere encouragement during your relationship with them. Consider for a moment what some of the experts have had to say about what humans need—or at least what they perceive they need.

Abraham Maslow

As mentioned in Chapters 1 and 8, humanistic psychologist Abraham Maslow proposed in the 1940s and 1950s that, after essential physical needs are met, people inherently begin to seek the approval of others, through family love, group membership, and the basic acceptance of others around them. This very human need for acceptance is an intense force in our lives—much more than we probably care to admit. Again, peer pressure does not end with prom tuxedos and acne medication. The desire to conform stays with us for a lifetime.

I'm a big fan of Maslow. Although his theories have been adjusted, questioned, and flat-out challenged over the decades, I think his understanding about how innate forces push us, as well as how these forces fall into a predicable pecking order, is dead on. The cool thing I like about Maslow is that, back when many psychologists were focusing on psychoses and the sick mind, Maslow delved into psychology as it affected everyone, including very successful people. Furthermore, he became famous as he carried his theories into the business world, giving lectures and suggesting what great things motivational leaders could achieve if they accepted the human side of both themselves and the people they managed. Maslow was—and still is—da man!

Victor Frankl

I also like the refreshing thoughts of Victor Frankl, a neurologist and Holocaust survivor, who suggested that, when people live lives that seem to lack meaning for them, it is, indeed, a very empty existence. The good news, said Frankl, was that people are very much in control of their own sense of purpose and forming significance in their lives. He argued that people's attitudes can be channeled in such a way that they are able to find meaning and a positive outlook in any given situation.

David Burns

David Burns, a medical doctor and a pioneer in the study of cognitive behavioral therapy, is a very popular writer of self-help books. He proposes that we often have these natural brain warps, called *cognitive distortions*, which dramatically magnify our negative feelings about not getting what we want. By identifying these distortions and recognizing their poisonous effects, Burns suggests that we help ourselves feel a lot better before we even change our situation.

Repeated Excellence

David D. Burns, M.D., suggests that we wouldn't be so depressed and apprehensive about what we *don't* have in this world if we didn't allow the Ten Cognitive Distortions to make things much worse in our minds than they really are. In his books *Feeling Good* and *The Feeling Good Handbook*, he identifies those games our own minds seem to play with us. They include extreme thinking and generalizing, where we tend to look at things in all-or-nothing fashion. They also include mind-sifting, where we concentrate only on negatives. These distortions incorporate overblown predictions. Finally, they include self-pigeonholing, where we label ourselves in broad terms as failures or losers. Again, once we recognize the folly of these mind games, we feel better about ourselves and our situations.

Dale Carnegie

Finally, human interaction pioneer Dale Carnegie indicated back in the 1930s and 1940s that one of the greatest human needs is the need to feel important, and that making someone feel significant is an essential first step in motivating that person toward a particular behavior.

Respect the Fragile Nature of People

I once worked with a gruff old boss who I'm pretty sure could have ripped me in half with one hand tied behind his back. He was a big, crusty guy that everyone loved and respected—and feared, if just a little.

And so, I was surprised when I once described how I planned to counsel a team member who had done a poor job during a machine "conditioning," or scheduled maintenance, and he indicated that the chewing-out I was planning would be too rough.

"Why's that?" I asked, perplexed. "He really screwed up big-time today."

"Yes," said this brusque old man. "But people are fragile, and you don't want to break him."

People are fragile. Well, that was the last thing I had expected to come out of that curmudgeon's mouth. But he was right. People are, undeniably, very delicate, and words often can and do hurt. The motivational leader is sensitive to this human condition and is comfortable with the task of keeping people's *self-esteem* elevated and secure as much as possible.

def•i•ni•tion

> **Self-esteem** is a person's personal feeling of self-worth. It includes one's self-assessment regarding knowledge, ability, accomplishment, and personal control over one's destiny. A person with low self-esteem often feels disheartened and powerless.
>
> Although one might think this term is relatively new in this age of promoting high self-esteem, it is, in fact, over 100 years old. United States psychologist William James defined self-esteem in a large text on psychology he wrote in the late 1800s.

"Is everyone such a soft touch?" you might ask. "Are we *all* that vulnerable and spineless?" The answer is yes and no. Yes, all people, to some degree, are anxious enough to want to conform and be accepted by others, so much so that they feel hurt when it doesn't happen. But no, not all people react the same way when they feel rejected or demeaned. For example, some psychologists believe that older people—with plenty of experience at being accepted or rejected by groups—are more interested in how they feel about themselves than in how they are accepted into groups or by their peers. And certainly there are those self-actualized souls out there who are so comfortable in their own skin that rejection or the desire for conformity is minimized.

However, even if someone is durable on the inside and durable on the outside, treating him with anything other than respect and thoughtfulness is likely to be a disadvantage in the long run. When someone's previously established outlook, judgment, credibility, or sense of worth/importance is challenged, the immediate, very human response is to become defensive, perhaps hostilely so (after all, a good offense is the best defense). Rather than having to worry about disarming someone after confronting him, why not be disarming from the start, through the soft, concerned, compassionate approach?

> **One Step Back**
>
> I like the analogy about the nails in the wood fence. That is, when we hurt someone, it's like driving a nail into a fence. If we apologize and make amends, it's like removing the nail. Yes, the nail is gone, but the hole will always be there. It is better not to drive in the nail in the first place.

Value the Encouraging Word

Okay, so we've established that people covet a sense of sanctuary, acceptance, respect, admiration, importance, and purpose. And we've reviewed the expert notions that these needs are common and generally predictable. Finally, we've recognized that even the thickest-skinned people have vulnerable self-esteems.

So what conclusion does this lead us to? It means that, as a motivational leader, you need to place a very, very, very high value on the encouraging word. You constantly need to offer a kind word, approval of what's going on around you that individuals are doing, and acknowledgement of jobs well done.

Offering the encouraging word means providing constant reinforcement and cheering people along who might not openly seem to need encouragement.

"Hey, Jane, way to go!"

"You're doing a great job, John. Keep up the good work."

"This is way above and beyond the call of duty, Jane. Thanks so much."

"That's a wonderful discovery you made, Jane! Perhaps you could tell the team about it tomorrow."

Offering the encouraging word also means continually reminding your team members that they are an important part of the organization. Remind them that they are needed, that they bring a great deal of knowledge and experience to the organization, and that you don't know what you'd do without them. And be sincere. You should—because with today's management matrices, there's a good possibility that they know a *lot* more than the managers do (including you) and if you treat them like the experts and important people they really are, they just might teach you a thing or two out of appreciation.

"Jane, when you get a chance, I have a problem that requires your expertise."

"John, isn't next Tuesday your 15-year anniversary here? We'll have breakfast as a department, my treat, and you can have the rest of the day off."

"Jane, I shared your important discovery with my boss yesterday, and I made sure he knew that you had uncovered it. That piece of information is going to save this organization a lot of money. Thank you again."

Do these things read really corny? Sure. Do they sound cornier when you say them aloud? Probably. But trust me, if you mean them from the heart, they won't sound corny to the individuals you say them to. They will feel special, respected, and important, and one small component of your role as motivational leader, for one second, will be fulfilled.

Build a Sense of Community

It's tough to talk about the workplace as a community. Oh, it used to be okay to do that, back in the days when you began with a company and stayed with it for 30 years. Departments formed bowling teams, held picnics, and joined swimming clubs together. And, on a professional level, new hires were addressed as if they were newly adopted members of the family. I vividly remember, as a very young man, joining a Fortune 100 company, where I was led to a room and shown a chart of how I was expected to progress over a 30-year career. This new-hire greeter showed me one point on the chart, at the 10-year mark. "Here's where we would like to send you to school and make you a department manager."

> **Best Voices Forward**
>
> Albert Einstein believed that the value of "community" could not be overstated. "One should guard against preaching to young people success in the customary form as the main aim in life," he said. "The most important motive for work in school and in life is pleasure in work, pleasure in its result, and the knowledge of the value of the result to the community."

Boy, have *those* days gone the way of the do-do bird! With the cost of employment benefits out of control in the United States, there's little financial incentive for corporations to keep people around long-term anymore (even though you and I know there are other, real-world reasons to keep good, long-term talent around). Furthermore, with temps and even contracted professionals in the mix, there are times when a sense of community is impractical, even geographically so.

However, to the extent that your organization allows for a continued sense of community, you should, as the motivational leader, try to make it happen. After all, if people inherently seek approval and a sense of belonging, as the experts suggest they do, then why not tap into it? It makes sense to make people feel good, "at home" in a sense, about where they work.

I'm reminded of some Eastern cultures where, if an employee shows up to work upset, everything comes to a grinding halt as the work community comes together to ease that "family member's" mind. The notion may seem silly to us hard-boiled Americans, and I would imagine most of us would rather keep our private lives private, but the notion of people feeling that comfortable, that much of a member of a team—well, to the motivational leader, wherever she may be living, that's the acceptance, respect, and worth she needs to strive to cultivate through encouragement and kind words.

Appeal to the Tough Audience

Sometimes, it seems like great leaders don't really define themselves as such until they face the really tough challenge or persuade the really skeptical team. Now, I'm not suggesting that in order to be the quintessential motivational leader, you need to seek out vast fires to extinguish (or giant windmills to conquer) or to search for strong disbelievers that you can convert into admirers. I am, however, proposing that the entire world isn't waiting for you to decide you're going to be a leader, eager to follow you wherever and whenever you choose to guide them. In fact, you're probably going to encounter different and challenging fits along the way, and *that's* when you're going to impress people with what you're made of.

As you make your way through life as a motivational leader, practice the people skills discussed in this text, including celebrating team membership and cheering on the team, establishing rapport, staying approachable and eager to listen to what others have to say, practicing positive listening skills, and offering resolute decision-making when people yearn for sure-footed guidance. Hone these skills as you prepare for the day when you meet your ultimate challenge—the tough audience.

The tough audience might come in any one of many forms. It could be the disheartened team, still smarting from the ill will generated by a previous boss. It could be the individual team member, unsure of herself and insecure about her work capabilities. It could be the harsh customer, one step away from giving you up as a merchant or contractor. It could be the ruthless co-worker, cynical toward you and your many successes. It could be the callous supervisor, more eager to see you do things the old-fashioned way rather than entertain your thoughts on how things could be done better.

In all of these situations, your reaction should be the same: kill 'em with kindness! Respect the person, be empathetic toward her opinion, disarm her with a smile, listen, listen, listen, and seek common ground whenever possible. If you sense that a leadership vacuum has presented itself, step in with enthusiasm and make the frank, law-abiding, tough decisions. And if the person tagging along seems uncertain at times, offer the kind, encouraging word. Show her that you care about her success as much as you care for the team's success and your personal success. Make that team member feel good about who she is and where she's located in the organization and what she's contributing. Turn that tough audience into one that throws flowers at the end of your heartfelt presentation.

The Least You Need to Know

◆ The leader who recognizes human needs and offers encouragement in deference to these needs is likely to be a highly successful boss.

◆ Psychologists over the last century have suggested that people are naturally wired to seek the support of others and to seek feelings of worth and importance.

◆ The motivational leader respects the fragile nature of people's self-esteem—that is, their personal feelings of self-worth.

◆ Ultimately, the human condition, with regard to the need for acceptance, respect, personal worth, and self-esteem, means that you need to constantly offer words of encouragement to your team members.

◆ Even in employment environments with temps and contracted professionals, you should seek to cultivate a community-like, family type of work setting.

◆ When faced with resistance, you should respect the opposing view, be disarming with a smile, listen intently, and seek common ground.

14

Establish Trust and Credibility

In This Chapter

◆ Setting up trust by delegating

◆ Establishing a process for turning over tasks and authority

◆ Entrusting others

◆ Dealing with issues of integrity

◆ Finding how trust and reliability mesh

◆ Learning that credibility pays off big-time

Motivational leaders establish trust and credibility within the team and throughout the organization by always being truthful and by regularly handing out authority and responsibility to team members. They understand that delegating doesn't mean relinquishing control, but through a fortunate irony, it does mean ultimately gaining more control. Trustworthiness has a nice way of building on itself, and job-related dependability is wonderfully contagious. In this chapter, we'll look at how delegating works most efficiently and effectively.

Understand Why You Should Delegate

Hey, if you've been a boss, you've undoubtedly been burned by trusting someone. Typically, you send someone you *think* is dependable to get something done. "That's all taken care of," you ensure *your* boss—only to find out later that it is, indeed, not a done deal at all. The team member you sent off has let you down and, in the process, has embarrassed you in front of your supervisor.

No wonder we hate *delegating*. If you want something done right, you've got do it yourself, right? And, in fact, we all have a tough time countering that argument, especially since most managers are very comfortable with their own knowledge and proficiency. On the other hand, the trouble with using this belief as an all-encompassing management philosophy is that you will, at some point, end up with way too much to worry about. More importantly, if you don't learn how to get comfortable with delegating, you're going to consistently lose wonderful opportunities to build trust (yours and your team members') and credibility (yours and your team members') throughout your leadership experience.

def•i•ni•tion

Delegating is the process of authorizing and entrusting to others something that you are responsible for completing. It is, in a sense, turning team members into delegates for the team leader. It is important to note that delegating work and authority doesn't equal delegating the responsibility. In the end, the team leader is still accountable for all the work and authority that has been handed out to others.

Many managers, unfortunately, hold on to the idea that if all of their team members are around, within sight, at the same time, then things are getting done and all is right in the world. Delegating, however, means that team members are *not* around. They are away doing all sorts of horrible things—like getting important tasks accomplished! Such a concept frightens the heck out of many managers. They have something of a phobia regarding letting people go to achieve wonderful things—things that are important to the team and to the organization.

Sacrificing, or giving away, authority is also a scary notion. And, to be sure, it's understandable. Just about every irrational fear studied by psychologists involves the perceived loss of personal control over a situation. When a manager assigns a role or a task, she is giving up some of her authority but absolutely none of her responsibility. (At first glance, it doesn't seem like much of deal, does it?) It looks a lot less risky to do the work herself or to maintain such a tight grip on overseeing the task that it no longer falls under the definition of delegating.

One final drawback of delegating: it takes time, energy, and a lot of organization. Determining who gets what tasks, listing those assignments in a planner, keeping track of them, monitoring the progress, providing advice and feedback along the way—it all seems so one-sided.

However, delegate you must. It is an important way to show your team members that you trust them, that you respect them, and that you're interested in their learning job-related aptitude that the entire team can benefit from. It is also a wonderful way to generate an aura of trustworthiness between you and your team members, as well as among the team members themselves. Too much drudgery involved? Perhaps at first, but there's plenty of reward—including the reward of unhampered time. I'd argue that for every minute you spend delegating and following up, you reap four minutes of free time that you would otherwise have spent micromanaging those tasks or completing them on your own.

Once your process for delegation is set in motion, it doesn't require constant rethinking or reinventing. A good friend of mine, John Shattack, once said to me about delegation: "You know, you don't have to constantly steer a ship if it's headed in the right direction." He was right—if you own up to your personal anxiety over delegating and can get over the hump of launching a method for delegating, the ship will point right, and you can then move about it, tending to workers and guests who aren't in the immediate area of the helm.

Know the Process of Effective Delegation

If delegating is the key to creating trust, credibility, and more unrestricted time for yourself, let's look at some measures you can take for starting this magnificent, motivational leadership process.

Steps for Effective Delegation

First, begin with baby steps. Don't show up one morning spellbound by the idea that you're going to hand half of your work duties and authority to your team members. Even if your team members don't balk or retaliate, they surely won't embrace your marvelous new idea. Instead, start with quietly putting together a list of your team members, their capabilities, and your upcoming duties and projects. On the notepad, consider which capabilities complement which tasks.

Start with a task or two that are not too complicated and shouldn't take longer than a few days to finish. Also, make sure it is something that you would be completely comfortable doing yourself. That way, you'll know if it's being done right.

Assign the task, using all the important, one-on-one communication stuff that has been discussed up to this point in the book. Let that person know that you really are counting on him or her. Treat the task as if that person has always been expected to do it.

Keep tabs on the project, perhaps offering some advice (but not too much) along the way. Evaluate the job after its completion. If the team member did a bang-up job, let him know.

From there, begin adding tasks and people. Keep track in your planner. Most importantly, don't let less-than-perfect employees off the hook. One of the quickest ways to breed resentment in a team is to only delegate tasks to the best workers. Give the ones who need development things to do and keep counseling them along the way.

From there, move on to bigger projects that take longer. Avoid assigning daily duties. That is, if something is supposed to be done every day and it's part of your job description, and you don't want to do it anymore, then ask to have your job description reconfigured. Handing someone your daily duties simply means you have more to check up on, countering the time advantage you get from handing out projects. On the other hand, assigning limited undertakings, with beginnings and endings, provides the neat bookends to the time that you are handing yourself, and it provides the proper scenario for entrusting, mentoring, and evaluating team members.

Repeated Excellence

I embrace many of today's gadgets and all the conveniences they bring. However, I prefer a daily planner—or calendar book—with paper pages, to an electronic planner. Why? Several reasons, but the one that's most important is that, with an electronic planner, you lose the magnificent impact of a moving pen.

With a traditional planner, when you assign a task to someone and suggest you'll be checking up on its progress, you can immediately open the book and write in the date and time when you'll be following up. The sight of that pen inking a team member's name, task, time, and date can be very imposing. That person knows you're not going to forget. And it suggests that you take the chore seriously.

This view of a moving pen also works nicely when someone asks you for something. By jotting it down at once, you project the image of a leader who cares and will follow up on a team leader's question or concern. Contrast that wonderful image with the unfortunate one of the boss who lets things go in one ear and out the other.

Some Pointers for Effective Delegating

Make sure that you utilize your team members based on their strengths and not simply because of their pliability, geniality, or willingness to say yes. I'm not a big fan of the manager who likes to staff his team with weak people in order to make himself feel smarter and more in charge. As a kid, when you were the captain of a team during recess, did you only pick the weak kids, hoping that you could command them? Of course not. So don't do the same when delegating. Place the strong talents with the corresponding tasks. If a team member shines in that task, consider yourself a very blessed team leader. And pay attention: you might learn a thing or two!

Speaking of being a recess team captain, don't ever be afraid to lobby for people with more talent than you have. Rather than avoiding brilliant teammates, you should be negotiating for them and rejoicing when you have them. Again, one of the goals of the motivational leader is to establish trust and credibility within your team. That's a lot easier when you're managing All Stars.

And if you don't control who's on your team, embrace the process of delegating by learning and gaining an appreciation for the specific, special talents of each team member. Go into the process with the view that each person on your team can do at least one thing a heck of a lot better than you can. Delegate, let that person show you how it's done, and sharpen your credibility by asking the right questions and learning a little bit more about a skill that your organization considers important.

A nifty thing about delegating is that it forces people out of their own little worlds and prompts them, from the vantage point of their newly assigned tasks, to see what's going on in the big-picture world that surrounds them. It also teaches them to appreciate the big impact of their contributions—like ripples across the lake that is the larger organization.

I'm a big believer in explaining to people, as tasks are being delegated, how their efforts fit into the process and what's going on at different points along the way. I remember, as a manufacturing manager, being in charge of a team that had to repair, relabel, and repackage some paper goods that had been damaged during the initial production process. I went into grand detail explaining how the damage had been caused and how the company was hoping to prevent it in the future. "You're wasting your time," a colleague said to me. "All they care about, or need to know, is how to fix what's broke."

In fact, the team *did* care and always asked questions related to the entire mill. And for good reason—each member of this team had worked at various other stages in other departments over the years. Discussing quality with them often meant that they would discuss it with their old buddies, where the mistakes were occurring and where the leadership was trying to make an impact. My guess is that sometimes a conversation with old, respected colleagues during lunch carries more of an impression than the pestering of senior bosses.

By starting with small projects, celebrating the strengths of your team members, keeping track of assigned projects, and keeping team members aware of the big picture, you turn delegating into a powerful method for building team confidence and turning your team and yourself into reliable, convincing forces.

Know the Paradox of Effective Delegation

Flash bulletin: the days of job security are over! Oh, you already knew that? Okay then, let's move along.

One reason some managers these days are afraid to entrust team members with authority and workload is that they believe it will eventually lead to their downsizing. That is, if I seek to instill trust and credibility within my team and I start sharing my knowledge, my projects, and my authority with you, then I put myself at risk of having the larger organization fire me and turn over parts of my job description to you (with or without a raise). That fear has, to some extent, prevented some managers from turning over even the most mundane tasks to others.

I remember working a management job where the supervisors never really went on vacation. When one supervisor took some time off, two other supervisors simply absorbed one-half of that shift. In effect, all we were doing was switching hours and calling it vacation. I once suggested to one of the more senior co-managers that we train some team members to occasionally take over the supervisor's duties. That way, we could take real vacations and not have to worry about covering each other's hours.

My associate looked around hastily, making sure no one else was around. "Don't *ever* say that again," he said. "We don't want anyone here learning our jobs. If they can do without you for one vacation, they can do without you forever."

Best Voices Forward

Longtime leadership expert Max De Pree, of the De Pree Leadership Center, suggests that motivational leaders must expose themselves to the risks involved with relinquishing some authority if they are to grow and eventually gain power. In his milestone book, *Leadership Jazz*, De Pree writes: "Leaders have to be vulnerable ... [They] have to offer others the opportunity to do their best." De Pree says such "vulnerability" means delegating, sharing accountability, and cultivating innovation.

Man, that was intense. But the assumption is worth considering. When you delegate, are you delegating yourself out of job? And, as a result, aren't you, in essence, becoming less influential as a motivational leader?

My personal experience (and my experience discussing the situation with first-tier managers) suggests, counterintuitively, that delegation actually helps, rather than hurts, whatever sort of job security still exists these days. For all sorts of reasons, being able to delegate—even visibly so—makes you more in demand as a motivational leader.

First, consider the more traditional, opposing viewpoint—that keeping your knowledge and your duties tightly guarded makes you termination-proof. It doesn't work. If you think hard enough, you're sure to recall someone in your organization who thought he could never get fired but did. I vividly remember a boss at a previous job who was the only person who knew a certain process for blending. "They can *never* let me go," he often boasted. "I'm the only one who knows how to do this." But downsize him they did, and the organization never really missed a beat. Someone else picked up the blending process and, less than a week later, it was as if he had never worked there. Pretty creepy, especially considering how much he had made himself suffer trying to keep secret all his amazing talents.

Now, apply the counterintuitive viewpoint to that same scenario. Suppose that this boss had shared his expertise with others and taken a proactive role in getting his team involved in the mixing process. Suppose he had delegated special mixing projects to people on his team. My sense is that he would have gained a reputation for being enthusiastic—motivational, even!—and for being interested in the development of people on his team. Would it have saved his job? Who knows? But it certainly would have put him in a better position than the personal disaster of his self-preservation strategy.

Why might the act of delegating actually add to a person's leadership within the organization rather than subtracting from it? It probably has much to do with the close connection that delegation has with training. Leaders who cultivate reputations for being good trainers are often considered beneficial, if not indispensable. The involved, capable delegator is hardly deadwood to the organization. The delegator is involved, interested, impacting. The delegator has a handle on the tasks needed by the organization and the individual strengths of team members who can carry them out.

Furthermore, with delegating, one-on-one "face time" becomes a high priority. Delegating work intrinsically means offering feedback—lots of it. It would be very easy for you, as a manager, to shelter yourself in paperwork, silly daily tasks, and work-related anxieties. Delegating tasks forces you to put yourself on the front lines and get in the pathways of people on a daily basis. So put yourself where the action is. Your team will see it, your bosses will notice it, and you'll become a hot commodity.

That's the wonderful paradox of delegation: rather than diminishing your importance by handing over authority and undertakings, delegating enhances your control over people and your status within the organization. Offering a piece of your authority to your team members doesn't conflict with motivational leadership; it's motivation leadership in force.

Add the Overlooked Ingredient: Integrity

Is it possible to consider trust and credibility—or to engage in any sort of leadership discussion—without reflecting on the value of honesty? Possible, yes, but also sinful. Possible because the business world today seems to be more and more about political scheming and word/number gamesmanship than ever before. Sinful because that's exactly the *opposite* of what young, aspiring managers should be talking about at today's business schools. From Dale Carnegie's *How to Win Friends and Influence People*, written over 70 years ago, to Jack Welch's *Winning*, milestone books about influencing the actions and behaviors of people

> **Best Voices Forward**
>
> Dan Rice, who manages over $1 billion in assets at US Trust, suggests that it's easier to be honest with your team if you treat them like you report to them. "If you act like you're working for them, you'll always be more up-front with them," says Rice. As for losing the trust of your team, Rice likes the old saying: "Credibility is like virginity: you only lose it once."

consistently emphasize the importance of being genuine about what you say.

Step back, just a moment, from the virtuous aspects of integrity, and consider its practical aspects. Every time you fabricate a fib or false-hood for the sake of advancing your cause—even if it's a righteous cause—you can, without fail, anticipate having to create two more lies in order to cover the first. From there, the process mushrooms, until there's such a web of pretense that you must either be a master orga-nizer to keep track of all your deceptions, or you must surrender to the notion that, very quickly, you're going to gain a reputation for being a phony. Ask anyone for the major attributes of a motivational leader: I'll bet you that "phony" doesn't make anyone's list.

Here are two more things to consider. One, managers go to jail for being deceitful—sometimes, for very long times. Two, as they're being led away, they very, very often insist that they did absolutely nothing wrong. (I'm thinking specifically of Enron's chief operating officer, Jeffrey Skilling, and his arrogant statements before Congress and before a judge after his conviction and sentencing for corporate fraud and con-spiracy.) What does that mean? I suggest that these unfortunate souls, over many years, became so good at concocting lies that they begin to fool themselves. White lies become crimes. Sugar coating becomes deep labyrinths of conceit. And notions of righteous ends justifying the double-dealing means become disgraceful, entrenched corruption simply for the sake of self-preservation. No leader begins a job by saying, "I think I'll be a conniving felon!" The process begins with a mild itch that festers over the years into an uncontrollable cancer.

So if you can't be convinced to stay truthful for the sake of goodness and morality, do so for the no-nonsense reason that it makes you a much better leader and that you will, in the long run, still be around when others are shown the door (in some cases, one with bars on it).

Raw integrity doesn't just foster trust and credibility in its own right, but it lends itself well to the faith that develops when delegating author-ity. When you say to a team member, "I trust you with this task," you basically are saying, "I trust that you will honestly keep me updated on its progress," and "I trust that you will complete the task in a truthful way." When a team member says to you, "I won't let you down," he's also saying, "I trust that you have honestly explained what this task is about and why it's important," and "I trust that you have given me a task that you sincerely believe I can accomplish and will appreciate when completed."

One Step Back

Before making wrong, untrustworthy decisions, make sure that you know how to spot them. Sometimes right and wrong aren't completely evident and mapped out by thick, identifiable boundaries. Shades of gray can creep in and make the right course of action occasionally tough to identify.

West Point teaches the Three Rules of Thumb for figuring out if a particular deed is, indeed, dishonest or unethical.

1. Does this action attempt to deceive anyone or allow anyone to be deceived?

2. Does this action gain or allow the gain of a privilege or advantage to which I or someone else would not otherwise be entitled?

3. Would I be satisfied by the outcome if I were on the receiving end of this action?

In a book I wrote a few years ago, *West Point Leadership Lessons*, I discuss the U.S. Military Academy's take on integrity, its Honor Code, and how reliance on everyone's word is the necessary foundation for anything else good that's going to happen in an organization. Again, I argue that today's motivational leader desperately needs to be straightforward in thoughts, words, and deeds. Without integrity, everything else falls apart.

Discover the Multiplying Effect of Trust

By telling someone, "I trust you," through delegating authority and tasks to people, through showing honest confidence in them and not micromanaging them, you will find that their sense of trust, credibility, and confidence is mirrored back to you and, magnificently, builds on itself throughout the team. This multiplying effect ultimately means more control for you as the motivational leader.

Again, a nice irony about handing out trust is that it means more hands-on control, not less. Remember, entrusting and building credibility take planning. You need a list of tasks and responsibilities that you're entrusting to others, and you need to maintain control over that list. You need to plan one-on-one mentoring time with each team member to assign these tasks and, later, to review how that person is carrying out those duties. You need to maintain a current inventory of each team member's strengths and areas requiring development. You need to keep a tally of the tasks themselves, as you are ultimately responsible for their completion, and you need to be able to report to your boss—at any given moment—the status of each task. You need to be involved, which is great, because an involved, trusting leader is a leader in control.

John Barry, the senior loss prevention manager and special projects manager for IKEA (the only company in North America that handles its job promotions 100 percent from within the ranks), says that taking a chance on people and showing them that you trust them is a wonderful way to develop future leaders. "Take a chance on that person's ability," says Barry. "And, while you're at it, sell the rest of the team on your confidence that that person can do the job. The up-and-coming manager will appreciate it, and the company will have a new, loyal leader."

Not everything regarding the building of trust and credibility is touchy-feely marvelous. Some of it is very bottom-line and practical. For example, the multiplying effect of trust translates into more people knowing how to get things done and, therefore, more work getting done all around (by you and your team members).

The multiplying outcome of trust also feeds nicely into the *coaching effect*, where the mentor learns more than the student. About a hundred years ago when I was a young artillery lieutenant in the U.S. Army, our unit had to test very potent gunpowder that had never been fired in combat. In fact, it was suspected that the jolt from firing this charge would require rotating the soldiers on and off the cannon as it was fired. Understanding the risks involved, I reviewed the written procedures and had them down cold the night before firing those charges.

def•i•ni•tion

> The **coaching effect** is the increased know-how that often occurs when leaders prepare for their jobs. The outcome is that they become better experts about tasks, as managers, than they were when they were team members, similar to a football player's becoming more knowledgeable about football once he makes the transition to coach. The coaching effect implies that, the more a leader learns about a task that she's about to delegate and supervise, the more of an expert she becomes on that particular duty.

The next day, sensing that some officers would avoid being around when these powerful concussions went off, my soldiers playfully said, "Sir, come on over and fire a few!" Ah, they didn't think I would! But I knew the routine—at least on paper—and after supervising the firing of a few volleys, I assumed the right spot at the gun. Pulling the lanyard that fired the cannon, I felt a detonation so strong that it forced the breech back and down nearly into the sand, hurling a 50-pound round many miles away and onto a target. As James Earl Jones might say, "*That* is power!" Knowing that I would have to supervise and, in a sense, coach the firing off of the powder that day forced me to learn and be the expert on it, creating a very safe and commanding sense of trust and credibility.

Trust and credibility, through delegating and coaching, become compounded within the team because, at some point, your visits to your team are no longer checking up on them, but genuine dropping by, where your new priorities are concern for your people, mentorship for those who show great potential, and self-improvement for you as a boss, as you ask and learn more about your organization. The more you trust them and they trust you, the more you hand out and walk away from. The more they accomplish, the stronger the trust and internal credibility. And so on.

Again, the marvelous paradox of delegation is that the process means anything but losing touch. The manager who delegates is *the* exemplary hands-on, motivational leader. Without delving into the process of delegating, you'll never fully discover your own potential, because you'll always be too busy handling tasks that could be handed out and checking up on people for lack of trust and two-way credibility.

Learn That Credibility Is Contagious

One of the nicest indirect compliments to ever receive is when you accidentally overhear someone say, "Give it to (insert your name here)'s team. They know their stuff, and they're dependable." If you're not walking on Cloud Nine after hearing something like that, well, then you're not really a motivational leader. Turn in your badge at the door.

Of course, job credibility begins with you. Make sure that you know your stuff. Before turning over a task to team members, make sure that you can accomplish it yourself. That way, you know the time, effort, and ability involved when you hand it over to others.

Gaining an in-depth understanding of even menial tasks makes you a credible leader and one people know can't be duped. It also presents you as a team player, as well as a team leader. Don't ask anything of your team that you wouldn't do yourself. Working a task competently in the presence of team members lets them know that you not only have empathy for them, but that you also have an *understanding of them*, as well as what's expected of them.

By making yourself credible, you find that it spreads, pulling people out of their own little worlds and tapping into the skills and reliability of one another. They begin to gain both an individual pride and a team pride, especially as they start to appreciate the effect each task has on the big mission—like ripples in the organizational water.

The Least You Need to Know

◆ Building trust on a team often begins with delegating tasks to team members and having faith that they will get the job done.

◆ Begin the process of effective delegating with small tasks, not terribly complicated and lasting no longer than a day. From there, move on to bigger and longer tasks.

◆ An interesting paradox of delegating is that it tends to make you more of a hands-on leader rather than less of one, as it promotes mentoring, shows you know your stuff, and augments your influence over your team in an inspiring way.

◆ Integrity is not simply a pie-in-the-sky concept. It is an indispensable part of establishing trust, promoting credibility, and being a truly motivational leader.

◆ Trust within a team has a nice way of building on itself; as you begin to trust your team members, they begin to trust you and each other, more work gets done, and the trust spiral continues upward.

◆ If you learn a task and carry it out competently before handing it over to a team member, you portray credibility, a trait that's very contagious within a team.

Chapter 15

Practice Charisma and Inspire Others

In This Chapter

◆ Learning, not inheriting, charisma

◆ Uncovering charm school secrets

◆ Making one person feel important

◆ Rousing the crowd

◆ Showing them a magnificent place

◆ Looking at charisma and inspiration vignettes

Motivational leaders understand that possessing charisma and the capacity to inspire people are important tools in the leadership toolkit. They know how to be more charming and rousing and how to make people around them feel important. In this chapter, we'll consider practical steps for becoming more inspiring and agreeable to others.

Know That You Weren't Born with Charisma

Hopefully, this far into your reading, you're convinced that motivational leadership is more science than art—more learned technique than inborn talent. So, what about *charisma?* Is it possible to develop this mysterious, magnetic charm and personality? Well, I'm sorry to say, the bad news at this point of the book is that, if you're not born with charisma, you unfortunately don't ever stand a chance of having it.

def•i•ni•tion

Charisma is the ability to allure and fascinate other people. It is a personal magnetism that makes people take notice of you and remember you in a positive way after you've left the room. It creates an eagerness to like and a willingness to obey. Popular opinion suggests that charisma is a relatively unique ability. Leaders who garner large numbers of devotees are thought to have large amounts of charisma.

Just kidding!

Charisma, an important tool in the motivational leader's toolbox, is just as attainable through knowledge and practice as any other leadership device.

Admittedly, there are some things you can't do much about, such as the natural looks you were born with, the shrillness of your voice, or the gait of your feet in motion. But being able to work with what you've got holds a lot more potential impact than God-given beauty. Haven't you ever seen those paparazzi photos of swimsuit models without their makeup on and hair done up? They look just like you or me. Okay, maybe not me. The point is that it's all about preparation, confidence, and attitude—the natural beauty is really very secondary.

If you can put just enough effort into your hair and clothing to make yourself well turned-out, then being charismatic will carry you further toward being that superb, influential leader.

Much, much more than personal appearance, charisma is the power to generate positive emotion for you in others. It makes people accept you a lot quicker, like you almost instantly, and want to follow you almost automatically. After you've left the room, if you are charismatic, people will feel good about your having dropped by. The charismatic leader gets people emotionally involved in the professional endeavors of the day.

Ten Steps for Being More Captivating

There are some reasonably practical steps toward creating an aura of charisma around yourself. You can start using them immediately, and they will bring you instant results. One or two of them take a little practice or getting used to.

1. **Wake up with a smile on your face and try to keep it on for the entire day.** After an initial, awkward phase, you'll start to like it, and you'll be surprised how well people around you take to it.

2. **Address each person you come into contact with by his or her name.** Privately write names down in your planner as you learn them. If you don't know someone's name—even the person who vacuums the carpets at your office in the evening—find it out. People, deep down and without really knowing it, love, love, love to hear the sound of their own name.

3. **For each time you offer your opinion throughout the day, ask four other people for their opinions.** Listen sincerely to what they have to offer. Write their ideas down in your planner.

4. **Put your cell phone on silent-vibrate ring and don't answer it in the middle of a conversation with someone.**

> **Best Voices Forward**
>
> In his quintessential guide on getting people to think positively of you as a person of influence, Dale Carnegie, in his book *How to Win Friends and Influence People*, writes about the crucial but often overlooked value of a smile. Carnegie tells of a department store flier that asked its sales clerks to try and maintain a smile, even during busy times of year like Christmas. "It enriches those who receive it, without impoverishing those who give it," read the smiling directive. "It happens in a flash and the memory of it sometimes lasts forever ... It is rest to the weary, daylight to the discouraged, sunshine to the sad, and nature's best antidote for trouble... For nobody needs a smile so much as those who have none left to give!"

5. **When someone approaches you, practice active listening skills.** Pretend each person is the most important person you're going to meet that week.

6. **Carry breath mints.** Use them often (especially if you're a smoker or coffee drinker).

7. **Throughout the day, energetically describe the ideal way you'd like things to be for your team and your organization.** Tell people what's happening, and how they can contribute toward making this vision real.

8. **Proudly own your situation.** "Yes, that was my call!" "Yes, that's my responsibility!" "Yes, we're the ones to go to for that. What can we do for you?" Enthusiastically take responsibility for your actions—whether that results in accolades or criticism. People will judge you by how quickly, openly, and positively you react to a critique.

9. **Share compliments with your team.** "Well, my team deserves the credit. I'll let them know your kind words." But don't share the blame. "Well, I was in charge that day, so it happened on my watch."

10. **Be open and candid.** People's radars are better than you think they are. They know if you're lying or hiding something. Offer your thoughts candidly but courteously always.

Treat Someone Like the Person of the Moment

General Colin Powell, the well-liked and much-admired former Secretary of State, is not the type of person you'd think would have time to schmooze. After all, he was the Chairman of the U.S. Joint Chiefs of Staff and also a National Security Advisor. It's tough to imagine him making friends at the water cooler.

And yet, that's exactly what some people say defines Powell's charisma. He loves to go out into crowds and shake hands. Thousands, probably millions, of people have met him in such a way in his various positions in life. Dr. Sheila Murray Bethel, a business consultant, best-selling leadership author and lecturer (bethelinstitute.com), was appointed by Powell to the Board of Advisors for his "America's Promise Alliance With Youth" and has worked with him extensively. In her speeches, she speaks about feeling like you're the most important person in the room whenever Powell is talking with you. "It's his magnetism," she says. "It's what defines him as a great leader.

That's what the charismatic, motivational leader does: she talks to people, one-on-one, with such warm, personal regard that each person, at that moment, believes he or she is the most important person in the room. Her sincere show of interest, along with the listening skills mentioned in Chapter 11, is engaging and tends to create a team of followers and devotees.

Treating an individual like you are genuinely interested in what he or she has to say and offer magnifies your charisma a hundredfold.

One Step Back

If an invisible person were in the room, and someone else were talking to that person, and you could neither see nor hear that person, would it make you uncomfortable? Sure. And that's what psychologists say is rude and unnerving about cell phones. They have a way of barging in on conversations or people's time together in offices and restaurants. The person holding the cell phone doesn't think anything's wrong, but the other person in the room is subliminally uncomfortable with this new "invisible person" on hand.

Charisma and cell phones don't go together. If you want to be a charismatic person, don't treat your cell phone like it's the most important person in the room. Keep it on the silent ring and ignore it if you're talking with someone. If you're expecting an important call from your boss, or if you're the emergency contact that people call, let the person you're speaking with know up front that you might have to pick up.

Be More Inspirational

If being charismatic seems out-of-reach to some people (even though it shouldn't), then being inspirational probably seems downright unrealistic.

But, again, many of the things we find inspiring about motivational leaders are things that any boss could do, if he were to set his mind to doing it. That's the difference, isn't it? Many bosses simply don't care—and it catches up with them down the road.

Here are some ways to inspire your team. They are not as cut-and-dried as the charisma steps just mentioned, and they are not things that you can begin doing immediately. But if you think through these methods, write down some things, and attempt to apply them to your management setting, you might find yourself becoming another MacArthur over time.

First, constantly talk to your team about the big picture. Remind people that they are part of something greater than themselves. And remind them that the big picture is made up of important, exciting goals. Sell it, sell it, sell it!

Second, talk about your long-term vision enthusiastically, even if the possibility of ever seeing this vision realized seems remote at the time. And if the vision ever starts to come into focus, formulate yet a new, exciting, vibrant vision.

Third, let people know what's going on. If a priority is important to the larger organization, portray it as important to your team. If it's considered urgent to the larger organization, make it urgent to your team. If it's something they can do simply to help you out, tell them it is so. If more bosses started sentences with "Could you folks do me a favor?" then the world would be a much better place.

And finally, don't accept mediocrity, or even satisfactory, performance. Ask that your team members aspire to greater levels of accomplishment, professionalism, and decency. Ask them to take their values and way of thinking to a higher level.

Champion the Grand Ideal

Show your team a magnificent place where they can go. Keep this over-the-top, grand ideal in their minds. Tell them why this aim is important.

As mentioned in Chapter 9, there are, without a doubt, strong parallels between selling an appliance to a customer and selling a grand ideal to your team. The idea is to create an interest, show a need, remind them how this need can be met, and continue to encourage them as they work toward this goal.

Repeated Excellence _____

Brian Tracy (briantracy.com), one of my favorite speakers on the subjects of influencing people and improving sales, notes that without sensing a need, most people will neither do what you want nor buy what you're selling. In other words, no need = no sale.

The same could be said for "selling" a grand ideal to your team. If they perceive that they don't stand to gain anything from this lofty set of goals (either as a team or an individual), then it will be difficult to get them to do anything other than go through the motions.

Remind your team as often as possible what's in it for them if they attain the grand ideal (a more successful, more stable company to work for, perhaps more time off, team recognition, personal growth, tangible rewards for good performance, etc.). These reminders are what will prompt their support and hard work.

Make sure that your team members contribute to modifying or shaping these bold objectives. The more they own them, the more likely they are to work toward them. And make sure the grand ideal isn't so outrageous that it can never, ever be attained. Keep at least a small dose of reality in the mix (but just a small dose).

Be bold, daring, and spirited and champion this grand ideal throughout the organization. Be so enthusiastic that people think of you when discussion of this organizational goal comes up. Sell the grand ideal, and service it well after it has been sold.

Read These Inspirational Leader Stories

Here are two quick stories about motivational leaders who made a difference by practicing the methods of charisma and inspiration mentioned in this chapter.

For charisma, it's tough to match former U.S. President Bill Clinton. Although his extramarital behavior—as well as his apparent lying about it under oath—almost toppled his presidency, Clinton remained, and still remains, an extremely friendly, charismatic figure in American politics. The smiling, the handshaking, the addressing people by name, the intensive listening and nodding as people speak—well, he's really something. I remember when Clinton was first elected and sworn in as president in 1993. He formed a line leading into the White House— some people had won tickets early on; others simply stopped by while jogging—and made a point of meeting and greeting thousands and thousands of well-wishers. Although the line moved fairly rapidly, each time he shook someone's hand and repeated his or her name, you could tell that he had won another supporter for life.

As for inspiring people, there are few stories more compelling than that of Mahatma Gandhi, leader of independence for India in the early part of the twentieth century. In both South Africa in the early 1900s and India in the 1920s through the 1940s, Gandhi promoted a grand ideal: that tyranny could be overcome through nonviolent protest and civil disobedience rather than through war and aggression. To object to South Africa's registering of Indians, Gandhi encouraged Indians to refuse registration and then accept the punishment nonviolently. The South African government jailed, beat, and killed thousands of Indians over a seven-year period. But eventually, sensing international outrage, the government negotiated with Gandhi and gave the Indian population something they never could have achieved through violence—a more respectful existence without having to register. Gandhi used the tactic again to gain India's independence from the British following World War II. In spite of many years of imprisonment for Gandhi and his followers and his family, he boldly sold a nation on peace, spirituality, and a grand ideal of independence and meaningful existence.

The Least You Need to Know

◆ Just as motivational leadership is more science than art, charisma— the ability to enchant and captivate others—is also an ability that can be acquired and practiced rather than a personality trait of birthright.

◆ Becoming more charming involves smiling, listening, using people's names, ignoring your cell phone whenever possible, taking responsibility, sharing compliments, and being candid.

◆ When you are having a conversation with someone, treat that person as if he or she, at that moment, is the most important person in the world.

◆ Inspiring people is easier if you continually talk up the big picture, create a long-term vision, ask for exceptional deeds, and keep people updated about where they stand in the organization.

◆ Supporting the grand ideal is easier if you convince your team that they need and should desire the related, lofty objectives and that these objectives are attainable.

◆ Charisma and inspiration involve building admiration through sincere handshakes and greetings and presenting people with grand, noble, and righteous aims.

Chapter 16

Be Someone's Guru

In This Chapter

- ◆ Becoming a guru in the Western world
- ◆ Defining yourself through your disciples
- ◆ Attracting the secret sponsor
- ◆ Helping people enhance their own jobs
- ◆ Being a guru gets you certain advantages
- ◆ Learning about formal mentoring

Motivational leaders recognize the value of a meaningful, mentoring relationship. They embrace the idea of serving as an eager, available guru. When selecting their disciples, motivational leaders should gravitate toward those who can add their talents to the organization, who can benefit from the mentoring, and who desire a guru-disciple relationship. Gurus can help disciples enhance their own jobs, as well as boost their own influence in the organization. In this chapter, we'll learn the process for becoming a guru and what it means for both the team and the leader.

Know What a Guru Is

Okay, so this young, aspiring manager climbs a nearby mountain, where a guru is supposed to tell him the secret to great motivational leadership.

When he reaches the top of the mountain, he approaches an old man with a long white beard, sitting high up on a rock, and says, "Oh, wise one, they tell me you know the secret to becoming a successful and inspiring leader of people."

"Yes, there are actually three secrets," says the guru, handing the manager a brown bag.

The manager opens the bag and finds eyeglasses, baby powder, and a laxative. Perplexed, he asks, "Uh, what the heck is this?"

"Put on the eyeglasses," explains the guru. "You will always appear intelligent. Rub the baby powder in your hair to add some white. You will always appear distinguished. And swallow the laxative. You will *always* appear earnest and concerned!"

Hopefully, the *guru* in your professional career has given you better advice than the one in the above joke. And with any luck, you have discovered the benefits of serving as someone else's personal guru—especially someone on your team who you can mold and give counsel to.

Motivational leadership includes the largely forgotten but wholly important duty of serving as someone's guru and, if you're lucky enough to have one of your own, continuing on with that relationship as long as it's rewarding.

Being a *guru* means taking a team member under your wing with the hope of providing guidance and early career development. It starts with identifying someone on your team who reminds you of yourself as a young worker or young manager (not physically, but attitude and aspiration-wise). This team member might work for you or she might not. (However, I recommend that the best guru counseling occurs when it involves someone whom you directly supervise.) Without displaying open favoritism toward this team member, you show a professional interest that includes sharing career-building guidance, tips on being a manager someday, and trade secrets along the way.

def•i•ni•tion

In Buddhism and several other Eastern religions, a **guru** is a worshipped teacher, considered a necessary instrument for attaining religious enlightenment and self-actualization. In Western societies, a guru, or mentor, is considered a personal advisor and expert in the professional field where the student is seeking knowledge and advancement. Often, the guru also serves as an advocate, showing concern and putting in a good word for the student when one is needed.

As a guru, you don't want to stay hidden atop a high mountain: you want to be constantly approachable and interested in listening when this team member occasionally brings you her problems and asks for advice. You keep tabs on her progress throughout the months, maybe even years. If she's worthy, you might put in a recommendation when her promotion is being considered. When this team member ultimately departs your team for bigger and better things, maybe even reaching greater professional heights than you, you can observe and admire from afar, knowing that you had much to do with her success story. Oh, and don't be surprised if, even from her high post, she still sometimes calls for a sympathetic ear and some mature words of wisdom.

For you, the motivational leader, serving as a guru makes certain that you pass on to others some of the hard-earned lessons you have encountered along the way, along with some of the bedrock values that perhaps your guru shared with you a hundred years ago. It's a nice way of knowing that a part of you—and what you're all about—will continue into another generation.

Define Yourself Through Your "Grasshoppers"

Today's guru is defined mostly by her disciples. And so, for you to define yourself as a modern guru, you must decide who you want to teach, mentor, and look out for. Choosing the right disciples—team members who stand to contribute the most to your team—can make over a team in dramatic ways. The process of selecting your students, your "grasshoppers," should be a fun and worthwhile endeavor.

The first step toward characterizing yourself as a modern-day guru is to determine who is interested in your guidance.

If there's one thing you've gathered in this book up to this point, it's that the vast majority of organizational psychology and leadership experts agree that people are infinitely more likely to do something if they *want* to do it. So sharing your wisdom, even if it entails nothing more than passing along old philosophies and experience, can turn tedious in no time if you don't take pleasure in it and if it does not create a sense of personal worth for you, the motivational leader.

As you begin to select your disciples, consider first those who come to you seeking mentorship. The biggest reason most people do not get what they want out of life, on personal and professional levels, is that they simply do not ask for it. If someone appeals to you, their team leader, for guidance, consider the request on the surface as a desire to exceed. It takes a lot of nerve these days to approach someone looking for answers: many of us—even new, young employees—feel as if we are already expected to *know* all the answers. Additionally, in a fast-paced society, few of us step back from the daily business of putting out fires to consider the bigger issues of business success and triumphant motivational leadership. The team member who approaches you and says, "Yes, I would like to learn about these bigger things" sets himself apart from others. There is no greater joy for a guru than to be in the presence of eager learners.

One Step Back

Watch out for people who claim to want to learn from you but are merely seeking to place themselves in front of influential people. Fortunately, such ulterior motives often make themselves apparent. Shallow people have a funny way of eventually exposing what they're up to. Of course, it is possible to want to learn *and* be in the presence of important people, like yourself. But always scrutinize the request of someone seeking your mentorship. If he or she is hoping to exploit your guidance sessions without really wanting to learn from them, then the process will become tedious for both of you, and it will end soon enough. The idea is to stop wasting your time and advice beforehand.

Next, consider those prospective disciples who are most likely to benefit from your time and effort as a guru. Who in your organization has the raw skills necessary to be a great team member—and perhaps a successful motivational leader—someday? There is no sense wanting to sculpt if the marble isn't of a good quality. Look for these people in your organization:

- ◆ People who display unrefined talent
- ◆ People who have strong analytical skills
- ◆ People who act in a professional manner
- ◆ People who work well with others
- ◆ People who have the most to offer immediately to the organization
- ◆ People who are most likely to be around long enough to impact the organization in the long term
- ◆ People who you believe might be the organization's leaders in 20 years

Your prospective disciples should be fast, enthusiastic learners, displaying a capacity to absorb your advice, analyze it, and take it to heart. They should be open to criticism (yes, it's tough for all of us)—not the type that spends their entire time in defensive mode. They should be vibrant, eager minds ready to draw on your energy and good thoughts.

You serve as the most effective guru if you are mentoring someone perhaps one or two levels down from you. The person does not have to be directly in your "chain of command." It should be someone who is friendly and able to listen. Of course, there's a nice son/daughter effect if you see an earlier version of yourself in this disciple.

The guru-disciple arrangement can be a very nice ray of sunlight in the otherwise dreary, impersonal world of business, for both you and your grasshoppers.

Be the Hidden Advocate

"Hey, wait a minute," you protest as you read this chapter. "Why would I want to be a guru if people are simply going to take what I learn and leave?" Admittedly, there is a potentially uncomfortable aspect of being a guru. That is, the people who get the most out of your mentoring are sometimes the first to leave the team—and you—through promotion or personal advancement. A gifted disciple that you take time to teach might not be around for long.

> ### Repeated Excellence
>
> Gurus have a funny, almost paranormal, way of always being around and always having an impact. A personal mentor of mine, a U.S. Army major who encouraged me as an enlisted soldier 23 years ago to apply to West Point, is still in the Army and still keeping a watchful eye on my career teaching young Army leaders as a civilian. The different times we have run into each other over the years, and the times when his advice and help have been there *exactly* when I needed them, are so coincidental as to be unbelievable in a novel or movie script.

So avoid being a guru, right? No sense in developing gifted people only to lose them in the process, right? Create a set of defensive strategies, aimed at keeping good people around, right?

Wrong!

You should enthusiastically serve as a guru for the good people in your organization. And, I would argue, you should also enthusiastically set them free when other opportunities present themselves—even opportunities outside your team or organization.

Sound crazy? Not really. There are several practical reasons you should quietly serve as a career coach for your best people.

First, your disciples will be a lot more relaxed and willing to learn from you if you simply acknowledge up front that you want to be their career coach—even if it means losing them someday. If you both openly discuss the possibility that new opportunities are on the horizon, you put to rest any discomfort they might have over hidden agendas or lack of loyalty. Let's face it, most good people do not aspire to be the best entry-level employee. An exceptional team member is always in training for, and possibly considering, the *next* good thing to present itself. Put your disciples at ease. There is nothing wrong with team members developing themselves for future positions. And it's the generous guru who offers advice along the way.

Unquestionably, there are members of your team, as we speak, attending school at night or perhaps pursuing college online. Are these people working a full-time job plus a college schedule simply because they want to be better at what they are *currently* doing? Perhaps. There's nothing wrong with simple self-improvement. On the other hand, as someone who has worked a full-time job while carrying a full graduate course load for years and years, I can assure you that there are probably grander notions in the minds of these people. Working while going to school is not easy, and those willing to endure its rigors usually have their designs on a bigger lot in life. If your larger organization is lucky, perhaps one or two of these self-enriching people will seek positions as motivational leaders.

I have worked at several companies where my bosses and gurus openly stated, "So here's the deal: you learn here, you help us out in the process, and you move on." That candor was refreshing, and it made their career-advancing advice all the more worth listening to and appreciating. By freely admitting to and bringing up the potential for advancement, you display your relaxed nature and sincerity as a mentor.

Another reason for serving as a guru, in spite of the possibility of losing good people, is that your disciples, if they are to be properly developed, need to see past their current horizons. In other words, if the people you mentor are not already focused on their potential, then as a guru you should focus them on it. You should plant in your people's minds the notions of promotions and advancement and of becoming motivational leaders some day. You should put the thoughts in their minds that, down the road, they can do bigger and better things with their lives. People always try harder when their sights are set higher. And it helps if you portray those sights as realistic.

The third reason for serving as a guru, regardless of the prospect of losing good people, is that openly discussing with them the possibility of leaving the team does not necessarily *mean* they will. Sometimes, team members find the self-development and personal fulfillment they desire right where they are. Feelings of respect, recognition, and prestige—all the things mentioned up to this point—have a nice way of keeping people around. Also, promotion within the team, pay adjustments for accomplishment, and open acknowledgment of good performance go a long way toward retaining good people. Although, as a guru, you may not be directly responsible for promotions or raises, you should make sure that your colleagues who award these things are aware of a good disciple's performance.

Repeated Excellence _____

Dozens of Major League Baseball players have come from Seton Hall University in South Orange, New Jersey, including John Valentin and Mo Vaughn of Boston Red Sox fame. Subsequently, the names of all these players are often invoked during practice and throughout the season. Why? If you are coaching a college baseball team, do you want your players focused on being good *college* baseball players? Certainly not. You want them focused on the majors and reaching for the stars. Building on that dream and selling them that image makes them great college baseball players—and possibly more!

Here's an interesting thought. Isn't it possible that some team members might stick around, in ironic fashion, simply because you recognize the possibility of losing them? By conceding this plausibility, you essentially tell your disciples: "I fully acknowledge that you are good enough to be sought by others." Such an admission on your part is a heck of a compliment to hard workers, and sometimes, just knowing that others recognize and appreciate their level of performance is enough to keep them on board.

By openly accepting the potential for the advancement of disciples off your team, you present an honest comparison between what else exists for them and what they currently have. Often, people grow to appreciate and become more enthusiastic about their current positions after screening other opportunities—even briefly.

So don't avoid being a guru, and certainly don't be protective of your people or selfish with your mentoring advice. By not being afraid to set good people free, you create a set of disciples that, as part of your team, will make you look good, and feel good, as a guru and motivational leader.

Promote Job Enrichment

I like telling the story of Jim, an old paper machine tender of mine. Was I his guru? No way. I was his foreman and nothing more. However, he did have a guru—Bub, whom I considered a guru, too (and was also my boss).

Anyway, I once watched an interesting guru-disciple encounter take place between these two men. We had a paper machine that was specially retrofitted to manufacture a wide array of paper products. However, shutting the machine off to change from one product to another was time-consuming, and the down time cost the mill money. One day, Jim approached Bub with an innovative scheme. He suggested modifying the machine to change from one product to another *without shutting the machine off!* Bub liked the idea—it was potentially a time-saving and money-saving idea, and he told Jim to give it a try. However, there were some restrictions. First, Bub said that modifying the machine while *in process* had to be done safely. Second, he insisted that any innovations could not be damaging to the equipment. And finally, Bub said that the grade change had to be completed within 30 minutes—making more than 30 minutes' worth of off-grade, substandard paper would have offset the time benefits of keeping the machine running. Other than those constraints, Bub's guidance was "Go for it!"

Hey, you can write the rest of this story. Jim and the crew seized the opportunity to shine. After a few trial runs, they were able to change from one paper product to another, with the machine still running, in under 15 minutes, as compared to 45 minutes or more using the old method of pulling liquid paper stock off the machine. As other crews watched and learned, they came up with their own nifty ways to change product on the fly.

At any point during this mentoring, Bub could have disturbed this job enrichment by over-dissecting Jim's idea, micromanaging it, or trying to standardize the procedure once a particular crew came up with the "best" way of accomplishing the task. On the other hand, Bub could have stifled the process by offering too little guidance or no guidance at all, which could have led to unsafe or destructive practices on the machine. Furthermore, if Bub had provided no guidance, it might have been taken as a lack of interest.

Instead, Bub the Guru offered lots of latitude and created innovation, all by simply setting forth a few straightforward parameters and remaining interested, supportive, and flattering. In the end, his time parameter of 30 minutes became the time to beat, rather than a goal to meet. Bub's goal of enriching the jobs of this crew within some loose but well-defined limits worked like a charm.

Same crew, different story. Once every two weeks, on that same paper machine, our mill would shut down for *conditioning*—which was essentially a good fixin' and scrubbin'. During these half-day conditionings, the crew foreman (including me) would schedule what each worker had to do down to the minute. As Murphy (the guy who wrote that unfortunate Law) would have it, unforeseen problems would arise, people would have to be pulled off other tasks, and our thoroughly planned-out schedule would fall apart.

With Bub the Guru's help and advice, our team eventually came up with a very loose schedule of tasks. As long as the tasks were accomplished, the crews could pair up any way they liked and complete the jobs in any manner or order. The positive results were staggering. Machine conditionings were accomplished in about two thirds of the time laid out in our original, complicated time lines. More potential machine problems were unearthed and addressed. My team members teamed up with those they got along with and got more done. Again, by formulating time and task standards and following Bub's loose constraints, we were setting goals to be met and times to be beaten. The result was that more got accomplished and people's jobs were enriched.

Best Voices Forward

As you serve as a guru to people who want to grow at your workplace, be sure to set limitations just restrictive enough that they seek clever ways to do things better within those parameters.

Remember that the emphasis here is on creating job enrichment by promoting personal innovation within some structure. As an old boss of mine, John Pastor, once said, "Let people know the rules—so that they can beat them!"

I would love to say that the above examples are the ways things are going in today's corporate workplace. But both academic and anecdotal evidence suggests that innovation within well-defined boundaries is *not* the thing that is happening these days. I would argue that today's business world is embracing just the opposite—*no* innovation within the blurry lines of poorly defined control and boundaries. Hey, it's tough to come up with new, clever, smarter ways of playing the game when you don't know what the rules are.

My argument is that the forceful but somewhat removed guru is a wonderful, job-enriching paradox—someone who celebrates freedom within structure.

So be a guru who provides flexible but well-defined rules for your disciples. You won't have to worry about enriching their jobs and making them more rewarding—they'll do it for you

Expect Something Back—It'll Come

Besides developing great raw talent, serving as a guru brings you personal rewards. Certainly, there is the sense of accomplishment that comes from seeing people advance. Living vicariously through the professional accomplishments of your students is no small psychological reward. And besides, it's not all that indirect: people will know that these success stories are "yours." "Undeniably, it's self-promotion," a good friend of mine, Ron Green, once said. "You definitely promote yourself by promoting others toward success."

Be a Guru to Yourself

By serving as a guru to others, you essentially serve as a guru to yourself. Nothing makes a leader more tuned in to self-improvement than helping others improve. Good advice requires philosophical consideration and preparation—sometimes lots of it. Such advice might involve your research, analysis, and personal reflection. After all, a guru doesn't just blather silly advice (like in those jokes) but instead offers sound counsel as a master of the subject in question.

If you are to approach a disciple's concerns about, for example, career development, chances are that you have already considered these questions on a personal level, assessing your own career development and the steps you followed and continue to follow along the way toward becoming a master motivational leader. You now know what things

Best Voices Forward

Nobel Prize–winning playwright George Bernard Shaw suggested that mentoring is as good for the guru as it is for the student. He once said, "I'm not a teacher—only a fellow traveler of whom you asked the way. I pointed ahead—ahead of myself as well as you!"

work, what things create setbacks, and what choices might ultimately bring career fulfillment and happiness. In order to be comfortable with the idea that disciples will approach you for nuggets of wisdom, you become obligated to take the time and effort to develop—and master—decision paths for yourself.

Here's an example. Once, a team member of mine openly approached me about promotion into a management job in another manufacturing department. What nerve! Nah, it was okay. Believing in the concept of setting good people free, I offered him some ways that he might position himself more assertively toward getting that promotion. I suggested that he might create a resumé-like list of recent accomplishments and then provide that list to the department supervisor he hoped to work for someday, possibly even updating the list periodically. My lesson: selling yourself, even within your own organization, can be almost as important as doing a consistently good job.

As it turned out, not long after he began those lists, I decided to follow it myself. I created a monthly newsletter to my team, reminding them how well they had performed the previous month and what new, innovative things they had achieved. Choosing a few people within the larger organization I was hoping to work for someday, I ensured that each of them received a copy of my newsletter. This bulletin served many positive purposes. It helped *sell* the team on themselves, as they took account, in writing, of the good things they had done recently. And it permitted me a good amount of subtle, shameless self-advertising. And so, serving someone else as a guru translated into serving myself.

More Specific Ways That Being a Guru Benefits You

Here are some other, more tangible ways that being a guru generates a positive return on your time and energy invested:

- **Being a guru helps you choose your successor.** You're not going to be around forever. Being a guru helps you select the person who might replace you. And if your long-term success in the organization is defined by the team you leave behind, then having a role in how that team continues might be important to your legacy.

- **Being a guru helps you encourage loyalty.** My good friend Ron Green observes the most beneficial side effect to mentoring your team members up to their next assignments: loyalty from your disciples. "Advising people to the point that you're advancing them out the door creates an atmosphere of indebted loyalty," he says. "You can ask people to work long hours and to make all kinds of sacrifices. If they sense deep down that you care for them personally, they will always be devoted to you and your objectives." Green adds that most people possess very sensitive radar when it comes to detecting caring bosses. In other words, if you say you're interested in helping your disciples advance their careers, you'd better mean it, because they'll know if you're full of it.

- **Being a guru means being in control.** Another benefit to mentoring is that it translates directly into influence. As you channel the attitude of your disciples, you hold some sway over them. If your ultimate goal is to direct the activities of your team members toward organizational objectives (and, of course, it should be), then certainly serving as a guru has some very utilitarian applications. As you guide others in their personal development, you guide them in their conduct and perspectives. In the process of becoming good disciples, your followers also become good workers—useful, integral parts of your team. It may be somewhat self-serving, but it certainly is not selfish for a team leader to advance the team while advancing the individual needs of its team members. Again, by controlling the outlook of your disciples, you control their actions.

Encourage Formal Mentoring

Whatever happened to formal mentoring programs? Maybe it's part of corporate America's weird, current aversion to seasoned talent.

Or (an even more cynical notion), perhaps the corporate world invalidated mentoring by, at some point, formalizing it and therefore killing it. After all, in a formal mentoring program, a junior employee is arbitrarily assigned to a senior person. You could argue that this is the same as being told whom you had to take to the senior prom. Maybe a bond forms, maybe not. Without the personal chemistry that tends to accompany the voluntary quality of mentoring (for both the guru and the disciple), it's easy to see why these types of programs have a tendency to fade away.

Perhaps such formality is best left as ancient history. That is, perhaps a new team member *should* have relative freedom in choosing how to gather advice and from whom those helpful hints will come. Perhaps choosing one's mentor *should* be a relatively informal and innovative endeavor on the part of your team members.

> **One Step Back**
>
> Don't force people to serve as gurus. And don't force new guru-disciple relationships. Without the up-front aspiration to mentor or the desire for mentoring, the relationship, in all likelihood, will fail—or exist on paper only. However, it certainly *is* appropriate for you, the motivational leader, to demand that a new team member seek out and ask questions of people in your organization with experience. Indeed, a legitimate first assignment for a new hire might be to have this new team member go out, ask questions, and report back to you on what she learned from senior people in your organization. You might say, "In one month, come to me with five important idiosyncrasies you have learned about this organization and five ways senior people have suggested you deal with them. I don't need the names—just the advice." (Of course, don't be surprised if a guru-disciple relationship forms out of this initial venture.)

However, as this chapter has alluded to, there's a big difference between formalizing results and formalizing processes. Formalizing results places a requirement on someone but still encourages personal growth, innovation, and job enrichment. Formalizing processes sometimes just turns people off.

My concern is that, if you never bring up the idea of mentoring to your team members, it might never happen. Indeed, it may be silly to expect your team members to come rushing to you, admitting their naïveté, and begging you to find a guru. Many team members who begin jobs are positive that they already know all the answers. My favorite sign, seen in a restaurant: "Hire a teenager—while he still knows everything!" Such an attitude continues into employment and, for some, doesn't leave until it's too late.

The true spirit of mentoring lies in how mentors and students find each other and how they are creative in passing along and taking in experience-related information. So, assuming that you belong to an organization with no mentor program, how do you go about encouraging formal mentoring without making it seem, well, formal?

You might start by looking at the potential gurus available in your organization. They could be smart, senior people, connected directly to your team or not. They could be senior administrators with a clear, not-too-cynical perspective. In some situations, effective gurus could be managers retired from the company or experienced people who have since moved on but still hold the best interests of your organization at heart (perhaps someone who shifted into contracting but still works hard for your team).

It's theoretically possible for a guru to be at a level or tier *under* you, similar to the seasoned platoon sergeant who, while theoretically subordinate to the new, wet-behind-the-ears lieutenant, still takes the lieutenant under his wings and instructs him on becoming a successful young leader. I have benefited from similar situations in business, manufacturing, and academia. I learned a lot from a senior manufacturer who took me, as a new production manager, aside on many occasions and set me straight on a number of things. He explained peculiarities about that machinery I would never have learned from an operations manual. On a personal level, he told me what he respected about good managers and what he disliked about bad ones. And, when it came time to deal with a problem employee, he discreetly told me how other managers had effectively officiated in similar situations. Although, strictly speaking, he worked for me, he was a guru in every sense of the word.

The Least You Need to Know

◆ Being a modern-day guru means taking one or two good people in your organization under your wing and providing them with guidance and early career development.

◆ When selecting your disciples, you should consider who in your organization is the most interested in your guidance as a guru, who stands to gain the most from it, and who can best help your team and your organization.

◆ By molding your disciples for theoretical advancement away from the team, you develop the best people *on* your team.

◆ By providing structure and parameters, you paradoxically offer your disciples freedom. Once freed from having to find their limits, people will exercise creativity and innovation in order to stay within a provided set of guidelines.

◆ Being a guru helps you choose your successor, encourage loyalty, maintain control within your organization, and maintain control over the outlooks and actions of others.

◆ New team members should be encouraged, but not forced, to find gurus. And senior people should be encouraged, but not forced, to mentor.

Part 5

Manage Change and Adversity

In today's dynamic world, stagnation can be the same as death for an organization. The motivational leader recognizes the importance of sensing upcoming, new priorities and seizing upon tactically beneficial opportunities.

The motivational leader rallies the organization through the often difficult task of stimulating change. He carries out this tough deed by helping his team handle its fear of the unknown. He paints a picture of something better ahead for the team, and he pushes for change in the role of an assuring, convincing guide.

The ultimate motivational leader is also a transformational leader, sensing hidden talents and qualities in people and teams, and pulling them out for the benefit of everyone.

Chapter 17

Be a Cheerleader for Change

In This Chapter

- ◆ Anticipating resistance to change
- ◆ Selling your team on the change
- ◆ Ensuring that the change is worth the time
- ◆ Assessing your team's change capacity
- ◆ Staying calm in the storm of crises
- ◆ Instituting leadership greatness at the margin

Motivational leaders know how to stand out in an assured way during crises. They grab hold of initiatives and opportunities, and when others are seeking cover, they offer themselves as crisis managers and problem-solvers. They present optimism and help people adjust to their fears of the unknown future. They sell their teams on the need to weather a crisis or embrace a new, important organizational change. They get their teams involved in the solutions. They carry ideas through to execution and completion—where other would-be leaders simply stop at the

PowerPoint presentation. In this chapter, we'll look at what sets apart motivational leaders in times of necessary change.

Appreciate That People Dread Change

People innately are creatures of habit. Although there are those high-energy personalities out there who love something new and exciting every five minutes or so, the vast majority of us like to get into a comfortable groove and stay there. And when we find ourselves getting tossed around in our groove or, worse still, getting pried from our groove, our natural reaction is to resist and seek to find our groove again.

As mentioned previously, it's no wonder that so much anxiety-based discomfort stems from the fear of the unknown. We all know those people who would rather live in a crowded, unfriendly neighborhood, work in an underpaying, dead-end job, and tolerate a miserable jerk of a boss, day in and day out, than tolerate one moment of uncertainty in seeking something potentially better.

Interestingly enough, corporations aren't that much different than people. When corporations seek *change*, they so dread the implementation of the change and dealing with people's reaction to it that they often replace their leadership just to make it so.

def•i•ni•tion

The word **change** is derived from the near-identical French verb *changer*, meaning to cause something to turn into something different. Change as a concept has been given lots of theoretical consideration, going back as far as Greek philosophy and joining such terms as "truth" and "logic." Some schools of thought have considered change as ever-present and even-flowing. Others have seen change as random, devoid of fate. Others have considered change preordained. And still others have looked at change as a repeating process, suggesting that things always work their way back to the same reality. Such an idea is a nod toward Spanish essayist George Santayana's observation, "Those who cannot remember the past are condemned to repeat it."

What a shame. Without change, we would all still be living in caves and worshipping the sun. Progress means positive change. No change, no progress. Organizations that give in to change resistance are essentially accepting a short business life. Leaders who don't embrace a dynamic way of leading that welcomes and celebrates change are abetting this untimely death and are not fulfilling their true potential as strategizers, motivators, executors, and accomplishers.

As a motivational leader, you must avoid the temptation to resist change. Instead, serve as the seeker of ways to improve, to do things better and differently, and, when necessary, to completely revamp your team's goals and perspectives. It may even involve a change in your leadership style!

The fact is that any healthy, successful organization is a dynamic organization—an organization in flux. As a motivational leader, you need to recognize that people inherently resist change and that, when change is necessary, they need to be sold on its need.

Just as motivational leadership is a science and not an art, so, too, is the process of introducing, implementing, and monitoring change. However, much like being in charge, bringing about change is often done every way but the right way. It's no wonder that changing policy is often accompanied by changing heads: larger organizations, based on experience, have little faith in their leaders to make positive changes happen.

Perhaps you can begin a new trend at your organization, with your team—that of the change-savvy, change-driven, and change-dependable leader.

Know How to Introduce and Launch Change

Some people argue that the pace of change is accelerating. I'm not sure I subscribe to that notion. After all, it's hard to gauge anything from the perspective of the present. But I do believe that the capacity to adjust to change is more important now than ever. If for no other reason, the ability to contact anyone in the world and to send information instantly and materials near-instantly opens us up to a much wider array of possibilities, meaning a greater potential for change—and quick-paced change, at that.

Here are some ways to introduce change to your team in a way that might make it, at times, be a pleasant experience and not one of constant anguish.

The first, and most crucial, step to bringing about change is to convince your team that the change is needed and that their input for making it happen is important. Just as with selling a product or a service, when there is no need (or at least no perceived need), then that means no sale. Your team needs to buy into this change: if you try to surprise them with it and force it upon them, you are in for a very rough ride. Instead, you should set aside some time to ponder people's potential reactions and concerns, to gauge their potential defiance, and to speculate how you might address these things.

> ### Best Voices Forward
>
> Italian Renaissance political philosopher Niccolò Machiavelli wrote *The Prince*, a somewhat ruthless (depending on your interpretation) guide for people seeking to obtain and hold on to power. However, even when he advocated some underhanded tactics for gaining authority, Machiavelli recognized how difficult change is when people resist it.
>
> In *The Prince*, Machiavelli writes: "We must bear in mind, then, that there is nothing more difficult and dangerous, or more doubtful of success, than an attempt to introduce a new order of things in any state …. Hence it is that, whenever the opponents of the new order of things have the opportunity to attack it, they will do it with the zeal of partisans, while the others defend it but feebly, so that it is dangerous to rely upon the latter."

The second step toward instigating change is to convince your team members that they're going to benefit in some way from the change. This new set-up doesn't have to be all things to all people. But certainly a change that benefits the team or the larger organization has to serve the team members in some way. That's the aspect that needs to be emphasized. As my current boss Stephen Jacobs, with 40 years in education administration, says, "Find that one selling point and lead with it." In other words, convince people up front that they're getting something in the deal.

The third step for promoting change is to push past the passive resistance. Most people don't aggressively refuse to change. They attend their briefings, take their directions, nod their heads in compliance—and then they simply continue to do things their old way. It works like a charm. Often, bosses are too busy to micromanage the change or even to check up on its progress. "Just ignore it until the next big priority comes along," people say. "And then we can ignore that one, too." Again, the best way to defeat this complacency is to sell the change up front.

Quick note in this regard: don't confuse your team's ability to make a change happen with its willingness to do so. If, early on, your larger organization determines that people have the know-how to bring about a policy or structural adjustment, the discussion shouldn't end there. Determining how to approach, sell, and solicit input from people will take the change from conception to realization.

The fourth step is, along with your team, to map out exactly how they might help the change occur, when they might see the benefits of their role, and how these benefits will make themselves known. As discussed in Chapter 8, the Path-Goal Theory of Motivation indicates that the clearer the path, the more likely the desired action.

I'm not a big fan of meetings, but the idea of a subteam, set up to hear about, react to, and discuss the upcoming change makes all kinds of sense. It also serves to offer a sense of importance to the senior people on your team or in your organization and to open up a communication channel for handling feedback and concerns. Remember, there's going to be anxiety when the change is announced. Keeping people as informed and involved as possible will help take away some of the "unknown," thereby taking away some of the apprehension.

Finally, in keeping with the theme that any type of change must be "sold," the fifth step to bringing about change is to indicate to your team members that there are certain now-or-never aspects to the change. Don't make things up, but let them know what things will come harder later on if they don't make the change work now. Also, remind them that the earlier the change happens, the greater their say in how it goes down. This step could be compared to the scarcity strategy used in retail: while supplies last!

> **One Step Back**
>
> If you think that the best way to bring about change is to spring it on your team at the last minute, you had better think again. Keeping some unavoidable, difficult change a secret until it's time to implement it is sure to magnify the knee-jerk defiance and confrontation. And, more importantly, it will hurt your credibility as a team leader, with members of the team constantly wondering, "What's the boss hiding now?" It is better to give your team as much of a heads-up as the larger organization will allow (and perhaps convince the larger organization that such a heads-up is in order), and keep the information as free-flowing as possible.

It's worth saying again. Making change happen requires getting your team members to buy into the change the same way a salesperson gets a prospective customer to buy a product.

Oh, one more thing: implementation and follow-up. People who think they're motivational leaders come up with a new, wonderful way of doing things every day. *Real* motivational leaders maintain a daily planner, keep track of a plan's progress, let people know when they're going to be checking up, and then make good on those follow-ups. Change doesn't break down at the conception stage. It breaks down at the where-the-rubber-meets-the-road execution stage.

Don't Change Just for the Sake of Change

Change isn't always better, and change simply for the sake of change is a drain on time and a quick way to turn people off. Sometimes, the old way is the best way.

Unfortunately, as businesses constantly seek to build the better mousetrap, the newest, touted way of doing things often gets the attention of the big bosses who jump into the water without first checking how deep the lake is. That's a pity. People get numb to hearing about the new and improved way of doing things, and they learn fast that if they nod their heads but ignore the directive, it's likely to pass like a teeny-bopper fad.

Don't allow yourself to get caught in this "new always equals better" trap. The price of change is high, and so if you don't think you're going to make a "profit" on your time and energy invested, then don't do it.

Besides, pushing change on your team when change isn't necessary will hurt your credibility as a motivational leader.

> ### One Step Back
>
> Don't cause a change simply for political or career gain. If you go looking for highly visible, but unnecessary, ways to change things (in order to brag about them later on), you might be setting yourself up for a big fall. If your team senses that you're simply grandstanding, you won't have their support. And change without a team's support is like leadership without a team's support—it generally doesn't exist.

Make sure that you know exactly what you're getting into. What is the proposed change all about? What's the reason for it, and to whom does it extend in the organization? Beside your own efforts, what are the costs? How much overtime is involved? What material resources are required? What will the initial damage to morale be? What is the opportunity cost—that is, what other important things is your team being pulled away from? How dynamic is this change—will it go on forever and drain the life out of your team? All are important questions that should be answered before you go forward.

Again, consider the time involved. Some organizational sociologists suggest that change generally takes twice the amount of time most managers think it will take. The primary reason is that managers are big, big, big in coming up with great ideas, but they're small, small, small-minded when it comes to planning and implementing. It's as if the idea were more important on the PowerPoint slide in front of the conference room than it is in actual practice.

People need time to take in the idea of change, and they need to be informed about, sold on, and involved with the change if it's going to become a worthwhile reality. *Real* change includes time and energy for adjustment.

Measure Your Team's Change Success

It's important that you occasionally appraise your team's ability to handle change. No need to wait for the next change to come along—it'll be here any second. Follow that change from announcement to full implementation and rate each part of the process along the way.

How interested were your team members in contributing to the change process? How much did they want to "own" the change along with you and your bosses? After their contribution, was a good, understandable, doable plan in place?

There's an important strategy behind every good plan of attack, and it often includes instant feedback and adjustment. During the last change, how quick were your team members to provide input, and, if something needed readjusting, how quick were they to offer some ideas on how the plan could be fine-tuned?

Do I keep bringing up investment of your time and energy? There's a reason. If you maintain a stock portfolio, I'm guessing that you check the market each day. I wouldn't be a bit surprised if you didn't log on to an Internet business page or two and see where those stock prices were going. Why? You want to make sure you're getting a return, and, if not, you want to consider whether or not it's time to get out of a particular investment. The same goes for your team's handling of change. If on any given day you're seeing positive returns on your efforts (and theirs), then staying with the investment is warranted. But if you're not getting anything out of it, then you need to consider: a) helping your team adjust the way they're handling the change, or b) deciding the change itself (if you're in a position to make that decision) is no longer worth it.

It's a tough feeling, figuring out that you're not getting a profit on time and energy invested. I suggest that this is the point where many managers decide they're going to force-feed the change to resistant people—out of stubbornness, out of spite, out of refusal to admit defeat, and out of ego.

If you're the motivational leader who gives it your all, it's tough when you realize that the "all" doesn't always come all back. But don't seek retribution or a corner where you can go and sulk. Instead, decide where the change has gone wrong and see if it can be salvaged.

Does the problem come down to one or two *Sad Sacks?* Or, worse still, one or two *USS Defiants?* A poisonous personality or two can unquestionably pollute the change process, just as it can contaminate any aspect of teamwork and team existence. And, as mentioned elsewhere in this text, the solution involves one-on-one talking, listening, more listening, and handing some of the ownership over to that person. It also involves helping that person feel important—and a vital part of the solution. "You're an important part of this," you need to say. "I'm counting on you."

> **Best Voices Forward**
>
> Woodrow T. Wilson, president of the United States from 1913 to 1921, is famous for saying, "If you want to make enemies, try to change something!" But don't take his reference to mean that you should avoid change in order to keep all your friends: they aren't real friends if that's what you need to do to keep them. Instead, Wilson was observing how unfortunate it is that people are creatures of habit, and that they'll fight to stay in their routine.

If your team's change-success rating continues to stay low, keep listening, stay concerned, and page through this book once again. Determine those areas where motivational leadership could best help the team and the change process. Seek advice from your mentor. Don't worry, you'll get there. Again, nothing is more difficult than leading change. Once you conquer that, other stuff will seem easy.

Get Comfortable Managing Crises

If you, as the motivational leader, find yourself saying, "Things will be okay if I can just make it past this crisis," well, I've got some bad news for you. It's never over, and there's *always* going to be another crisis.

Instead of wishing your life away, try to become acclimated to these crises, these daily change-traumas. Better still, look at them as an opportunity. "Sure, take lemons and make lemonade, right, Scott?" you ask cynically. Well, no, not really (although it is nice when you can turn adversity into something positive, but enough Pollyanna stuff for now). What I mean is that, from the perspectives of influence and career, you should seize initiatives whenever opportunities present themselves. And they present themselves more often during crises than during any other time.

When all hell is breaking loose, try to be the first in line taking on new responsibilities to handle the crisis. Try to be the first in line with practical solutions. In fact, if a crisis is imminent, try to be the first in line letting your larger organization know it's coming (and have some potential solutions at the ready when you let them know about it).

Like U.S. Trust vice president Dan Rice says, "The easiest time to differentiate yourself from other managers is during a crisis. Be the contrarian, the optimistic innovator, with a new idea for handling the problem and the concrete plan for getting it done." School administrator Stephen Jacobs agrees: "During a crisis, people just want something that works, and they want smart leaders to come up with it and to share it with others."

Look around you. Take your cues from people who seem to possess the gift of good timing in a crisis. It's not an art; it's a science, right? So take these people to lunch and pick their brains. Find out how they manage to see trouble around the corner and react to it before other people even know it's coming. You'll be surprised how much practical, meat-and-potatoes advice they offer you.

Repeated Excellence

I believe the general belief in business is that great salespeople and great sales managers are often asked to be general managers and operations managers as a reward for the financial success they have brought their corporations. I argue differently. I suggest that great salespeople are often asked to run operations because they know how to convince people about the need for positive change—to the point where they instill in people the importance of the change and the urgency in making it happen. In other words, selling people on organizational change is the same as selling products to customers. Think I'm wrong? Listen to a Brian Tracy lecture on good salesmanship and then, at another venue, listen to a Brian Tracy lecture on motivational leadership. The parallels will astonish you—but they shouldn't!

As mentioned in Chapter 1, there are all kinds of good reasons to become a motivational leader. At the top of the list is a leader's unparalleled potential to make a difference in his or her own little world. Motivational leadership is all about wanting to have a positive impact.

Again, it seems silly to some—those ghosts and self-preservationists who'd rather hide in shadows and hope no one will notice them. But to the person who seeks to feel openly significant and valuable (which, really, should be everybody), longing to make a difference is the unquenched thirst.

Tyge Rugenstein, a colonel in the U.S. Army and commandant of West Point Prep School in New Jersey, suggests that crises tend to make or break leaders. "When you gain a reputation for getting things done in crisis," he says, "it translates into a lot of respect for you as a leader." Rugenstein also argues that such a reputation tends to serve as an example and an inspiration for others. "Such credibility becomes contagious," he notes. "It goes from a point where people know a particular leader is going to get things done in a pinch to where people start counting on the whole organization that way."

As a motivational leader wanting to manage during crises and make a difference, you surely place yourself on an endangered species list. You're just what today's business world needs but is finding tougher and tougher to come across. Today's corporate crusader is initially seen as a bit of joke, maybe something of a chump. But, invariably, that leader becomes the go-to person everyone wants to have around. Fantastic challenges and rewards await the leader who wants to take the helm. Take on a crisis. Seek responsibility. Be that great manager who not only wants to make a difference but also longs to do so. Save the world!

Work the Margin Between Good and Great

A common theme among leadership experts seems to be that they agree on the slim margin between good and great. That is, the best leaders aren't dramatically greater than everyone else; they simply do a lot of little things better than the next guy. I wish I could tell you how many times I've gotten what I wanted in life because I was just a tad better than someone else who wanted the same thing. Like football coaching legend Vince Lombardi said, "The object is to win—to beat the other guy. Maybe that sounds hard or cruel. I don't think it is." Me either.

Says Colonel Tyge Rugenstein: "There's something of a domino effect, where you start out knowing a little more than your competitors, and these small victories compound. Soon you're consistently ahead and others are playing serious catch-up."

As you seek to be a cheerleader for change in your larger organization and for your team, remember that the expectations on you are probably low. Some companies have so little confidence in their leadership during times of necessary change that they simply clean house and bring in new big bosses, charged with implementing these new, important happenings.

In order to make yourself known, you simply have to be a *little* better than that. Just get a *small* change accomplished. Be just a *tiny* bit more effective in implementing change than the team leader down the hallway. Be just a *slight* bit quicker in suggesting solutions and seizing the initiative during crises. Those tiny bits, like raindrops, will form a whole lake of difference in how you present yourself as a motivational leader.

So be that cheerleader for change. Get people on board. Tell them what great things lie ahead if they'll go along with and be part of the change. Show a drawing. Post signs that list the potential benefits for all to read about and get fired up over. Be excited!

The Least You Need to Know

- People inherently fear the unknown, which also means that they are generally opposed to change. Motivational leaders must work against their own human tendencies and the human tendencies of their team members and serve as advocates for positive change.

- Bringing about change begins with selling your team members on the need for the change.

- Don't change simply for the sake of change. If you have a say in whether or not a change is going to happen, ensure that you know what you and your team members are getting into.

- Regularly evaluate your team's ability to adapt to change. Rate their acceptance of the change and their interest in contributing positively to the change process.

- Motivational leaders set themselves apart from others by standing out during crises.

- If you work at being just a little bit better than expectations and a little bit better than your competitors during times of crisis, these small margins of victory will compound into big conquests.

Chapter 18

Choose a Transformational Outlook

In This Chapter

◆ Uncovering the hidden, magnificent team

◆ Getting people to impress you

◆ Starting from a point of high expectations

◆ Reaching for an available reality

◆ Being the renowned leader

◆ Finishing with some concluding thoughts

Sometimes motivational leaders seek a higher form of existence as transformational leaders. Being transformational means helping people and organizations tap into their hidden gifts and forever change in positive ways. It means discovering buried potential in others and making them feel good enough about themselves to develop it and to excel. It means setting very high expectations and being eternally optimistic about their realization. Being transformational also means caring so much about the personal and professional development of others that they work and accomplish things just to get their leaders' approval. In this chapter, we'll consider motivational leadership from its capacity to dramatically impact people's views of themselves.

Go from Motivational to Transformational

Okay, so you think you've got this motivational leadership thing down. In fact, you're so "motivational" at this point that you're able to motivate people to improve for themselves and for the larger organization. So that's all there is, right?

Indeed, in the world of leadership, if you've accomplished all that, then you have reached a very special place. But there is one more step, one more ultimate plateau to reach as a leader. At some point, you should evolve from motivating people to *transforming* them.

def•i•ni•tion

There's a difference between changing something and **transforming** it. If you change a team member or change your team, you improve them in some way that is noteworthy but generally unremarkable and perhaps temporary. However, if you transform a team member or transform your team, you uncover something new and exciting—something you suspected was there all along but had to work a bit to reveal to the larger organization. A transformational leader, therefore, is someone who draws out and makes use of the most dramatic potential in people.

What does being transformational mean? It means altering people and places in such a way that they are forever changed and forever enriched. Every team has the potential for greatness. Every team member has the potential for accomplishing great things. As the transformational leader, you can see that underlying potential, almost like wearing x-ray glasses. And as someone who can spot that talent and point it out to people, you help them become aware of it and you help them access it. Uncovering wonderful, previously unseen attributes and abilities and forever changing people and organizations in the process—that's what being transformational is all about.

Helping others discover their hidden gifts will continue to define you as the leader who's in it to make a difference. As mentioned before, larger organizations are only mildly interested in managers who can keep a humming machine humming. They are much more interested in leaders who can approach a broken machine or a machine running in fits and starts and turn it into a humming machine.

To that end, you shouldn't necessarily avoid the organization with problems or the team with problem personalities—especially if the situation shows long-term promise (or frankly, if there's short-term money involved in coming on board). The transformational leader looks for opportunity amid crisis. It may be true that "if you break it, you bought it." But if you didn't break it and you *fix* it, then you probably *own* it in all kinds of wonderful ways. Garnering a reputation as a Mr. Fix-it or Ms. Fix-it is a nice approach for making your presence in the larger organization at least a bit more locked in—and your marketability to other organizations a lot stronger.

Traits of the Transformational Leader

What characteristics does the transformational leader possess?

First, the transformational leader enters a situation immediately (but privately) looking for ways to make things better. No one likes the boss who comes charging in like gangbusters, trying to change everything. And no one likes the new boss who starts changing things simply for the sake of change. On the other hand, entering a new management situation thinking *How can I simply maintain the status quo and survive?* is no good either. If you quietly enter a new leadership job looking at what might be gradually and agreeably changed when the time is right, then you possess the important, initial trait of a transformational leader.

Second, the transformational leader embarks on an assignment with a very, very high expectation of success. He sets very high standards for his team, and he celebrates and rewards loudly and often whenever those high standards are met.

Third, the transformational leader goes looking for team qualities that he believes are already there but simply need to be brought out. The same goes for personal capabilities. He believes that there is a great destiny—already in existence on some predetermined timeline—and that his team simply needs to choose the right course of action and place itself on that right timeline, the right destiny-line, in order to discover this grand success story.

Fourth, the transformational leader gives attention to what his team members and his larger organization think about him, at least as far as advancing the team is concerned. That's not to say you should try to be liked. But ensuring that people respect you and that they appreciate the time and effort you put into their personal successes sometimes completely alters the way they do business. If people think enough of you, they will work very hard, oftentimes for no other reason than to impress you. At that point, you are the one leader in the organization everybody wants to see stick around. Let's consider this last point a bit more.

Have People Work Just to Impress You

Well, it certainly looks good in writing, but is it really practical? That is, is it possible to get people to do good things at work simply to get your, the leader's, attention?

We know that people react predictably and in predictable ways to certain incentives and motivators. But is a boss's approval a motivator? For the transformational leader, absolutely! If you are the type of leader who tells someone, "I see the potential for greatness in the things you do," and you convince your team members that they *can* do amazing things, then when those things get accomplished, you'll be the *first* person they'll want to tell. After all, you were the one who saw greatness when others only saw a cluster of workers. And you were the one who had visions of grand things when others were only looking for a paycheck. Expect greatness, tell people that you see it in them, and they will try for those things, first, to convince and impress themselves, and, second, to show you that you were right!

My good friend, Roger Vaughan, a senior sergeant in the U.S. Army with combat experience in Afghanistan and Iraq, suggests that transformational leaders get people to work especially hard for them by running interference from the things that normally get in their way. "My soldiers don't need me in order to do a great job," he notes. "They already know how. What they need me to do is to control the stuff that gets in their way. For example, I make sure their promotion paperwork is in order. I make sure pay problems are taken care of quickly. I handle any personnel paperwork that seems to be jammed up. I try to help them with personal problems that are troubling them."

Best Voices Forward

People skills legend Dale Carnegie, in his milestone work *How to Win Friends and Influence People*, notes that, if you don't offer encouragement and accolades to team members in an effort to draw out their hidden talents, then you as a leader are not living up to *your* hidden potential. "Yes, you who are reading these lines possess powers of various sorts which you habitually fail to use," he writes. "And one of these powers you are probably not using to the fullest extent is your magic ability to praise people and inspire them with a realization of their latent possibilities. Abilities wither under criticism; they blossom under encouragement."

Vaughan says that when workers are burdened with administrative problems or problems that fall outside their normal work pursuits, they become saddled down and preoccupied. When leaders keep their teams focused on the tasks at hand, team members often return the favor by working hard and making sure their leaders know it. "A happy, untroubled worker is more likely to be my most diligent worker," says Vaughan.

As mentioned in Chapter 8, when you show people what they have the potential to accomplish and you explain to (or remind) them how they might get there, they are much more likely to take up the charge.

The main proponent of this path-goal theory, Victor Vroom (still researching and writing wonderful articles on leadership after 40 years of pioneering discovery on the topic), recently offered some new thoughts with business leadership expert Arthur Jago. They argue, rather persuasively, in an article for the *Journal of the American Psychological Association*, that since organizational success depends so much on other people's discovering their own talents and on other people's working together collectively, perhaps leaders occasionally get too much of the credit for positive results and too much of the blame for negative results. "Although army generals, orchestra conductors, and football coaches receive adulation for success and blame for failure," they write, "successful performance is typically the result of coordinated efforts of many [and the consequence of many outside variables] …. All of these factors can have large effects on organizational effectiveness, making it difficult to discern leadership effects."

Vroom and Jago aren't suggesting that leaders are total victims of circumstance, but they are strongly arguing, and I agree, that no man is an island—especially leaders. There are extenuating circumstances and extenuating people galore. But if others play so dramatic a role in the success of a team or an organization, then motivational (and transformational) leadership is more important than ever. If you, as a leader, depend so much on others for your achievement, then the last thing you need to do is go into a new situation, like gangbusters, and start barking commands and demands. Instead, get people on your side. Take care of the things that might get in the way of their getting things done. Make them appreciate you to the point where they do great work simply to return the favor and impress you.

Take the Tough Initial Stand

Some quick thoughts on taking the initial, rigid stand. Throughout this text, it has been implied, rightfully so, that the best leaders are beloved leaders. But I should emphasize once again that that doesn't mean you should start off as everyone's buddy. Just the opposite. As you talk to team members and learn about them (their interests, concerns, talents, and hidden gifts), you should set your initial expectations of them very, very high—about as close to unobtainable without actually being there.

Establish yourself as a leader of unwavering principle, as a leader with rigid standards. Will there be letdowns? Sure. Will there be extenuating circumstances? You bet. And will there be all kinds of learning experiences (some pleasant, some unpleasant)? Undoubtedly. But you shouldn't go into a new leadership situation telling people how much they're going to fail and learn from it. Instead, you should meet a new team telling them that the stretch goal is perfection and greatness, and that you think they have the potential to get there.

Repeated Excellence _____

In the U.S. Army, there's a tough job called *advance party*. Believe me, it's no party. This small group of soldiers, with one or two junior leaders, must go forward by themselves, sometimes into enemy territory, confirm that the area is safe, and begin setting it up (determining gun positions, map surveying the directions of fire, and so on). Often, the most junior soldiers are sent off as an advance party, and, as a result, it's considered one of the least desirable jobs.

I served in the Army as both an enlisted soldier and, some years later, as an officer. I worked advance party in both capacities. As a soldier, I remember our platoon leader—a very demanding leader—often telling us, "You soldiers are doing an important job. We appreciate it, and we're counting on you." Did it make a miserable, sometimes dangerous mission more desirable? No. But it did make it infinitely more bearable, and I recall us setting up those advance positions more diligently whenever he said it. And so, as a young lieutenant leading an advance party, I too reminded my soldiers how important their mission was and how much people appreciated them and counted on them.

My good friend Roger Vaughan, just mentioned, agrees that setting lofty goals and encouraging people toward them is a transformational way to lead. "Set the prize high and far off, and keep their eye on that prize," he suggests. "From there, it's persistence, perseverance, encouragement, and then more of the same."

Once the stage has been set and you know what your team can accomplish and what direction they're headed, you certainly can ease back a bit at a time. But it's a lot easier to start off firm and exacting and then loosen up than it is to start off loose and expect to tighten things up later on.

Sell Destiny

Italian Renaissance sculptor and painter Michelangelo was convinced that works of art were not created but were simply revealed by the artist. Each piece of canvas was a painting waiting to be divulged. Each piece of stone was a breathtaking statue, hidden under the excess granite that only needed to be whittled away.

Similarly, modern-day horror novelist Stephen King believes that all good stories already exist, in their entirety in some alternate reality, and that the writer simply needs to bring them into this world for all to enjoy. King insists that he begins most stories without having any idea how they're going to end! Although a writer of nonfiction texts, I can certainly relate. I have picked up my old books from time to time and read parts of them, having no idea how I wrote them, how they got finished, or where any of the good ideas came from. From my vantage point, they had been there all along, and the angels had helped me draw them out. (Of course, I still cashed the checks!)

Even if you're not spiritual, there's something very comforting about the idea that a certain path—a certain life's course—is there, waiting for you to select it. That's not to say all you have to do is sit at home, pop open a beer, and wait for life to happen to you. But it is to say that, if tremendous, forthcoming accomplishments are already there—in some locked-in future reality—then your tendency to want to work toward them and seek them out is a hundred times greater. And the same goes for your team. People are much more inclined to try for something that is already there, or work to preserve something they think they might already have, rather than to put effort into something that might or might not generate results.

Sell your team on their place in this almost divine outlook. Sell them their destiny! Tell them that they are destined for greatness. Tell your team members, one-on-one, "I see truly great talent in you, waiting to come out. You just need to work on it." Make sure that the ability you're referring to is talent that the person does, indeed, inherently hold. You want to be high energy and encouraging, but you don't ever want to be insincere. If you are, people will sense it in a second.

Again, what you're trying to do is have your team reach for an available reality that might or might not make itself real, depending on their determination. "It's there for the taking," you should tell them. Sell them that destiny. Sell, sell, sell!

Be optimistic. Offer constant encouragement as your team and its members go for that brass ring. Convince them that they have the innate ability, the determination, and the unique inventiveness to make it so. Reward their persistence. Reward their innovation.

> **One Step Back** _____
>
> Don't confuse the terms *fate* and *destiny*. Although often used inter-changeably, the word *fate*, from the Latin word *fatum* meaning both "fate" and "death," leans more toward one's uncontrollable fortune. When one speaks of fate, the implication is that there is nothing anyone can do to stop (or start) this ultimate providence. The word *destiny*, on the other hand, is from the Latin word *destinatio*, meaning "a determin-ing." In other words, you have some control over your destiny. Saying it is your destiny to become a leader, no matter how predetermined it may be, still involves your will and determination to make it happen.

Be the Remembered Leader

You know, it wouldn't hurt to start every day looking in the mirror and asking yourself, "If I were to leave my organization today, how would I be remembered?" A leader shouldn't be consumed by his legacy. But he should lead with an underlying interest in how he will be remem-bered. If reality is 50 percent perception, then people's memory of you will define who you are as much as anything. Word travels fast—and to places that will always surprise you. It's a small world, and the world of professional leaders is smaller still. Odds are that, if you ever leave your organization, your reputation will follow you.

Remember, no matter how irreplaceable you might think you are, you can almost certainly be replaced within your organization. Companies are about numbers—not about convenience or inconvenience. And unless your leaving is going to mean a dramatic drop in profits over a year's time, your company really isn't all that concerned (if it's con-cerned at all) about the hassle your absence is going to cause others.

The key isn't to set yourself up as the all-knowing, inimitable person-in-charge. Instead, your goal is to convince others—above and below you—that: a) at any given time, they are doing better having you around as a motivational leader, and b) if they ever lose you, your tal-ent, energy, vision, and way with people will be remembered and sorely missed. Be the leader who is instantly missed the moment you leave. It's like that old vaudeville saying: "Always leave 'em wanting more."

That's not to say every organization is appreciative—or even attentive. Many companies are outrageously out-of-touch when it comes to viewing effective motivational leadership as an asset. In fact, many businesses, once they sense they have a good person on board, reflexively assign him everything and work him to death—or at least until he leaves.

Some years ago, a very effective (and overtasked) leader where I worked said to the company, "Listen, I've been offered an extraordinary opportunity from another organization. But I like it here. So here's a small list of things I'm asking for in order to stay here." The company balked. But the moment they lost him, they realized the huge vacuum he had left behind. Here's the kicker, and the big insult to this great person: they used his minimum-things-I-need-to-stay list to write the job description for his replacement! Wow, talk about business being mean.

The good news, in my humble opinion, is that the pendulum is beginning to swing in the opposite direction. Companies are starting to figure out, the hard way, that it sometimes costs much less to retain and indulge its proven motivational leaders (and its good team members) than it does to hire, train, and take chances on new ones. Just as motivational leadership has its quantitative, measurable, and learnable aspects, good leadership, as an asset, has a value that some organizations have learned to gauge and monetarily appraise. As the motivational leader, you not only prove yourself to be people-effective but also cost-effective.

But setting yourself up as the appreciated, will-someday-be-missed leader is more than simply numbers. There's an aura you can surround yourself with that conveys a worth to people not quite as calculable. If you gain a reputation for being high energy, always enthusiastic, and decisive in a pinch, then you certainly add a premium to your organizational worth. If people start to know you as being highly organized and able to juggle several tasks at once, your value increases further. And if you become known for listening to, caring about, and connecting with people, then your perceived value multiplies even more. Are these perceptions fair? You bet they are—you and I know the merit of having good bosses around. The secret is to project perceptions that are on par with what we know to be true.

The cool thing about a good reputation (or the unfortunate thing about a bad reputation) is that it has a funny way of growing and magnifying. The good stories will change and exaggerate and collectively morph into this incredible caricature of a motivational leader. What should your response be? That's easy. When the legend becomes greater than the person, then the person simply needs to rise up to the legend. If tall tales of your great deeds and can-do attitude become overblown, just show some modesty—and then live up to the image!

Just the fact that you care about how an organization and its employees remember you, in and of itself, helps define the type of motivational leader you become. You don't want to be known as people's friend or flunky. But you do want to be known as the boss who cares enough about people to make *them* care.

So be the remembered leader. Be remembered as smart but unpretentious, firm but fair, caring but demanding, optimistic but with a nod toward reality, inspirational but down-to-earth, and forever appreciative but not obsequious. Be remembered as the motivational leader whose team everybody wants to be on—the leader nobody wants to see leave.

Some Final Thoughts on Motivational Leadership

Warren Bennis, who is leadership research personified, recently wrote in the *Journal of the American Psychological Association* that the more we learn about the human mind, how it functions, and how it reacts, the more likely we are to someday map out a fully understandable model for motivationally leading others. In fact, Bennis compares it to perhaps mapping all the DNA pairs in the human genome. Although we do not know what this ultimate model will look like, writes Bennis, "we do know it will be interdisciplinary, a collaboration among cognitive scientists, social psychologists, sociologists, neuroscientists, anthropologists, biologists, ethicists, political scientists, historians, sociobiologists, and others."

In the meantime, Bennis argues that there are already some constants in the theory of leadership. For example, he suggests that motivational leaders "create a sense of mission, they motivate others to join them on that mission, they create an adaptive social architecture for their followers, they generate trust and optimism, they develop other leaders, and they get results."

Man, that says it all, doesn't it? All common attributes, and all things that you can learn and live.

As you continue on your journey in learning and practicing the science of motivational leadership, remember that it *is* a science and a skill. It *can* be learned and implemented successfully. You *can* make an impact on individuals and teams in ways that dramatically improve output and performance. You *can* draw out the hidden gifts in people and make them want to work for little reason other than they want you to notice and approve. And you *can* make a name for yourself as the consummate leader that your organization wants to keep around and that other organizations seek to invite.

Let the journey begin (or continue, if you've already begun). I hope this text serves as a worthy roadmap. And I wish you, from my heart, the very best of luck as you make your way to your destiny.

The Least You Need to Know

- Being transformational means altering people and organizations in such a way that they are forever changed and enhanced. It means drawing out the potential greatness that you see in people and in teams, and helping them discover and make use of these hidden gifts.

- People react dramatically when you tell them that you see in them a potential for greatness. You can help them find that greatness by clearing out the obstacles that often preoccupy people and keep them from seeking their full promise.

- As the transformational leader, you begin by setting very high initial expectations and establishing yourself as a leader of principle. You continue your undertaking with persistence and with your encouragement of others.

◆ As the transformational leader, you should sell your team on their destiny and convince them that greatness already exists—it simply needs to be drawn out. That is, it's there for the taking.

◆ Start each day by asking yourself, "If I were to leave my organization today, how would I be remembered?"

◆ Motivational leadership and transformational leadership include a series of skills that can be learned and practiced: generating goals, getting others to join in, building an environment where people can work and grow professionally, building trust and hopefulness, and helping people and teams to meet their objectives.

A

The Motivational Leader's Checklist

Certainly not an exhaustive list, this inventory of action items is for the prospective motivational leader who wants to keep track of his or her leadership development. And for the experienced manager, it serves as a reminder of what attitudes and actions best influence others in a positive way.

Your Image and Your Daily Routine

❑ You desire to become a motivational leader and to enjoy all the status, recognition, sense of control, and personal triumph that goes with it.

❑ You are comfortable with the notion that motivational leadership is an ability that you can learn and improve upon over time.

❑ You want to enhance your team members' view of you and themselves.

❑ You are committed to radically revamping your personal goals, image, and outlook.

❏ You constantly exhibit high enthusiasm, reminding your team that they are part of a big, important picture.

❏ You are boldly decisive, while you remain flexible and approachable.

❏ You work to connect with people, one person at a time.

❏ You faithfully maintain a daily planner.

❏ You are firm but fair.

❏ You work to present yourself as a "product" that your team members and your boss are comfortable "buying."

❏ You consistently "own" your mistakes and the mistakes of your team, but you share all compliments with your team.

❏ You calmly display confidence in yourself and your team.

❏ You dress and groom yourself in a way that's a cut above the rest.

❏ Through your job knowledge and your professional behavior, you serve as a model for others to admire and follow.

❏ You limit the number of promises you make, but you follow up on your promises religiously.

❏ You accept the volatility of your business, and you seek to learn new trends and needs within your profession.

❏ You are ready to present yourself as a solution.

❏ You combine your self-confidence with a genuine concern for others.

❏ You appreciate it when your team members teach you things.

❏ At any given time, the loyalty you show your team members equals the loyalty you show your supervisor.

Your Earned Respect and Your Power

❏ You seek to free yourself from the obstacles others create and that you create for yourself.

❑ You have inventoried your position power (from the organization) and your personal power (from expertise, likeability, and respect).

❑ The majority of your power comes from the entrustment and cooperation of the people on your team.

❑ You quietly keep track of professional friendships, connections, favors, and favors returned.

❑ You keep your power focused on the needs of the organization so that the power does not corrupt.

❑ You keep an open flow of vigorous debate and dissenting opinions.

❑ You have made ethical behavior part of your organization's training program.

❑ You fight cruel peer pressure, ultra-polarizing opinions, and groupthink within your team.

❑ You promote team identity and team pride without obstructing original thought or personal responsibility.

❑ You regularly accept blame and seek new responsibility.

❑ You offer ownership of situations to your team members as a reward, celebrating a sense of independence and self-rule.

❑ You offer your team members worthwhile incentives.

❑ You can make the right, if initially unpopular, decision.

❑ You do not offer the same rewards over and over again to the point where they are ultimately resented and result only in minimal compliance.

❑ You emphasize reward for good performance over punishment for bad performance.

❑ You promote the notion of intrinsic rewards by consistently complimenting your team members and telling them they're doing a great job.

❑ You punish or counsel impartially and in a way that encourages improved performance rather than simple resentment.

Your Instinct and Your Communication

❏ You try to offer your team a picture of the future that inspires and motivates them.

❏ You have a vision statement that your team members and your customers helped create.

❏ You have a mission statement that your team members and your customers helped create and that serves as a brief but pointed description of how your team will reach its vision.

❏ You and your team members have agreed on measurable aims and the amount of time needed to accomplish them.

❏ You say "corny" things.

❏ You try to lead your team "from the trenches" rather than hide in your office, offering the right amount of "breathing room" to your team members.

❏ You don't put yourself in a position where you compromise your air of authority and responsibility. For example, you don't drink with your team members.

❏ You regularly show an interest in the individual professional and career goals of others.

❏ You keep your number of meetings and your meeting times to a bare minimum.

❏ If a meeting is absolutely necessary, you utilize an unyielding agenda, a narrow set of goals, and an assistant to help you keep the meeting on track and finished on time.

❏ You promote teamwork, especially in light of people's eagerness to belong to and identify with a group.

❏ When listening to someone, you use good body language and pro-active listening skills.

❏ You shun secrecy and pettiness, preferring strong working relations and very open lines of communication.

❏ You like to "manage by walking around."

❏ You tightly schedule your day, but your schedule regularly includes time for speaking with your team members one-on-one.

Your Ability to Inspire

❏ You appreciate the things your team members inherently desire: health and security, group acceptance, respect and admiration, sense of purpose, and the feeling of importance.

❏ You regularly fight the Burns's Cognitive Distortions.

❏ You respect the fragile nature of people's self-esteem.

❏ You strive to cultivate a community-like, family type of work setting.

❏ When faced with resistance, you respect the opposing view, are disarming with a smile, listen intently, and seek common ground.

❏ You regularly delegate tasks, recognizing that you're still responsible for the work.

❏ You constantly encourage trust and integrity, and you display your trust in your team members.

❏ You serve as someone's guru.

Your Ability to Manage Change

❏ You begin all leadership assignments by setting very high expectations and establishing yourself as a leader of principle.

❏ You recognize that people inherently fear the unknown, which also means that they are generally opposed to change, and you work against that tendency.

❏ Before beginning a new policy, you "sell" your team members on the need for the change.

❏ You don't change things simply for the sake of change.

❏ You continue to regularly evaluate your team's ability to adapt to change.

❏ You step up to the plate during organizational crises.

❏ You work at being just a little bit better than expectations and a little bit better than your competitors.

❏ You seek to be a transformational leader, pointing out to people their hidden, potential greatness and helping them discover and make use of their hidden gifts.

❏ You regularly tell your team members that you see in them potential for greatness.

❏ You start each day by quietly asking yourself, "If I were to leave my organization today, how would I be remembered?"

Appendix B

Suggested Books on Motivational Leadership

A Primer on Organizational Behavior (Sixth Edition), by James L. Bowditch and Anthony F. Buono (New York: Wiley, 2004). My all-time favorite book on how groups collectively think and act. This book is a very easy and entertaining academic read. It goes into great detail about several of the theories of motivation mentioned in this text, and it offers an inspiring discussion about transformational (as opposed to transactional) leadership.

Client-Centered Therapy, by Carl R. Rogers (New York: Houghton Mifflin, 1951). This is Rogers's discussion of his Rogerian method of active listening, what he called "the reflection of attitudes." It is a milestone work in psychology that introduced the notion of using specific techniques to garner revealing information from people by providing them with the opportunity to talk and reflect.

Decision for Disaster: Betrayal at the Bay of Pigs, by Grayston L. Lynch (Washington, D.C.: Brassey's, 1998). This book expands on the topics of groupthink and bad decision-making in detail, as it discusses the disastrous Bay of Pigs planning process during cabinet meetings in the Kennedy Administration.

The Essential Drucker: The Best of Sixty Years of Peter Drucker's Essential Writings on Management, by Peter F. Drucker (New York: Collins, 2003). Drucker really changed the way people thought about how bosses and workers should interact. Here are some milestone articles chosen by Drucker himself.

The Feeling Good Handbook, by David D. Burns, M.D. (New York: Penguin Plume, 1989). Is it too corny to say a book changed my life? Too bad—this one did. Burns's discussion about what we desire and how our minds play tricks on us when we don't get it is amazing and revealing. This book is a follow-up to his groundbreaking work on cognitive behavioral therapy, titled *Feeling Good*. Both books are still very popular and still on bookstore shelves.

How to Land Your Dream Job: No Resume! and Other Secrets to Get You in the Door, by Jeffrey J. Fox (New York: Hyperion, 2007). This book was initially released in 2001 under the title *Don't Send a Resume*. It expands on the notion of the leader as a "product." A wonderful, quick read on how you should present yourself to your bosses (prospective and current) and to your colleagues.

How to Make Meetings Work, by Michael Doyle and David Strauss (New York: Berkley, 1993). I personally believe that the most effective business meeting is the one not held. But if you *must* convene a meeting, I recommend this handy text, still in print and still in bookstores. It expands on the topics of maintaining a tight meeting agenda and not letting things get off track or out of hand.

How to Win Friends & Influence People (Reissue Edition), by Dale Carnegie (New York: Pocket Books, 1990). Originally written over 75 years ago, this text remains perhaps the best book ever on getting people to respect you, support you, and do what you ask them to do. It expands on the topics of "selling" your team on a vision and constantly encouraging your team members. If you have a CD player in your car, I highly recommend the uncondensed audio book version, read by Andrew MacMillian (New York: Simon & Schuster Audio, 1999).

Leadership: Audio Success Suite (Audio Book), by Brian Tracy, Zig Ziglar, Chris Widener, and Dr. Sheila Murray Bethel (Renton, WA: Topics

Entertainment, 2006). These CDs are funny, inspiring, and they offer some very practical advice from the best motivational speakers in the business. They expand on some of the ideas mentioned in my text from these four great tutors (the brief thoughts that I shared with their permission). An enjoyable listen while driving.

Leadership in Organizations (Sixth Edition), by Gary A. Yukl (Upper Saddle River, NJ: Prentice Hall, 2005). A rather expensive scholastic text. But if you ever want to immerse yourself in the academic study of leadership as a science, there really is no better starting point than Yukl's milestone work. The book expands on the different theories regarding leadership and power. It is exhaustive and painstakingly documented. A superb academic work.

Leadership Jazz, by Max DePree (New York: Dell, 1993). I don't really subscribe to DePree's "leadership is an art" philosophy, but I do agree that being creative with how you relate to people can be rewarding, especially at work. DePree's advice is very practical, and his book is entertaining and worthwhile.

Learning to Lead: A Workbook on Becoming a Leader (Third Edition), by Warren G. Bennis and Joan Goldsmith (New York: Basic Books, 2003). It's tough to recommend just one book by Bennis, an icon in leadership research. But this brief, enlightening workbook really does the trick. The worksheets will help you learn about yourself as a prospective motivational leader.

Managing with Power: Politics and Influence in Organizations, by Jeffrey Pfeffer (Boston: Harvard Business School Press, 1994). The title is misleading: this isn't a modern-day *The Prince*. Instead, it discusses power from the standpoint of overcoming obstacles and getting things done and helping others do the same. It expands on the idea that power has more to do with clearing a path to success than with dominating others.

Obedience to Authority: An Experimental View (First Edition), by Stanley Milgram (New York: Harper & Row, 1974). Certainly not a rose-colored look at happy, motivational leadership, this text is nevertheless a very important academic work regarding people's tendency to follow authority. Milgram conducted his sobering experiments at Yale, still controversial and much-discussed today. This book is his account of those experiments. It expands on the topic of most people's inherent desire to conform and follow directions. I'm not into playing mind games with people, but this text shows us what we're made of.

The Psychology of Selling: The Art of Closing Sales (Audio Book), by Brian Tracy (Niles, IL: Nightingale-Conant, 2002). Any of Brian Tracy's audio-book stuff on leadership and sales is a pleasure to listen to in the car, and his advice is very practical and extremely useful. When I was in sales, Tracy was all I listened to.

See You at the Top (25th Anniversary Edition), by Zig Ziglar (Gretna, Louisiana: Pelican, 2000). Still giving fantastic lectures in his eighties, Ziglar is a real treat. This book is his milestone work. Also, anything on audio book from Ziglar makes for a pleasant drive to work.

Stop the Meeting, I Want to Get Off!: How to Eliminate Endless Meetings While Improving Your Team's Communication, Productivity, and Effectiveness, by Scott Snair (New York: McGraw-Hill, 2003). This book focuses on how to run your team without meetings. It looks at how some very successful business people have managed big groups and big companies with few, if any, meetings as part of their daily routine. It expands on how meetings are inherently flawed and why they should be used as a last resort for informing and influencing team members. I wrote it—I hope you like it.

Victims of Groupthink: A Psychological Study of Foreign Policy Decisions and Fiascoes, by Irving L. Janis (Boston: Houghton Mifflin, 1972). A second, revised edition published in 1983 includes a discussion of the Watergate cover-up. This book, in chilling detail, discusses the innate desire of many people to conform within their group—even very intelligent people who quietly sense a storm brewing.

Winning, by Jack Welch and Suzy Welch (New York: Collins, 2005). Whenever I read advice from Jack Welch, former head of General Electric and perhaps the most successful CEO in history, I always get the feeling that he's holding back. But, having admitted that, I very much enjoy reading all his articles and books. This recent text, written with his wife Suzy Welch, is more a discussion about leadership as a science than was his 2003 autobiographical work, *Jack: Straight from the Gut*.

C

Suggested Biographies and Autobiographies of Motivational Leaders

The Autobiography of Martin Luther King, Jr., by Martin Luther King, Jr., edited by Clayborne Carson (New York: Warner, 2001). An interesting and inspiring mix of papers and speeches from the Nobel Peace Prize–winning civil rights leader.

American Caesar: Douglas MacArthur 1880–1964, by William Manchester (Boston: Little, Brown & Company, 1978). Entertaining biography about MacArthur, one of history's greatest military leaders.

Elizabeth I, CEO: Strategic Lessons from the Leader who Built an Empire, by Alan Axelrod (Upper Saddle River, NJ: Prentice Hall, 2000). Leadership lessons linked to the fascinating life of the young queen of England who led her nation through war, growth, and crisis.

Faith of My Fathers: A Family Memoir, by John McCain with Mark Salter (New York: HarperCollins/Perennial, 1999). Inspiring story about John McCain as a young Navy pilot, who endured years of torture rather than leave his men behind in a Vietnamese POW camp.

Jesus CEO: Using Ancient Wisdom for Visionary Leadership, by Laurie Beth Jones (New York: Hyperion, 1995). Short, lesson-like stories about Jesus tied into modern-day management scenarios.

Moving Mountains: Lessons in Leadership and Logistics from the Gulf War, by William G. Pagonis with Jeffrey L. Cruikshank (Boston: Harvard Business School Press, 1992). Pagonis went from leading the movement of people, weapons, and supplies in the Middle East to handling the enormous task of moving merchandise at Sears. He is an amazing man and the quintessential motivational leader. I recommend this autobiographical account of his management style.

Memoirs of the Second World War, by Winston Churchill (New York: Mariner, reprint 1991). Autobiography of Winston Churchill, prime minister of Great Britain who kept his country motivated and confident during their harsh challenges in World War II.

My American Journey: An Autobiography, by Colin Powell, with Joseph E. Persico (New York: Ballantine, 2003). Autobiography of Colin Powell, former U.S. Secretary of State and Chairman of the Joint Chiefs of Staff.

My Life, by Bill Clinton (New York: Vintage, 2005). Autobiography of the only U.S. president to balance the federal budget two years in a row. Raw politics aside, that *had* to take some type of motivation and teamwork.

Patton on Leadership: Strategic Lessons for Corporate Warfare, by Alan Axelrod (Upper Saddle River, NJ: Prentice Hall, 2005). Great business book tied into the life of General George S. Patton, Jr., who was a much more charismatic and caring leader than those soldier-slapping movie scenes suggest.

Portrait of a President: John F. Kennedy in Profile, by William Manchester (Boston: Little, Brown & Company, 1967). Manchester's leadership profile of one of America's greatest presidents.

The Right to be Human: A Biography of Abraham Maslow, by Edward Hoffman (Los Angeles: Tarcher/New York: St. Martin's Press, 1988). Maslow was a forerunner of humanistic psychology in the 1940s and

1950s. His famous Theory of Motivation and Hierarchy of Human Needs was unique at the time in that it touched on psychology as it affects everyone—rather than focusing on psychoses. He carried his theories into the business world.

West Point Leadership Lessons: Duty, Honor, and Other Management Principles, by Scott Snair (Naperville, IL: Sourcebooks, 2005). Short, lesson-like stories about West Pointers and the leadership lessons they brought with them into various management situations. I wrote it—I hope you like it.

When Character Was King: A Story of Ronald Reagan, by Peggy Noonan (New York: Penguin, 2002). Inspiring story about Ronald Reagan, perhaps the most people-person president in U.S. history, written by his former speechwriter.

Glossary

360 evaluation   A method for providing a leader with criticism and advice from all levels surrounding the leader—above, below, peer, and even self. The 360 evaluation form often includes comments about a leader's capacity to give direction, offer encouragement, and consider the opinions of others.

accountability   The state of being responsible for and answerable for an activity.

achievement-power-affiliation theory   Motivation model, hypothesized by David McClelland in the 1960s, suggesting that people are motivated by the need for accomplishment, the need for control, or the need for bonding with others.

autonomy   The state of being independent and self-directed.

blame   The state of being accountable in a way deserving of censure, discipline, or other penalty.

charisma   The ability to allure and fascinate other people, creating an eagerness to like and a willingness to obey.

coaching effect   The increased know-how that often occurs with mentoring. The more a leader prepares to give advice regarding a job, the more of an expert he or she becomes regarding that position's duties.

coercive power The power generated by the ability to apply punishment, withhold awards, or reduce awards. A type of position power.

cognitive distortions Hypothesized by modern-day psychiatrist David D. Burns, M.D., these are thought alterations that make things seem much worse in most people's minds. Examples include immoderate thinking, where people look at things in extreme ways, and overgeneralization, when people think that something negative will go on forever.

commander's intent A leader's explanation of what needs to be achieved, why it needs to be achieved, and what forces exist that might keep it from happening. A commander's intent message is meant to allow second- and third-tier managers to operate within a set of guidelines that allows independent decision-making and innovation.

conformity Behavior that coincides with the behavior of others and with norms.

connectional power Power gained through personal connections. A type of position power.

delegating The process of authorizing and entrusting to others something that the team leader is responsible for completing. Delegating work and authority does not equal delegating the responsibility.

ecological power Power gained by controlling the technical, electronic, and aesthetic environment of team members. A type of position power.

entrusted power Power essentially handed to the team leader by being accepted by his or her team members.

environmentally-based theories A group of motivational theories that consider motivation from the vantage point of rewards, punishments, and expected outcomes for work.

equity theory of motivation Motivation theory, proposed by J. Stacy Adams in the 1960s, suggesting that people are motivated when they perceive fairness within the workplace. That is, if they believe their reward/effort ratio is the same as (or better than) the reward/effort ratio of others, they will continue to work hard.

expectancy theory Motivation theory, hypothesized by Victor Vroom in the 1960s, suggesting that, for a reward to work, team members must be convinced that the action will lead to the reward and that the reward is worthwhile.

expert power Power gained from holding a highly specialized skill or expertise in a particular area. A type of personal power.

extrinsic rewards Material, tangible rewards that draw people to complete tasks.

farsightedness The ability to see the long-range, big-picture impact of new happenings in a profession or in an organization. The ability to predict the long-term effect of things such as hiring and policy trends.

forming, storming, norming, performing Mnemonic (memory aid) developed by Bruce Tuckman in 1965, who suggested that teams begin a process by learning about each other, followed by creatively conflicting, followed by reaching consensus, followed by completing tasks.

group dysfunction The collective negative tendencies of a group, including the call for conformity, groupthink, loss of personal responsibility, and polarizing (or extreme) viewpoints.

groupthink The phenomenon that occurs when members of a group surrender to conformity, allowing plans (often bad ones) to develop without dissent. Once a plan takes form, the group members often commit to it passionately and completely. Investigated as a psychological concept in the 1970s and 1980s by Yale research psychologist Irving L. Janis.

guru A worshipped teacher, considered a necessary instrument for attaining personal and professional enlightenment; a mentor.

hierarchy of needs Motivation model, hypothesized by Abraham Maslow during the 1940s and 1950s, suggesting that people tend to go from more primitive, basic needs and then, as each need is met, to more enlightened needs.

influence theory of power A theory of power suggesting that power is a constant within an organization. That is, there is a finite amount of power in each organization that can be gained, lost, or shared.

informational power   Power derived by one's control over information. A type of position power.

intrinsic rewards   Internal feelings of satisfaction produced by a job well done.

management by objectives (MBO)   Process introduced by Peter Drucker in the 1950s, where the team agrees to measurable aims within specific time periods.

Milgram experiment   A controversial psychology study at Yale in the 1960s conducted by social psychologist Stanley Milgram. In the experiment, the majority of subjects were ordered to administer electric shocks to someone behind a screen. The shocks were faked, and the victim was an actor. The study was unsettling in that it suggested that most people were predisposed to follow authority, despite the consequences.

mirroring   A tactic used in active listening where the listener "mirrors" some phrases back to the person speaking to provoke more openness and more revelations. Mirroring is part of the counseling technique that famous psychologist Carl Rogers in the 1950s called *the reflection of attitudes.*

mission statement   A team's written description of how it strategically plans to meet the ideal portrayed by its vision statement. It typically includes descriptions of team strengths, customer communities, and specific goals and objectives related to both.

motivation   The state of having incentive, of being driven to action.

motivational leader   A supervisor who uses the process of inspiring and persuading others with a compelling combination of actions, attitude, and persona.

negative reinforcement   A shunned thing that, in the name of avoidance, causes a particular behavior.

norm   A model or standard for social behavior; an expected behavior among people in a group.

path-goal model of motivation   A theory of motivation, hypothesized in 1974 by Robert House and Terence Mitchell, suggesting that team members are collectively more inclined to do something when they are given a clear, well-described path to the desired outcome.

personal power Power gained through personal attributes such as expertise and the ability to make friends, demonstrate loyalty, and stay politically astute. Defined in the early 1960s by John French and Bertram Raven.

planner A notebook, appointment book, or electric organizer for jotting down notes, scheduling follow-up items, and recording noteworthy events.

polarization The tendency of a group to form very extreme opinions.

position power Power related to a manager's job description and the formal authority that he or she is handed in that job. Defined in the early 1960s by John French and Bertram Raven.

positive reinforcement A desired item or response that causes a particular behavior.

power The ability to exercise influence or control. The capacity to get things done effectively and unhampered.

process theories of motivation A group of motivation theories that consider the before-and-after effects of specific motivators over time, as opposed to snapshot effects.

punishment Anything unlikable enough that it prompts someone to reduce the behavior connected to it.

rapport A working or business relationship steeped in mutual trust, empathy, a sense of kinship, and warm personal regard.

referent power Power to persuade others through charisma, personal interaction, and other personality qualities. A type of personal power.

reward power The capacity to get things done by offering company-sanctioned rewards. A type of position power.

safe-and-silent slant The act of staying silent in a meeting, sensing the social dysfunction that's going on in the conference room.

self-esteem A person's personal feeling of self-worth. It includes one's self-assessment regarding knowledge, ability, accomplishment, and personal control over one's destiny.

self-promotion Actions involved with "selling oneself" to superiors, colleagues, and subordinates. The actions are charismatic and confident, with a nod toward humility.

self-view theory of leadership A theory of leadership suggesting that the motivational leader inspires people by helping them improve how they view themselves. For instance, highly charismatic and inspirational leaders bring about high levels of confidence in their team members.

situational theory of leadership Also called *contingency theory*, a theory of leadership, hypothesized in 1988 by Kenneth Blanchard and Paul Hersey, suggesting that certain types of leadership should be matched to certain group situations. For instance, if leader-group rapport is low but task understanding is high, the leader utilizes very specific instructions and rigid monitoring.

social comparison theory of motivation Motivation theory, hypothesized by Leon Festinger in the 1950s, suggesting that people are motivated by comparing their situation to that of other people. In some cases, workers can perceive very tough work as enjoyable if they think others around them are enjoying it as well.

social impact theory Psychological theory suggesting that a person's behavior is influenced by the group he or she is in, with the size of impact depending upon the forcefulness of the people in the group, their proximity to the person, and their number. This theory argues that a large, tight-knit group with powerful opinions holds dramatic control over each group member.

static-content model of motivation A group of motivational theories that considers what is happening in someone's mind at any given moment, as opposed to what motivates a person over time.

SWOT analysis A method, created in the 1960s by Albert Humphrey, for assessing the status of a team or a project. SWOT is the acronym for the four things examined: strengths, weaknesses, opportunities, and threats. Strengths and weaknesses are considered internal factors; opportunities and threats are considered external factors.

technical proficiency Expert knowledge in the area that one manages. This aptitude runs contrary to "generalist" management, where the leader manages all types of people and all types of different projects without knowing much about them.

"the shadow up" A phrase that insinuates that all employees, even at entry levels, have the capacity to influence their organization.

traits theory of leadership   A theory of leadership suggesting that motivational leaders share the same personal attributes, many of which they were born with, including intelligence, composure, energy, and enthusiasm.

transformation   The act of improving something in a way that is significant and long-lasting. A transformation often involves drawing out hidden potential in people.

vision   Keen intuition; a mental picture of a prosperous future.

vision statement   A team's written description of what it wants to be in the short-term or long-term future, providing an idealized mental picture of what good things could happen.

Index

Numbers

360 evaluations, 51-52

A

abuses of power, avoiding, 68-69
accolades, sharing, 34-35
accountability
    blame, compared, 83-84
    culture of blame, avoiding,
      87-88
    importance of, 84-85
    ownership, importance of,
      88-89
    owning, 85-86
    veracity, power of, 86-87
Achievement-Power-Affiliation
  Theory, 97
Adams, J. Stacy, 99
Adler, Alfred, 116
advance party, 239
agendas, setting, 25-27
Ahner, Chuck, 26
Aldrin, Buzz, 19
Apprentice, The, 53
Armstrong, Neil, 19

B

backing up electronic organizers,
  25
Barry, John, 188
Barry, Karen, 144

Bay of Pigs Invasion, 77
behavior, organizational behavior,
  72-73
    dysfunctionality, 74-75
    groupthink, 75-78
behavior theory, 11
Bennis, Warren, 9, 243
blame
    accountability, compared, 83-84
    avoiding, 87-88
    owning, 34-35
Blanchard, Kenneth, 11
Bloomberg, Michael, 65
Book of Proverbs, 114
born leaders, myth of, 8
Bowditch, James L., 96
Brenner, Rick, 84, 87
Buono, Anthony F., 96
Burns, David, 170
Bush, George H. W., 112
businesses
    loyalties, balancing, 52-54
    needs
        discovering, 44-46
        meeting, 46-50
    visions, embracing, 50-51

C

Cameron, James, 150
Carnegie, Andrew, 145
Carnegie, Dale, 128-129, 138, 170,
  185, 195, 237
Castro, Fidel, 77
championing ideals, 198-199

change
   aversion to, 222-223
   crises, managing, 229-231
   introducing, 223-226
   launching, 223-226
   successes, measuring, 227-229
   when to implement, 226-227
charisma, 194-197
   steps toward, 195-196
Churchill, Winston, 12
Civil Rights Act of 1964, 115
clear communication, importance of, 22-23
Clinton, Bill., 112, 199
clothes, importance of appearance, 38-39
coaching effect, 188-189
coercive power, 62, 65
cognitive distortions, 170
collaboration, encouraging, 146-147
cologne, wearing, 39
commander's intent, 20
communication
   clear communication, importance of, 22-23
   encouraging, 148-149
   open lines, 149-150
community, building sense of, 174-175
companies
   loyalties, balancing, 52-54
   needs
      discovering, 44-46
      meeting, 46-50
   visions, embracing, 50-51
company person, 50
confidence, importance of, 35-37
connectional power, 63
constructive relationships, establishing, 144

corniness, importance of, 129-131
counseling before discipline, 104
Covered Bridge Produce, vision statement, 120-121
credibility, importance of, 190
crises, managing, 229-231
culture of blame, avoiding, 87-88

D

De Pree, Max, 183
decision-making, precise, 20-21
deeds, Three Rules of Thumb, 187
defining visions, 118
delegation, 178
   effective delegation, 179-185
      credibility, 190
      integrity, 185-187
      trust, 187-189
   importance of, 178-179
delegation lists, creating, 160
destiny, fate, compared, 241
Development Sequence in Small Groups, 145
Dion, Celine, 150
disciples, defining yourself through, 205-207
discipline
   carrying out, 106
   counseling before, 104
   motivational traits of, 106-107
   verbal warnings, 104-105
Don't Send a Resume, 32
dressing appropriately, 38-39
Drucker, Peter, 60-61

E

ecological power, 63
effective delegation, 179-185
    credibility, 190
    integrity, 185-187
    trust, 187-189
Einstein, Albert, 174
Eisenhower, Dwight, 8
electronic organizers, backing up,
    25
electronic planners, advantages of,
    181
Emerson, Ralph Waldo, 130
encouragement
    expressing, 175-176
    importance of, 172-174
enthusiasm, importance of, 35-37,
    128-135
entrusted power and seized power,
    compared, 66-67
environmentally-based theories,
    98-99
Equity Theory, 99
evaluations, 360 evaluations, 51-52
Evans, Martin, 98
examples, setting, 39-40
Expectancy Theory, 98
expectations, gurus, 213-215
expert power, 63
expressions, corny expressions, 131
extrinsic rewards, 102

F

fairness, importance of, 27-28
farsightedness, 45
fate, destiny, compared, 241
Feeling Good Handbook, The, 170

Festinger, Leon, 99
Fifth Discipline, The, 61
firmness, importance of, 27-28
follow-up, ideas, importance of,
    90-92
formal mentoring, encouraging,
    215-217
forming phase (teams), 146
Fox, Jeffrey J., 32, 38
fragile nature, humans, respect-
    ing, 171-172
Frankl, Victor, 170
French, John, 61-62
Fuchs, Jeff, 49

G

Gandhi, Mahatma, 200
Gates, Bill, 4
Goldsmith, Joan, 9
good reputations, forming,
    241-243
Gorbachev, Mikhail, 130
grooming, importance of, 37-39
groups
    change success, measuring,
        227-229
    collaboration, encouraging,
        146-147
    communication
        encouraging, 148-149
        open lines, 149-150
    dysfunctional attributes, recog-
        nizing, 74-75
    enthusiasm, importance of,
        128-135
    follow-up, importance of, 90-92
    groupthink
        avoiding, 78
        recognizing, 75-77

meetings
    alternatives to, 159-160
    avoiding, 154
    detriments of, 155
    failures of, 158-159
    necessary meetings, 156-158
    running, 161-163
    scripting, 161
mission statements, creating, 121-123
objectives, managing by, 123-124
one-on-one management, 135-137
    time efficiency, 135-137
organizational behavior, 72-73
ownership, promoting, 89-90
people, viewing as assets, 80-81
polarizing nature of, 74-75
programs, promoting, 81
responsibility, assigning, 92-93
sense of community, building, 174-175
understanding, 79-80
vision
    defining, 118
    setting, 114-118
    vision statements, 119-121
groupthink, 76
    avoiding, 78
    meetings, 155
    recognizing, 75-77
gurus, 204-205
    disciples, 205-207
    expectations, 213-215
    formal mentoring, encouraging, 215-217
    hidden sponsors, 207-210
    job enrichment, promoting, 211-213

H

Heinlein, Robert A., 133
hidden sponsors, gurus, 207-210
Hierarchy of Needs, 97
Hillel the Elder, 91
Holy Bible, The, 114
honesty, power of, 86-87
Hopper, Grace, 53
Horner, James, 150
House, Robert, 11, 98
How to Win Friends and Influence People, 129, 185, 195, 237
human motivators, 100
human needs
    encouragement, 172-176
    sense of community, 174-175
    understanding, 168-172
Humphrey, Albert, 47
hypocrisy, avoiding, 40

I

ideals, championing, 198-199
ideas, follow-up, importance of, 90-92
individuals, motivating, 99
    discipline, 104-107
    human motivators, 100
    punishments, 101
    rewards, 101-104
influence theory, 12
informational power, 63
input, teams, gathering, 51-52
inspirational, being, 197-198
integrity, importance of, 185-187
intrinsic rewards, 102
introducing changes, 223-226
introversion, detriments of, 48-50

J

Jacobs, Jack, 91
James, William, 171
Janis, Irving L., 76
Jennings, Will, 150
Jeppi, John, 128
jewelry, wearing appropriately, 39
job enrichment, promoting,
   211-213
JPS Engineering, 123

K

Kamprad, Ingvar, 4
Kennedy, John F., 19, 76
Kerkorian, Kirk, 66
King, Jr., Martin Luther, 115
King, Stephen, 240
King Solomon, 114
knowledge-based research, 7
Koresh, David, 85

L

launching, changes, 223-226
leaders, qualities, 8-10
Leadership Jazz, 183
Learning to Lead, 9
legitimate power, 62
listening, importance of, 23-25
Lord Nelson, 131
loyalties, organizations, balancing,
   52-54

M

MacArthur, Douglas, 132
Machiavelli, Niccolò, 224
Mallon, Charles, 26

management, one-on-one, 137
   time efficiency, 135-137
Management By Objectives
   (MBO) process, 124
management
   crises, 229-231
   one-on-one, 135
Managing By Walking Around
   (MBWA), 159
Managing with Power, 103
Mandela, Nelson, 66
manicures, importance of, 39
Maslow, Abraham, 5, 97, 169
*Master and Commander: The Far
   Side of the World*, 131
MBO (Management By
   Objectives) process, 124
MBWA (Managing By Walking
   Around), 159
McCain, John, 138
McClelland, David, 59, 97
meetings, 154
   alternatives to, 159-160
   avoiding, 154
   detriments of, 153-155
   failures of, 158-159
   groupthink, 155
   necessary meetings, recogniz-
      ing, 156-158
   running, 161-163
   scripting, 161
Menoher, Charles T., 132
mentoring
   formal mentoring
      encouraging, 215-217
method-based research, 7
Michelangelo, 239
Milgram, Stanley, 73
mindset (motivation leaders)
   accolades, sharing, 34-35
   blame, owning, 34-35

confidence, 35-37
enthusiasm, 35-37
examples, setting, 39-40
promises, following up, 41-42
proper grooming, 37-39
self-promotion, 31-33
mission statements
creating, 121-123
model mission statements, 123
Mitchel, Charles, 24
Mitchell, Terence, 11
motivating
individuals, 99
discipline, 104-107
human motivators, 100
punishments, 101
rewards, 101-104
theories of, 96-99
motivational leaders, 3-5
choosing to be, 4-6
qualities, 8-10
recognizing, 18-19
motivational leadership
science of, 6-8
theories, 10
behavior theory, 11
influence theory, 12
self-view theory, 12-13
situation theory, 10-11
traits theory, 10
motivational speakers, 117

N

nails, manicuring, 39
Namath, Joe, 33
Napoleon Bonaparte, 131
needs, organizations
discovering, 44-46
meeting, 46-50

negotiations, importance of,
67-68
Neovista Consulting, LLC, 49
Nixon, Richard M., 77
norming phase (teams), 146
Nykwest, Larry, 39

O

objectives, managing by, 123-124
One-Minute Manager, 11
one-on-one management, 135-137
time efficiency, 135-137
organizational behavior, 72-73
dysfunctionality, recognizing,
74-75
groupthink
avoiding, 78
recognizing, 75-77
self-actualization, 97
organizations
change success, measuring,
227-229
collaboration, encouraging,
146-147
communication
encouraging, 148-149
open lines, 149-150
dysfunctional attributes, recognizing, 74-75
enthusiasm, importance of,
128-135
follow-up, importance of, 90-92
groupthink
avoiding, 78
recognizing, 75-77
interest, expressing, 143-144
loyalties, balancing, 52-54
meetings
alternatives to, 159-160
avoiding, 154

detriments of, 155
failures of, 158-159
necessary meetings, 156-158
running, 161-163
scripting, 161
mission statements, creating,
121-123
needs
discovering, 44-46
meeting, 46-50
objectives, managing by,
123-124
one-on-one management,
135-137
time efficiency, 135-137
organizational behavior, 72-73
ownership, promoting, 89-90
people, viewing as assets, 80-81
programs, promoting, 81
responsibility, assigning, 92-93
sense of community, building,
174-175
SWOT analysis, 47
teamwork, developing, 145-146
understanding, 79-80
vision
defining, 118
embracing, 50-51
setting, 114-118
vision statements, 119-121
outlook, committing to positive,
15
ownership
importance of, 88-89
promoting, 89-90

P–Q

Pagonis, Gus, 160
Pastor, John, 162
"Path-Goal Theory of
Motivation," 98

Patton III, George S., 138
Patton Jr., George S., 137
PDAs
advantages of, 181
backing up, 25
people, viewing as assets, 80-81
Perdew, Kelly, 53
performing phase (teams), 146
perfumes, wearing, 39
personal power, 62-64
Peters, Tom, 159
Pfeffer, Jeffrey, 103
planners
electronic planners, advantages
of, 181
keeping, 25-27
planning meetings, 161
polarization, groups, 74-75
position power, 61-63
positive outlook, committing to,
15
Powell, Colin, 196
power, 57, 61
abuses, avoiding, 68-69
entrusted power, 66-67
expert opinions on, 58-59
Drucker, Peter, 60-61
McClelland, David, 59
Senge, Peter, 61
Taylor, Frederick W., 60
Weber, Max, 59
necessity of, 64-65
negotiations, importance of,
67-68
personal power, 62-64
position power, 61-63
seized power, 66-67
word origin, 58
praise, sharing, 34-35
precise decision-making, exercis-
ing, 20-21

Primer on Organizational Behavior, A, 96
Prince, The, 224
programs, promoting, 81
promises, following up, 41-42
promoting ownership, 89-90
promoting programs, 81
proper grooming, importance of, 37-39
punishments, 101
   carrying out, 106
   counseling before, 104
   motivational traits of, 106-107
   verbal warnings, issuing, 104-105

R

rapport, importance of, 142-143
Raven, Bertram, 61-62
Reagan, Ronald, 46, 93, 116, 130
referent power, 64
relationships
   constructive relationships, establishing, 144
   rapport, importance of, 142-143
Reno, Janet, 85
research, 7
responsibility, assigning, 92-93
reward power, 62
rewards
   extrinsic, 102
   intrinsic, 102
   limitations of, 101-104
Rice, Dan, 185, 230
Robbins, Anthony, 117
Rogers, Carl, 25
Rugenstein, Tyge, 231
running meetings, 161-163

S

Schwab, John, 123
Schwarzenegger, Arnold, 58
science of motivational leadership, 6-8
Scott, Leonard B., 37
scripting meetings, 161
See You at the Top, 117
seized power and entrusted power, compared, 66-67
self-actualization, 97
self-esteem, 171
self-promotion, importance of, 31-33
self-view theory, 12-13
Senge, Peter, 61
sense of community, building, 174-175
setting examples, 39-40
Shattack, John, 179
Shaw, George Bernard, 214
shyness, detriments of, 48-50
situation theory, 10-11
Skilling, Jeffrey, 186
skills, fitting needs, 46-50
Skinner, B.F., 97
social comparison theory, 99
social impact theory, 79
Starship Troopers, 133
storming phase (teams), 146
strengths, assessing, 13-15
Sununu, John H., 112
SWOT analysis, 47
Sykes, Charles J., 84

T-U

tasks, delegating, 178-179
   effective delegation, 179-190
Taylor, Frederick W., 60

team members, viewing as assets, 80-81

teams

change success, measuring, 227-229

collaboration, encouraging, 146-147

communication

encouraging, 148-149

open lines, 149-150

enthusiasm, importance of, 128-135

follow-up, importance of, 90-92

forming phase, 146

input, gathering, 51-52

interest, expressing, 143-144

meetings

alternatives to, 159-160

avoiding, 154

detriments of, 155

failures of, 158-159

necessary meetings, 156-158

running, 161-163

scripting, 161

mission statements, creating, 121-123

norming phase, 146

objectives, managing by, 123-124

one-on-one management, 135-137

time efficiency, 135-137

ownership, promoting, 89-90

performing phase, 146

responsibility, assigning, 92-93

sense of community, building, 174-175

storming phase, 146

teamwork, developing, 145-146

vision

defining, 118

setting, 114-118

vision statements, 119-121

teamwork, developing, 145-146

theories of motivational leadership, 10, 96-99

behavior theory, 11

influence theory, 12

self-view theory, 12-13

situation theory, 10-11

traits theory, 10

Three Rules of Thumb, 187

time efficiency, one-on-one management, 135-137

Titanic, 150

tough audiences, appealing to, 175-176

Tracy, Brian, 46, 113, 117, 199, 230

traits, transformational leaders, 235-236

traits theory, 9-10

transformational leaders, 234-238

traits, 235-236

Truman, Harry, 85

Trump, Donald, 53

trust, importance of, 187-189

Tuckman, Bruce, 145

V

Valentin, John, 210

Vaughan, Roger, 236, 239

Vaughn, Mo, 210

veracity, power of, 86-87

verbal warnings, issuing, 104-105

Victims of Groupthink: A Psychological Study of Foreign Policy Decisions and Fiascoes, 76

vision

importance of, 112-113

organizations, embracing, 50-51

teams

defining, 118

managing by objectives, 123-124

mission statements, 121-123

setting for, 114-118
vision statements, 119-121
vision statements, 118
Covered Bridge Produce,
120-121
creating, 119-121
Voting Rights Act of 1965, 115

W-X-Y-Z

Washington, George, 8
Watergate scandal, 77
weaknesses, assessing, 13-15
Weber, Max, 59-60
Welch, Jack, 185
West Point Leadership Lessons, 187
Widener, Chris, 143
Wilson, Tom, 44
Wilson, Woodrow, 229
Winning, 185

Ziglar, Zig, 117

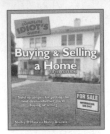

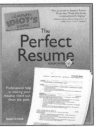

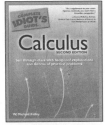